SKU0640289

contents

contents

parent's
guide
press

Los Angeles, California
www.pgpress.com

A Parent's Guide™ to

Homeschooling

Tamra B. Orr

A Parent's Guide™ to
Homeschooling

This book and all titles in the Parent's Guide series are available to fundraisers, educational institutions, parent or teacher organizations, schools, government agencies and corporations at a discount for purchases of more than 10 units. For larger purchases, Parent's Guides may be customized with corporate or institutional logos, specialized articles or other features. Persons or organizations wishing to inquire should call **Mars Publishing** at **1-800-549-6646** or write to us at **sales@marspub.com**.

JIHGFEDCBA

parent's
guide
press

Edwin E. Steussy, CEO and Publisher
Lars M. Peterson, Project Editor
Michael P. Duggan, Graphic Artist

PO Box 461730
Los Angeles CA 90046
www.pgpress.com

contents

contents

DEDICATION

To my loving parents who gave me a belief in myself and what I could accomplish and to my life partner Joseph for always being there and for our profound bond. To independent Jasmine for leading me down the right pathway, to delightful Nicole for renewing my faith, and to my sweet boys, Caspian and Coryn, for teaching me to never say never.

ACKNOWLEDGMENTS

This is to thank everyone for the part they played in the creation of this book. Thanks to people whose words I quoted; they often said it better than I ever could. Deep appreciation to my personal friends and other homeschooling parents who took the time to write down their thoughts and experiences to share with readers. A special thank you to my husband, who watched the kids, cooked the meals, and did the cleaning without too much complaining so that I could get this labor of love written.

FOREWORD

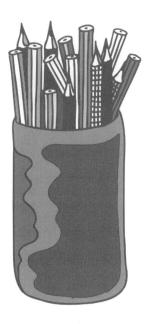

Foreword

If you could only choose one guide to home education, Tamra Orr's *A Parent's Guide to Homeschooling* should be it. In these 300 or so pages, Tamra offers the smart help and direction you need.

When you make the choice to homeschool, you open the doors to a whole new world for your children, one in which their particular learning styles can be directly addressed. From the visually acute, to the auditorially inspired, to the physically active learner, you release your children from the often-static standard classroom to an educational experience that pulsates with their own particular rhythms. And while you may want give your children this opportunity, you know that you're going to need help. Look to Tamra. Having successfully faced the challenges of homeschooling herself, she is ready to serve as your competent guide.

In Chapter One, Tamra discusses the history of homeschooling, introducing you to the long line of thought that informs today's philosophies. Here, you will discover writers like John Holt, who in the 1960s was one of the first to dramatically change my own beliefs about education. When

I read Holt's *How Children Fail*, I knew I was being taught the truth. Its much how I imagine most homeschoolers feel when someone notices the truth about how they learn—and then nurtures that learning.

Chapter Two answers the questions that inevitably arise when parents begin to homeschool. Tamra addresses these concerns with the sincerity, forthrightness, and authority needed to affirm this important educational decision. Even after your initial worries are over, this chapter can be repeatedly referred to for that extra dose of reassurance.

Of course one of the primary questions parents have is, "How do I get started?" which is the focus of Chapter Three. Tamra lays out the road map and then lets the experiences of other seasoned homeschoolers serve as the compass. In this section, we hear from the likes of Mark and Helen Hegener, Patrick Farenga, and Pat Montgomery, just to name a few, each offering advice on this essential first step.

In Chapters Four and Five, you will discover that, contrary to popular opinion, choosing homeschooling is not isolating. Community, local, state, and national groups can strongly support your family. Tamra shows us that the options for learning are actually expanded, not limited; the whole world becomes your children's classroom.

Chapters Six and Seven look at the changing needs of your children as they become college bound teenagers. Tamra also discusses special needs like Attention Deficit Disorder and other learning difficulties.

Rounding out the book is Chapter Eight, in which you will learn about the legalities of homeschooling. This section, could in itself, make a fine civics lesson!

And do not overlook the appendices. This extended array of publications, Internet sites, organizations, and even state-by-state contacts will keep you interested, motivated, and always eager to learn more.

With true excitement, I join Tamra and this book's contributors in welcoming you to the thrilling world of home education.

Ashisha
Articles Editor, *Mothering Magazine*
30 March 2002

Preface

Susan Evans and her family live in western North Carolina. She and her husband have raised their children outside of institutional schooling through high school and into adulthood. Besides being mother and wife, Susan has worked as a breastfeeding mentor to other mothers, a conference planner and speaker on a variety of family-focused topics, and as a writer. She was Coordinator of the National Homeschool Association, has written for *Home Education Magazine* and contributed to *The Homeschooling Book of Answers*.

I first met Tamra sixteen years ago when I was pregnant with my youngest daughter and her daughter, Jasmine, was a toddler. We were at a conference that supported and promoted gentle birth, mother/baby bonding, and close parent/child ties. The newsletter that she published at the time supported those ideals, as did the mother-to-mother meetings and workshops I was leading then. Our paths crossed several times over the years in other publications and in different non-profit organizations. Today, we are still in touch and singing the praises of those same ideas, having each raised and homeschooled four children—some of whom have successfully made their own way into the big, wide world and the rest of whom are still growing up.

The process of exploring such simple building blocks like informal support networks, workshops and conferences where parents communicate with other parents, as well as articles in magazines where family stories and parenting advice are shared should not be underestimated. Learning early on to listen to our children and creating and maintaining close bonds (both child-to-parent and parent-to-child) can make the most challenging years of parenting and growing up much less stressful and more rewarding for both parents and children. These patterns of behavior and bonds also provide a valuable base of support and friendship across the generations.

The pattern of perceiving parents in the position of primary caregivers, educators, and role models throughout their children's lives is sensible, efficient, and successful for families in the 21st century. Consider the current Rube Goldberg-ish machine of educational goals and standards: the very best public schools strive to be like good private schools (smaller class sizes, parental involvement, cross-age mentoring); the very best private schools strive to be like good free schools (freedom of movement around the classroom, independent studies, field trips into the community); the very best free schools strive to be like families (mixed-age classes, moving teachers from grade to grade with their classes). We've already got the families. Why don't we go with what has proven to work not only for countless generations in the past, but also for many families today?

In the average family with children, one can expect to find certain qualities when it comes to 'educational' topics. Whether taking a trip to the zoo, setting the dinner table, preparing for a visit to Grandma's, or explaining just where babies come from, there is immediate feedback in both directions as to the effectiveness of the communication. Children let their parents know right away if the approach, content, and focus of their lessons are on target. Parents can see, without testing, whether their children comprehend the information they are trying to convey.

Overlaying this reality with a look at institutional expectations in learning, it's easy to see some truths: there is no need to manufacture external rewards or sanctions for the children in a homeschooling family, or for their parents, by any bureaucratic body. The artificial concepts of 'grade level' and 'standard curriculum' are just that—artificial. The search for information, the accumulation of knowledge and understanding are intrinsically addictive for both generations. If children continue to ask questions, the explanations have not reached their 'grade levels' yet. If they have puzzled looks on their faces or don't respond to explanations, they're not ready for that material yet.

The contributors in this book have raised children thoughtfully and lovingly, and giving them a good hard listen is both wise and valuable. They have taken the time to publicly write and talk about their thoughts and experiences while actively doing the work of parenting. Tamra and her contributors have approached the issues and logistics of parenting in different ways; they've worked in different educational organizations and publications but have kept in touch over the years. I personally know almost all of her contributors and most of their children, thanks to the work we have shared. These children are bright, articulate, healthy, happy people. While I may not agree with all of their points of views—and some readers may not either—it is worth giving careful consideration to what each one has to say. They have walked the walk successfully and are graciously willing to provide us with a travelogue of their journeys.

Take a moment to compare the hands-on, 'down and dirty' parenting experiences presented in this book to the stereotype of academic researchers shuffling papers, sending out surveys, and considering hypotheses over pots of coffee in their offices. Sometimes, pondering descriptions of current problems being bantered about by governmental and educational policy makers makes one skeptical of 'expertism.' This book strips away pretense and posturing while putting forth ideas and possible solutions by real people, actual parents who have raised and educated their children according to the ideas of what families need in order to be strong and close, and what children need to be smart, healthy, and happy.

We have been at this job of raising our offspring, preparing them to carry on and increase the level, aesthetics, and spiritual understanding of the human race for thousands, hundreds of thousands, or millions of years. While there have been peaks and valleys in this effort, one consistency has been evident: in successful societies, parents have been intimately involved in the care, training, and education of their children. The true educational and sociological experiment with children has been the current one; where mass numbers of children have been moved out of their homes, away from their parents and siblings, and into institutions in order to increase their potential to become 'successful' adults. In the past, such Dickensian movements of children would have been used only in an attempt to make the best of a tragedy such as war, poverty, or orphanhood.

The view of homeschooling that is presented in this book is the ultimate in educational reform. It clears out the clutter and confusion, puts those with the most to gain (and lose) in charge of the process, and happily, no trees have to be cut down in order to evaluate and recognize the ongoing success of the process from year to year.

At a time when legislation is being regularly considered at both the state and federal levels to mandate evaluation, rewards and punishments for successes and failures in educating youth, Tamra's suggestions about raising and educating children should be looked at and seriously considered. Children's lives are not roads or bridges that need to be built, neither are they borders which need to be opened, closed, or monitored. Instead, the solution to many problems within families lies within the families themselves. Many families, many solutions, and again, most of them turn out pretty well. Tamra presents here a proven idea whose time has come, this time I hope, to stay.

INTRODUCTION

My personal journey to homeschooling is much like that taken by many homeschoolers. I started out with the simple step of becoming a mother and discovering quickly that everything I thought about children and how they should be raised was basically wrong. As in the words of John Wilmot, Earl of Rochester, "Before I got married I had six theories about bringing up children; now I have six children and no theories." My first child—now ironically referred to as my walking, homeschooling audio-visual material—opened my eyes to many aspects of being a parent that I had never even thought about before. The pathway my husband and I found ourselves following was not the typical, traditional one that we saw mirrored in our society's culture; instead, it was one that was based on what our hearts and our daughter's spirit told us. It wasn't always popular with friends and relatives, but we still knew it was the right direction to go and we leaned on each other when others tried to persuade us to detour.

One of the integral steps along that parenting pathway was discovering homeschooling. In 1988, it was still on the fringe and far from being the accepted model of education it is now becoming, but that was part of its appeal. When we first heard of it, we were intrigued. Both of us had had negative school experiences, and we didn't want this for our children. I had a brand new teaching degree under my arm and just knew that I could teach my daughter better than anyone else could. After all, I had already helped her with the hard stuff—she knew how to walk, talk, feed herself, and get dressed. We hadn't needed a teacher for that, so why did we need one now? The thought of having this six-year-old child gone from me all day was so bizarre and unnatural that I couldn't imagine how other parents did it. So, my husband and I made the choice to homeschool.

That was 18 years ago. Our walking AV material has been traveling the country for three years now, being remarkably independent and as she puts it, "Out seeing the world instead of just reading about it." Since then, three more children have come along to open our eyes about more things and

INTRODUCTION

to teach us more lessons than I can count. Through it all, our belief in homeschooling and what it does for a person, a family, and the world has only deepened. It is my joy that I can write this book and hopefully, through what you read and learn here, you might make the same choice for your family also. I can think of no better way to share the power of home education.

A note to remember as you read all of the "In the Trenches" essays—they represent a huge scope of homeschooling ideas, methods, feelings, and thoughts. Some will strike you as right; some as wrong. What these essays are meant to show is that there is NO ONE RIGHT WAY to homeschool; there are as many different philosophies and approaches as there are families. While one essay may advocate one direction, another might come along that supports the opposite road. I personally might have been cheering as I read one and shaking my head as I read another. These essays are simply intended to bring you into the minds of homeschoolers across the country and show you their incredible diversity.

Also, here and there throughout the book I refer to homeschooling as a movement. For some this word implies change; it infers options or choices. For others it means fanaticism or radicalism. Early in its development, the homeschooling movement was by necessity a politically oriented group working to move/change/alter/shift today's educational options. Not all of today's homeschoolers identify themselves as part of any political movement, though the changes that earlier pioneers have affected do benefit them. As used in this book, the homeschooling movement refers to the entire population of homeschoolers, whether they identify themselves politically or not, as well as the laws and culture that have grown up around homeschooling.

Homeschooling is a journey for all those who choose to take it. This book is a reflection of what I have learned on that journey, and I hope that it can act as a road map that makes your trip easier. There are no mandatory routes; detours are almost inevitable and can be the best part. Plot your course, grab your compass, and start the expedition. Wishing you many delightful discoveries!

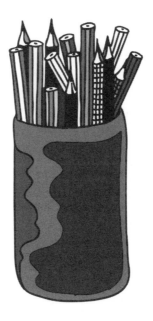

CHAPTER ONE

How Did Homeschooling Begin— and Where Is It Going?

> *"How we learn is what we learn."*
> —*Bonnie Friedman*

Consider this chapter your own basic 101 course in homeschooling. It will give you a good grounding in where homeschooling came from, who helped it along, and who has taken its tenets and made it a part of their lives.

CHAPTER ONE

How did homeschooling begin?

Homeschooling is not a new concept, but just a revival of the main form of education that took place in this country before the mid-19th century. Up until then, most children stayed at home and learned all the essentials of life, from how to make soap and milk cows, to how to read and write well enough to communicate. In 1852, the state of Massachusetts set the first state compulsory school attendance law and other states followed after that, much to the outrage of many families. As the world shifted to a more industrial society, mass-producing competent workers became a higher priority, and for this, school was deemed necessary. It stayed that way until the early 1960s when a few dissenting voices were heard. In 1964, former teacher and homeschool forefather John Holt wrote *How Children Fail*, a serious look at how schools were damaging children. A few years later, Dr. Raymond Moore, a former employee of the U.S. Department of Education, and his wife Dorothy, a teacher, began talking to over a hundred child development specialists about how schooling was affecting young children. Their groundbreaking research led to numerous books and their strong advocacy of homeschooling, which continues to this day.

In the early 1970s, there were an estimated 10,000 to 15,000 children being homeschooled in the U.S. In 1977, John Holt launched the Growing Without Schooling organization and the magazine *Home Education Magazine* followed a few years later. A landmark court case occurred in 1978 (*Perchemlides* v. *Frizzle*), when a Massachusetts court upheld the right of a family to homeschool their son. The 1980s brought even more momentum to the homeschooling movement. Changes in tax regulations forced many small, private, Christian schools to close, and a number of these families chose the homeschooling option over public school. Holt published his now famous *Teach Your Own: The John Holt Guide to Home Schooling* and the Moores published *Home Grown Kids*.

By 1986, all 50 states allowed homeschooling, as they do today. Two years later, David and Micki Colfax became celebrities when three of their

THE HOMESCHOOLING DECISION

four homeschooled sons were accepted to Harvard. This put homeschooling into the media more than ever before, as the family appeared on television talk shows and in magazine and newspaper articles.

As each decade passes, the interest in homeschooling increases. Studies are being done, books are being written, interviews are being conducted, and slowly, but surely, the concept of home education has become an acceptable one for many. In 1994, it even made the cover of *Newsweek* magazine, and it continues to be a topic that the media explores on a regular basis. As people read about the incidents of violence taking place in schools today, they are also beginning to wonder if homeschooling might be a safer option for their children.

How many students are being homeschooled?

The answer to this one boils down to this: it depends on whom you ask. The statistics are out there; unfortunately, that doesn't mean the truth is out there too. The statistics surrounding homeschooling are always changing and rarely accurate. Each organization that estimates the number of homeschoolers bases their estimate on different criteria and many of these estimates aren't reliable. One group, for example, may base their numbers on how many families are registered with state departments of education, while others might base it on a survey they have created and sent out. Others may base estimates on sales of curriculua or other homeschooling related products and services. The problem with this is that there are quite a few homeschoolers who don't register, take surveys, or buy a curriculum. These are homeschoolers who prefer to keep a low profile. They don't want others interfering in what they are doing and they suspect that much of the research being done will only end up doing harm to homeschoolers, instead of helping them.

CHAPTER ONE

These families are not necessarily being paranoid. There is a strong feeling among some that research on homeschooling might be detrimental both to the concept of homeschooling and to individual families. According to Larry and Susan Kaseman, authors and columnists in *Home Education Magazine*, almost all survey questions are based on the public school model of education. Researchers are looking for grades, hours spent teaching specific subjects, type of curriculum, etc. All of these concepts are public school concepts and may not play a part in a family's homeschooling style at all. This can make homeschooling parents begin to doubt themselves as they are led to look to the public school system as the one to emulate in their homes—an idea that is rarely, if ever, true. Instead of looking at what homeschoolers do well in their own style, these surveys look only at how they are doing in comparison to public schooled children. "Research is doing homeschooling more harm than good," the Kasemans write. "Homeschoolers seldom benefit from it. Instead, the benefits go to researchers, universities, experts, attorneys and others who use it in place of direct knowledge, alternative practices, and effective political action."

What all of this means, of course, is that, at this time, there is no study that can definitively state how many homeschoolers there are in this country. There are simply too many homeschooling families out there who are being overlooked. Knowing this, here are the top three estimates of homeschoolers in the country:

Brian Ray, President of the Home School Legal Defense Association, in his latest study for the National Home Education Resource Institute states that there were between 1.3 and 1.7 million children being homeschooled in the 1999-2000 school year. (Based on his own survey and the sales of curricular packages.)

Patricia Lines, from the U.S. Department of Education, estimates that there were 700,000 to 750,000 children being homeschooled during the 1999-2000 school year. (Based on data from all states that obtained records on homeschooling in 1990-91 and 1995-96.)

THE HOMESCHOOLING DECISION

The National Center for Education Statistics estimated that there were 850,000 children being homeschooled during the 1999-2000 school year. (Based on a rigorous sample survey of households.)

According to the Home School Legal Defense Association (HSLDA), if these numbers are even somewhat accurate, then there are more homeschooling students than there are public school students in Arkansas, Delaware, Hawaii, Montana, North Dakota, South Dakota, Rhode Island, Vermont and Wyoming *combined*.

Another question that is often looked at is how rapidly the movement is growing. Again, with so many homeschoolers lying low and not taking part in surveys and questionnaires, it's hard to be sure. However, the average rate of growth across the nation seems to stay right around 20 percent. Some states go as high as 65 percent (Maine) or as low as eight percent (Mississippi) and the rates fluctuate in each state every year.

What do the studies show about homeschoolers as a whole?

Keeping in mind, once more, that these statistics are based on some homeschoolers, but far from ALL of them, studies have shown that (as of 1999, according to the National Center for Education Statistics):

- 75% of homeschoolers are Caucasian; 25% are minorities.

- 62% of homeschooling families have three or more children (compared to 44% of public schooled families).

- 25% of homeschooling families have a college degree (compared to 16% of public school families).

- 80% of homeschooling children come from a family with two parents (compared to 66% of public schooled children).

- 52% of homeschooled children have one parent at home (compared to 19% of public schooled children).

- Incomes of homeschooling families and public schooling families were the same.

CHAPTER ONE

Why do parents choose this option?

There is no single answer for this question. Parents come to the concept of homeschooling for a myriad of different, often overlapping, reasons. Here are the primary ones cited by homeschooling families:

- *Dissatisfaction with public school system.* Whether they are upset with the curriculum, the teachers, the standards, or everything in between, parents almost always cite unhappiness with the school as one of their main reasons for looking at other options.

- *A noticeable decline in a child's spirit/enthusiasm/love of learning.* One of the warning signs that something is amiss with a child's education is when a child suddenly stops wanting to learn. Parents may see their children spending more time in front of the television than reading books, declining grades, increasing frustration with homework, or other telltale signs. A child may act more restless, unhappy, or bored at home, and may develop a need to be entertained, rather than entertaining himself. All of these are signs that there is a problem. A child is born with a drive to learn, and if that drive is fading, something is wrong.

- *A child in trouble.* This trouble could be anything from low grades to high absenteeism, or it can be a problem of behavior. Some parents find themselves looking at homeschooling after their children have been suspended or expelled. Others see falling grades or skipping school as a problem that might just be best handled at home.

THE HOMESCHOOLING DECISION

- *A child is not "fitting in."* Many children are shaped in ways that just don't fit the typical public school mold. They might have a learning disability; they might be gifted—or both. The majority of schools simply are not set up to address these situations as well as a loving family can. Many families prefer to educate their "gifted," "disabled," or "special" children at home, rather than to entrust them to a system that is designed to meet the needs of the average child.

- *Religious reasons.* A significant portion of the families who homeschool today do it for religious reasons. They want the basic tenets of their faith—whatever faith it may be—to be an integral part of their children's curriculum and overall life perspectives. By home educating, they can select lessons and other materials that support their religious stance, and they can build ethics and morals into it all without fear of exposing their children to concepts that they don't believe.

- *To keep a child safe.* Sadly, one of the reasons that homeschooling has seen a rise in interest in recent years is due to the horrible incidents of school violence. Newspapers run stories after each event remarking on the surge of interest in homeschooling. Parents may indeed fear that their children are at risk, although the list of fears often extends beyond the chance of a school shooting. Families may worry about their children being at risk from other things, including pressure from peers to take drugs, drink alcohol, or have sex. While homeschooling doesn't guarantee these things won't happen, it will almost certainly limit the opportunities and the temptations for them to happen.

CHAPTER ONE

- *Build family bonds.* Some families choose homeschooling simply because they don't like having the family separated for eight-plus hours per day. Siblings rarely see each other, and mom and dad are often too busy working, making meals, and doing household chores to spend one-on-one time with their children. Homeschooling means more time together to work not only on something educational, but to talk, wonder, dream, discuss, and share. Many times the outcome is a closer family that understands and likes each other. They all share common daily experiences, rather than spending the day separate from each other in different activities. Frequently, by being together everyday, siblings have stronger relationships.

- *Overall superior education.* Lastly, many parents truly feel that they can give their children a better education than the school can. They have the time and the interest, as well as an in-depth knowledge of their children's strengths, weaknesses, and learning style. They can design an education that fits the child rather than forcing the child to fit the style of the education. Homeschooling is flexible, affordable, and has a great student to teacher ratio.

THE HOMESCHOOLING DECISION

What myths surround homeschooling?

A number of common myths or misconceptions surround the concept of homeschooling. Many of them, just like the stories found in the tabloids, may have started out with a nugget of truth and then, somewhere down the line, become skewed and false. Here are a few of the most typical ones that still haunt the movement:

- *Only hippies homeschool.* When people originally heard about homeschooling several decades ago, they usually attributed the movement to parents who were refusing to leave behind the "question authority" attitude of the 1960s and 1970s or to families who lived in such remote areas of the world that they had no choice in the matter. While those families may have been the forerunners of home education, it is certainly no longer true today. Families of all kinds homeschool now; married and single, religious and secular, rich and poor, black, white, yellow, or red. They are from all ethnic and social backgrounds with any range of political leanings. They share one main thing; they are parents who are looking for a better educational option for their children.

- *Only Christians homeschool.* This is a common thought in recent years because many of the homeschooling families who are profiled in the media are from the Christian faith. However, perpetuating the myth means that people of other faiths or those who are completely secular are being ignored. While quite a few of the homeschoolers today do tend to follow one of a number of faiths, from Christian to Mormon to Wiccan, the number of secular homeschoolers is growing steadily and should not be overlooked.

CHAPTER ONE

- *Homeschooling is school brought home.* It certainly can be organized just like a classroom, from recess periods and report cards, to bells and pop quizzes. However, it can also be designed to be absolutely nothing like traditional school. Just like there is no one absolute way to parent, there is no one absolute way that families have to homeschool. The hours, style, curriculum, and every other detail depend entirely on the needs, interests, and personalities of the most important people in the picture—the parents and children. One of the biggest advantages to homeschooling is that the whole design of it is in your hands and under your control. You set the pace, the direction, the schedule, and everything else in the way that optimally fits your children and yourselves. For some families, this may mean something modeled directly after the pattern of public school; for others, it is directly the opposite, or somewhere in between.

- *You have to have a teaching degree to homeschool.* Thanks to a lobby of homeschoolers at Capitol Hill in 1996, this is not true. Congress had made a move to require all homeschooling parents to have teaching certificates, and families came out in droves to squash this idea. Many parents who do have teaching degrees have found their training to be one of the biggest obstacles they had to overcome when they began homeschooling. Their education classes had taught them how to teach, and their children were showing them how wrong much of that really was.

THE HOMESCHOOLING DECISION

- *Homeschooling is expensive.* It can be—but it doesn't have to be. Part of what will determine the cost of home-schooling in your family is your style. The more formal you are or the more you choose to imitate public school, the more materials you will need, and thus the more it may cost. There are many different places to obtain the curricula you will need, and not all of them are costly. Some are even free!

- *Homeschooling isn't legal.* As of 1986, it has been legal to homeschool in every state of the United States. The laws are governed by the individual states, however, so there are different restrictions and requirements you need to know about (as noted in detail in Chapter Eight).

- *Homeschooled children won't learn how to socialize.* Completely and utterly false. When confronted with this statement, one homeschooling father responded, tongue in cheek, that he planned to teach his children how to open the front door and answer the phone when they turned 13. The real world, where people of all ages, sizes, backgrounds, and styles live is not in a classroom. Homeschooled children learn about the world by being involved in it, rather than studying it at a desk.

CHAPTER ONE

What is homeschooling like for minority families?

According to the U.S. Department of Education, minorities (Asians, Hispanics, African-Americans, Native Americans, and Jews) make up one quarter (25%) of the total homeschooling population. Dr. Ray of HSLDA estimates that there are between 30,000 and 50,000 African-American children homeschooling in 2001. The problems these groups face are sometimes slightly different. A minority within a minority, they often deal with feelings of isolation and lack of support. For instance, some African-Americans have been condemned for homeschooling when their heritage includes such a strong fight to get into public schools. For some, homeschooling seems like a betrayal. Joyce and Eric Burges who founded the National Black Home Education Resource Association (NBHERA) in 2000 have adopted a slogan of "Homeschooling that J.A.M.S. (Joining America's Multicultural Society)."

The answer for many minority homeschoolers is participation in a specific support group. This is what the Minority Homeschoolers of Texas (MHOT) have done. Does this make the group somewhat exclusive? Not according to Johnson Obamehinti, MHOT President, who writes on the web site, "The idea of a minority support group is to celebrate the diversity within the homeschooling community." He says that support groups like the MHOT "serve as a means of motivation for many minority families that feel they are the 'only' ones in homeschooling. It also helps the children know they are not alone," he adds.

THE HOMESCHOOLING DECISION

What about homeschooling in other countries?

Homeschooling is taking hold in other countries, as well as the United States. It has reached to Australia, France, the United Kingdom, South Africa, Israel, and Japan, and continues to spread further each year. Homeschooling has grown rapidly in Canada—the Appendix includes information about the movement there, as well as basic information about the laws in each territory. Each country has its own educational battles to fight, of course.

In 1977 in the U.K., a homeschooling support group called "Education Otherwise" was formed by a few parents. It now has more than 3,000 family members or contacts across the country who are there to help new homeschoolers with their questions and concerns. They based the name of their group on their Education Act, which states that parents are responsible for their children's education, "either by regular attendance at school or otherwise." They have summarized the homeschooling legal situation in the U.K. with one concise statement: "Education is compulsory; schooling is not."

Similar groups are forming across the planet and can be found on the Internet through the search phrase 'international homeschooling.'

CHAPTER ONE

What does the media report about homeschooling?

Everyone knows that the media loves to focus on extremes. If it's extraordinarily wonderful or terrible, it comes out in the media. Rarely does a story on homeschooling just focus on the everyday, normal routines of a family. Susan's leap to reading chapter books or Steven's mastering of algebra does not make headlines. When stories do appear in the media, the reports often focus on the highs, or the lows, and as a result, the general reader doesn't get a very honest look at what homeschooling is like.

In recent years, the biggest stories to come out of homeschooling have been things like the Colfax's sons getting into college, homeschooler David Guterson writing the best selling novel *Snow Falling on Cedars*, the death of Jessica Dubroff—the seven-year-old homeschooling girl who was killed in a plane crash with her father in 1977, or the tragedy of Andrea Pia Yates—the mentally ill homeschooling mother from Texas who killed all five of her children. More positive news stories have centered on winners of national contests. In 1997, Rebecca Sealfon, a 13-year-old from New York, was the first homeschooler to win the National Spelling Bee, inspiring a rash of stories on homeschoolers. In 1999, homeschooler Rio Benin scored a perfect 1600 on his SATs, and homeschooler David Biehl won the National Geography Bee. In 2000, homeschoolers came in first, second, and third in the Scripps Howard National Spelling Bee. Stories like these inspire writers to take a look at homeschooling, and for the most part, they profile it positively. However, it is common for them to throw in some negative comments or postscripts from the public education sector.

THE HOMESCHOOLING DECISION

Are there any famous homeschoolers?

As Grace Llewellyn wrote in her book *The Teenage Liberation Handbook*, "One third of the men who signed the Declaration of Independence, the Articles of Confederation, and the Constitution of the United States had no more than a few months of schooling up their sleeves." In addition to them, here are a few other recognizable names:

- Ansel Adams
- Irving Berlin
- Pearl Buck
- Leann Rimes
- Hanson
- Samuel Clemens
- Thomas Edison
- Frank Lloyd Wright
- Beatrix Potter
- Jack London
- Alexander Graham Bell
- Orville and Wilbur Wright
- Douglas MacArthur
- Leonardo da Vinci
- Andrew Wyeth
- Albert Einstein
- Mozart
- Hans Christian Anderson
- Charles Dickens
- Agatha Christie
- C.S. Lewis
- Charlie Chaplin
- Will Rogers
- Clara Barton

CHAPTER ONE

Who are some of homeschooling's biggest advocates?

Can you imagine learning about astronomy and not knowing about Galileo? Could you possibly study electricity without learning about Edison? If you're going to learn about homeschooling, you had better get familiar with these names too. Here is a brief look at who they are, and why they are important to the homeschooling community.

John Holt

Often considered the true founding father of modern homeschooling, this former public school teacher was one of the first people to truly speak out against traditional schooling. From his own experiences in teaching, he knew that something was wrong, and he set out to find some solutions. In the process he wrote such influential and powerful books, including (but certainly not limited to) *How Children Fail*, *How Children Learn*, *Freedom and Beyond*, *Escape from Childhood*, *Teach Your Own*, and *Learning All the Time*. He became a true advocate of homeschooling and coined the word "unschooling" for teaching in a manner that was little like the traditional school model.

In 1977, Holt established *Growing Without Schooling* magazine, the country's first periodical about home education. It stayed in print until the end of 2001. Throughout his adult life, Holt was an outspoken and passionate friend to homeschooling. Although he passed away in 1985, his legacy continues at Holt Associates in Massachusetts, under the leadership of President Patrick Farenga. In Farenga's article, "John Holt and the Origins of Contemporary Homeschooling," he writes, "John Holt does not only speak to the choir of would-be and current homeschoolers, political parties or education theorists, his work speaks to adults and children in school as well as out of it; it addresses larger social concerns beyond school and continues to inspire thousands of people from all walks of life."

THE HOMESCHOOLING DECISION

Dr. Raymond and Dorothy Moore

Like Holt, this married couple was in on the modern homeschooling movement from its inception. Raymond, a developmental psychologist, and Dorothy, a reading specialist, did a great deal of research on the cognitive abilities of children and reached a controversial conclusion for its time. They believed that children were not ready for the basic academics (reading, writing, arithmetic, etc.) until they were about 12 years old. They called their philosophy "Delayed Academics" and wrote about it, as well as their other philosophies about parenting, in such books as *Home Grown Kids*, and *Home Made Health*. They produce *The Moore Report*—a monthly periodical, and many parents choose the Moore's basic principles as the foundation of their own homeschooling.

Charlotte Mason

Born in England in 1842, Mason focused her life on the issue of education and the role it should play in the lives of children. She authored a six-volume set of books now known as *The Original Home Schooling Series*. Today, 80 years after her death, many homeschooling families still follow her Christian beliefs, coupled with a strong emphasis on reading quality literature and appreciating nature.

John Taylor Gatto

Voted New York City's Teacher of the Year three times, and New York State's Teacher of the Year in 1991, Gatto is more than familiar with what is happening in today's schools. After 30 years as a teacher, he walked away and began advocating educational alternatives like homeschooling. His books *Dumbing Us Down: The Invisible Curriculum of Compulsory Schooling*, *The Exhausted School* and *The Underground History of American Education* demonstrate what is wrong with public school and what families can do to set it right.

CHAPTER ONE

Grace Llewellyn

Considered by many as the spokesperson for homeschooling teens, Llewellyn broke new ground with her books *The Teenage Liberation Handbook: How to Quit School and Get a Real Life* and *Education and Real Lives: Eleven Teenagers that Don't Go to School*. These books encouraged teens to take their educations into their own hands and "rise out" (as opposed to drop out) of traditional schooling. In addition to her books, Llewellyn is also the founder and coordinator of the annual Not Back to School Camp held in Oregon for homeschooling kids between 13 and 18.

There are other names out there to know: helpful and reliable authors like Cafi Cohen, Linda Dobson, Patrick Farenga, David Guterson, and David and Micki Colfax, just to name a few. Get familiar with who they are and what roles they had to play in the homeschooling movement. They can be wonderful guides on your new journey.

THE HOMESCHOOLING DECISION

In the Trenches

My Evolution in Homeschooling
~ Martha Lee

How I think about public schools has changed dramatically over the years since I began homeschooling my eldest son nine years ago, following an unpleasant kindergarten experience. I went from being afraid to do something so radical, to wondering how anyone can put up with the subtle disrespect schools give parents and children alike. I went from believing that schools are necessary, to knowing they are ludicrous! In recent years, I have been known to say things like, "My children have committed no crime so I decided not to incarcerate them!" When I drive past a public school now, they seem as foreign as prisons to me. After all, both are large institutions where people are kept in an orderly and often dehumanizing manner against their wills. I try not to fully admit my radical views to my three children, in the event our lifestyle changes one day and they are forced to go to school. Instead, I just focus on giving them their freedom and dignity to learn in a relaxed atmosphere of caring.

There are many things that schools provide that people think of as necessary, but are they really? Most parents worry about the socialization issue, for example. Will homeschoolers learn to get along with their peers? After nine years of homeschooling, I believe that too much of the socialization kids receive in school is actually quite detrimental. My kids have plenty of contact with peers through 4-H, scouting, church, neighborhood kids, family, friends, and relatives. I live in Lansing, Michigan, and we have a large homeschool support group that meets at the main library downtown. My friend and I founded the group three years ago, and now we have 80 families on our mailing list. Homeschoolers come from all over the greater Lansing area every week to this center of learning for socialization, board games, arts and crafts, and other activities where outside teachers teach subjects that are beyond the realm of the parents.

I once thought, will I know enough to be able to teach my own kids all the way through the challenging years of high school? I have seen other mothers do it, and I realize it is because they were learning right along with their children. Homeschooling parents are one intelligent and educated group of people!

What about tests, I asked myself. Can my children survive without them? A homeschooling friend of mine once ran into a truancy officer in the city. He asked her about testing and she replied, "Tests are for schools where there are 30 kids in a class, and the kids change teachers every year. It is the only way to keep track of where all those individual children are in their progress. I don't need them because I know exactly where each of my children is in their learning." The truancy officer never questioned her again.

CHAPTER ONE

I wondered about textbooks; did I need to go to the expense of providing the same ones the school did? I thought for years that textbooks were a necessary evil, but I don't think that anymore. In my family, we go to public libraries and borrow books on the same topics covered in science, history, and social studies and somehow, these books are so much more interesting. Textbooks almost seem designed to kill the interest of any curious mind. I found that most math textbooks, for example, have a great deal of unneeded repetition and busy work in them. I think they are created this way to keep children occupied in the classroom; more as a matter of crowd control than learning. My children and I prefer the math books that cover a topic fully from beginning to end; i.e. one that completely covers the concept of addition, subtraction, fractions, etc. We like to use many of the creative alternatives to textbooks in our homeschooling, and that's one of the nicest things about learning at home—there are so many choices.

One advantage to homeschooling that I hadn't anticipated when I first started was that homeschooled children do not seem to suffer the same burnout that their public school peers often do. They have more time to spend on outside interests like music or martial arts. My son's Tae Kwon Do teacher told me that his homeschooled students seemed more studious. Institutionally schooled kids have to deal with following rules all day—from sitting and paying attention to the teacher, to asking permission to go to the bathroom. They are surrounded with regimentation and coercion to follow the rules the entire time they are in school. My sons can go to their lessons with a fresher attitude, with noticeable results.

Learning styles can vary greatly from one child to the next, even in the same family. Schools basically use one primary method, but that doesn't work for all children. Some learn better while music is playing or while they are moving around. In our home-schooling environment, education is individualized to meet each child's needs and styles.

Discipline was a huge concern for my parents when we announced our plans to homeschool. It is sometimes easy for me to lose sight of regimentation and structure in homeschooling. Now, after years of observing my children and how they learn and work, I see that when they are interested in something, they dive into it with passion. Discipline becomes irrelevant. I make sure I have learning materials readily available, and when the urge strikes them, they pick the things up and begin to study on their own, with interest. What I am seeing is that when I do not impose outside structure, my children develop their own self-discipline, based on enthusiasm and not coercion. Children naturally enjoy doing things well when they are not being forced to do so. When they

THE HOMESCHOOLING DECISION

are led by their own sense of wonder, they learn easily and with happiness. Having grown up in a household where discipline was highly valued, it was a true lesson for me to recognize that it is okay to be flexible. My children can work for long hours on a project that fascinates them, or they can begin their writing lessons at 8 p.m. rather then 9 a.m. Why not? There is no need to schedule learning because my kids are doing it all the time.

I will never forget my son's compelling question his first week of kindergarten. He asked, "Do they love me at school?" I hemmed and hawed, trying to find the right answer to this difficult question, but he kept pressing me. "Yes, I know they like me and they want the best for me," he continued, "but do they LOVE me?" He had never been to preschool and had only been left in the care of grandparents or aunts for babysitters, so he was struggling to understand why he suddenly had to go and spend so much time with people he didn't know. After all of these years, I realize that there is no good reason to put children with strangers when they can do their schoolwork and learning at home in the company of those that love them most. What better way to foster self-esteem? My son's tender question put it all in perspective for me.

I often mention to my kids that homeschooling is not all it can be in the world, that as it evolves, it will improve. Communities will support it more one day, and it will become more widely accepted. As this happens, our very notions of education will evolve and improve, for the benefit of children everywhere. Homeschooling shook up my belief system, and I understand from an all-new perspective why government officials worry about education reform. Homeschoolers may well have a lot of answers to that problem, and one day, I believe, the 'experts' will even ask for our advice.

CHAPTER ONE

In the Trenches

On Our Journeys Through This Life
~ Lynelle Wilcox

Part of our reasons for homeschooling could be considered religious in an uncon-ventional way. We don't follow any organized religion, but we view religion as the beliefs, morals, and values that we live our lives by. By that definition, we are very reli-gious and believe that school systems tend to squash some of the very beliefs and values we consider important.

We place a lot of importance on individuality, personal responsibility, creativity, empathy, and respect for individuals, including—especially—our children. We want to instill these values in them. Most schools aren't equipped to do this and never will be. I'd even say it isn't their job to do these things . . .

I don't want my son Sean to have to be 'tough' just because he is a boy. I don't want my daughter Jamie to be treated a certain way because she is a girl. I don't want anyone telling them that they can't color elephants purple, skies yellow, or grass orange. I don't want anyone telling Sean that he should wear socks that match. I don't want anyone telling my children that any of their ideas are silly, stupid, not realistic, or impos-sible. I don't want anyone squashing their dreams and forcing their own reality, reli-gion, or views on them. I don't want them raised in an environment where it's more important to hold still, be quiet, line up, and behave that it is to live, love, and learn.

I want Sean and Jamie to retain their love, interest, motivation, passion, creativity, and individuality. I want them to learn from curiosity, not requirements. I want them to be able to focus on a project for as long as they want to and not have to switch gears every hour because it's time for the next subject. I want them to be exposed to more diversity, options, and uniqueness than a school could ever offer.

I want my children to learn how to think and reason and to question reality, author-ity, and facts. I want subjects to include hiking, biking, contemplating life, being in nature, considering moral integrity, honesty, self-fulfillment and values, discovering hap-piness in something other than things, setting life priorities, living a good life, devel-oping confidence, valuing truth and beauty more than stuff, keeping their word, inspiring people, motivating themselves and others, developing common sense and curiosity, and finding themselves, their hearts, their souls, and the whole connectedness of life.

THE HOMESCHOOLING DECISION

I want them to be able to speak their minds and open their hearts. I want them to trust their instincts, which requires having enough time to do so. And I want to be there to participate, help, and learn with them. I want to be there when the light bulb goes on in their heads. I want to be there when they figure out difficult problems and come up with creative solutions. I want to homeschool and live life with them because I love being with my children.

I hope that Sean and Jamie will know how to find peace with the world and themselves in spite of the chaos all around them. I hope that they know how to really connect with another person. I want them to realize that they can have some really terrible days but still see their cups as half full in spite of the terrible-ness; I want them to know how to find rainbows in the midst of sadness and know deep within them that there really is a pot of gold at the end of the rainbow. I hope that they are able to truly believe in things they cannot see, in things that aren't what they expected, in things that are more important than tangibles.

I hope that my children remember to make time to pick daisies, skip down the street, lie in a meadow, float in the water, do some cartwheels, make snow angels, make dandelion wishes and daisy chain wreathes, hike in a forest, climb up a mountain, and cuddle in bed as late as they want. I hope they can look in the mirror and really like the person looking back.

By choosing homeschooling, I have the chance to spend so much more time with my children—time to do, and live, and enjoy as much as possible in this journey through our lifetimes.

CHAPTER ONE

"I have never let my schooling interfere with my education."
— *Mark Twain*

From the Experts

Making the Decision to Homeschool
~ Mark and Helen Hegener

Do you remember when you first came across the idea of homeschooling your children? Did it just seem like a naturally good idea to you, or did you have to think about it for a while, try it on for size, find out more information about what might be involved, discuss it with a few people like your husband or your mother or your best friend, maybe even read a book or two on the subject in order to really warm up to the idea?

> **Mark and Helen Hegener** are the parents of five always-unschooled children, and the grandparents of five grandchildren. The Hegener family makes their home in north central Washington state, where they all enjoy horseback riding, gardening, sailing, and frequent travels. They have published **Home Education Magazine** since 1983, and have been founding members of three national homeschooling organizations.

Did the thought of teaching your own children fascinate you—or scare you? Did you envision you and your kids sharing mornings filled with reading, crafts, gardening, baking, music-making and afternoons filled with explorations, discoveries, enlightenments, and joy? Or did you wonder how on earth you could ever teach them chemistry or algebra, while envisioning a long nightmarish struggle, more akin to all your childhood homework assignments thrown at you all over again?

There are some people who can honestly say they took to homeschooling as a duck takes to water, but for the majority of parents the decision probably came only after a lengthy exploration of what's involved. For many it came even harder, with long agonizing nights of wondering if it was the right thing to do, heartfelt and sometimes heated discussions with family and friends, hours of poring over articles and books and magazines, search-

THE HOMESCHOOLING DECISION

ing for answers to their questions. Some parents started right out with optimism and high hopes, but too many others—most often the fathers—agreed to homeschooling only resignedly, half-heartedly, willing to try it, but just as willing to throw in the towel and send their kids to school at the first sign of difficulty.

Why is something so obviously good for parents and children so often approached with caution and concern? Why are some people so afraid of trusting their own feelings—their own good instincts—without validation from other people, and most often from the so-called experts?

We were involved with an online discussion group between several friends for a few years, and this very question once gave us all an opportunity to share our thoughts with each other. We had saved much of this particular thread of discussion as inspiration for our own writing, but in rereading our friends' contributions, we were struck by the power and eloquence of their writings... and we'd like to share them with you verbatim.

A close friend, Kathleen, wrote: "My point of view is simply that the system... whether you want to call that our government, or our school system, or something else.... has somehow taken away our basic human right to confidence in ourselves and acceptance of ourselves. When we equate 'all-rightness' with being like someone else, dissatisfaction and anxiety prevail. The product of those two are lowered self-esteem and inertia (unwilling to try for fear of 'failure').

"Adults are afraid to do everything. They rely on experts to doctor them, teach them, govern them, religion them. It is no wonder they are anxious about homeschooling. They have no confidence or self-esteem themselves. Making mistakes is how humans learn. We have to err to learn. Yet when we err... we cringe in fear and develop anxiety. I have come to know that not knowing something is no reason for anxiety. It is an opportunity to err gloriously."

One has to wonder why so many of us have lost our confidence... does it serve some greater purpose to have a compliant, pliable population, or is it merely a byproduct, an unfortunate happenstance?

CHAPTER ONE

Another friend, Deborah, shared thoughts which really struck home for us as publishers: "While I don't know how people develop confidence and courage in this culture, I do know that they won't ever get it from publications that promise 'The Answers.' One thing I've noticed in all my favorite magazines (all subjects, not just homeschooling) is that they ask more questions than they answer. There's a sense of a shared journey, travelers' tales on the road, instead of a leader shouting back directions to those behind. 'This is what we do' has a different attitude about it than 'This is what everyone should do.' Ideas instead of Rules. 'Why we love Math' instead of 'Ten tricks every math teacher should know!'"

Deborah's words also touched a chord in our friend Marylee: "I really like what Deborah says about 'shared journey.' When I was so anxious my first year homeschooling, I sought out 'experts' (and I mostly mean 'old-timers' who radiated confidence and common sense) to tell me things like 'trust yourself,' 'you know your kid and her needs better than anyone else,' 'trial and error is fine,' etc. I read as widely as I could, so that I could saturate myself with these thoughts, hoping to contain my anxiety. One of the main comforting messages that first year from the 'experts' was that anxiety was perfectly normal and would gradually fade as I developed more confidence. This helped me to remember that something only needs courage if it's frightening. Now that I'm more confident, I don't think of it as courageous to be homeschooling... but that first year I felt both more scared and more courageous."

The image of scared but courageous new homeschoolers seeking something different for their children is one every support group leader is familiar with. It does take a while to adjust to this strange new idea, to even learn what questions to ask. Our friend Suzanne writes that when she's answering new homeschoolers' questions she doesn't discourage them from using a curriculum or prepared materials if it's obvious they really want to. She adds: "My first recommendation is always for them to let their children be for awhile and for the parents to use that time to get more familiar with relaxed homeschooling, interest-based learning, unschooling. Sometimes the school-thing is so ingrained, they just can't. They want

THE HOMESCHOOLING DECISION

someone to tell them what to do for a bit until they do get that confidence. I've seen their troubled faces when they come to a meeting and want to know how to teach 'x' and are met with our bright chorus of, 'we don't teach, our children teach themselves, we unschool, it's easy, you don't need textbooks.' Maybe some of us unschoolers sprang forth fully 'unned' from John Holt's head, but I suspect that many more of us are still finding our ways."

Subscription information to the Hegener's Home Education Magazine: single issue $6.50 postpaid. One year/six issues $32.00 ~ Home Education Magazine ~ Post Office Box 1083 ~ Tonasket, WA 98855-1083 ~ 1-800-236-3278, email: HEM-Info@home-ed-magazine.com ~
www.home-ed-magazine.com

The oldest and most respected magazine about homeschooling, published by a second-generation homeschooling family since 1983. Winner of a Parents' Choice Recommended Award. Best subscription prices are usually found at their website. Many articles, columns, services, a monthly newsletter, a support group network, updated laws and regulations and much more—are online and absolutely free. Jean Reed, author of **The Home School Source Book**, writes: "If I had to choose only one homeschooling magazine to read, it would be this one!"

This takes us back to Deborah's observations of a sense of shared journey, and travelers' tales on the road. In our conversations, there were the inevitable allusions to homeschoolers as pioneers in education and family issues. We've always liked this analogy, as the pioneers had to be brave and courageous and confident souls, working together, supporting each other, blazing new trails, building foundations for those who would come later. Because those scared but courageous homeschool pioneers forged ahead, parents now have a wealth of support to draw from, but important questions still face us on the trail ahead. And the questions are changing, even as we're finding answers. Homeschooling is changing, evolving, and developing, and the decisions you make for your family—the ways in which you choose to help your children learn—are part and parcel of that change.

Welcome to the adventure! Welcome to homeschooling!

CHAPTER ONE

"The aim of education should be to teach us rather how to think, than what to think—rather to improve our minds, so as to enable us to think for ourselves, than to load the memory with thoughts of other men."
—Bill Beattie

From the Experts

Educational Alternatives: A Rainbow of Opportunities
~ Katharine Houk.

Once upon a time, the parents of a bright, creative, and expressive little girl had to make some decisions about how their daughter was to be educated. Because this was their first child, and because most people the parents knew simply sent their children to the local public school, the parents had to learn what would be best for their daughter through a trial-and-error process. As parents, they discovered that it was not always easy to find information about educational alternatives—and especially alternative education. Thus, as the years passed, the girl attended a small neighborhood urban public school; a large, experimental open-classroom downtown urban school; a small rural public school; a Waldorf private school; a small, private alternative boarding school; and engaged in home education.

> **Katharine Houk** is author of **Creating a Cooperative Learning Center: An Idea-Book for Homeschooling Families**, director of the nonprofit Alliance for Parental Involvement in Education, co-founder of The Alternative Learning Center, and is engaged in interfaith ministry. She lives in Columbia County in New York State.

THE HOMESCHOOLING DECISION

As a parent reading this book, you are in a different position than the parents in this once-upon-a-time story. The girl in that story was born in 1969; I am writing this essay on her thirty-second birthday. (She is my daughter, the first-born of my three children). Though it was a challenge, we were able to locate and/or create alternative learning situations that to varying degrees honored who she is.

Since those early days, I have learned a tremendous amount about educational alternatives, and have enjoyed helping hundreds of other parents seeking information. This essay will offer the reader practical information about finding out what is "out there" in the world of alternative education through offering pointers to resources. But first I must clarify what I mean by the term "alternative education."

The term "alternative education" carries a very particular meaning in this essay. First, I must explain what I do *not* mean by alternative education. The term "alternative education" has taken on a certain meaning within the public school system in the United States over the past twenty-five years. It is often used to refer to special schools within the public system where students who are failing in conventional classrooms are sent for remedial or intensive help. This essay does not focus on this type of school, nor does it include traditional private schools (in other words, those with methods and structures similar to a typical public school), parochial schools, military academies, "prep" schools, or some "drop-out" schools, which are similar in intent to the "alternative education" as defined by the public system. This is not to say that these educational choices are not available to people interested in home education, but, for economy of space, this essay focuses instead on those educational alternatives whose approaches differ from typical public education.

The alternative educational opportunities addressed here (which may include some public school programs) are those which have the following general characteristics in common. Of course, not all alternative educational options will exhibit all of these characteristics; the following list seeks to give a general flavor of the sorts of resources included.

CHAPTER ONE

- They are accessible by choice, rather than assignment.

- Each has its own distinct mission, philosophy, and goals.

- They include non-traditional teaching strategies, beyond the "lecture" method, and have innovative evaluation systems.

- They tend to focus on the needs of the individual students and the process of education itself, rather than on academic outcomes.

- They are often small, with much community contact and parental involvement.

- They often have high adult to child ratios, and strong systems to counsel and advise young people.

- They are participatory, creating governing processes and structures that involve students and parents, as well as school administration and staff.

- They often strive to be democratic and/or cooperative in the ways the schools or centers are run.

A rainbow of options exists between home education and traditional public schools on the educational spectrum. When my husband and I were first seeking information about alternative education, we turned to NCACS: the National Coalition of Alternative Community Schools (see resources listed below). That organization's *National Directory of Alternative Schools* (NCACS) lists on its latest cover: "Home schools. Free schools. Community schools. Cultural spaces. Charter schools. Open schools. Puerto Rican schools. African-American schools. Community centers. Holistic schools. Spiritual communities. Self-education. It's education for the people, by the people." This 2001 edition lists "groups and organizations which promote participant control, community building, holistic learning, and environmental sustainability." This resource, along with John Holt's books and magazine *Growing Without Schooling*, were vital resources for us in those early years.

THE HOMESCHOOLING DECISION

In order to remain succinct and to the point, in light of the hundreds of educational options available, this essay will direct you to resources where you and your children, in true home education style, can do the research yourselves. Whether you are interested in Quaker, Waldorf, or Montessori schools, experiential, outdoor or environmental education, early college, or alternatives to college, learning centers or resource centers for home-schoolers, in using the information listed, you'll be well on your way.

The NCACS is still available for people seeking alternatives, along with other clearinghouses for information: the Alliance for Parental Involvement in Education, Paths of Learning Resource Center on the web, and many home education organizations and web sites. Waldorf, Quaker, and Montessori organizations offer pamphlets, booklets, books, and listings of schools. If there are no alternative-type schools in your neighborhood, with a handful of parents you can start one. Resources and consultant help for starting schools and learning centers are available from the Alternative Education Resource Organization and the Alliance for Parental Involvement in Education.

One thing that I have learned through working with hundreds of parents and children is that there is no "one best way" for all children to become educated. People have a wide variety of cultural backgrounds, beliefs, temperaments, and values. Children, even within the same family, thrive with different amounts of structure, discipline, and adult input when learning. One size does not fit all. While it would be convenient to believe that all alternatives are flexible, some alternatives (including some styles of home education) can become every bit as rigid and oppressive as the crustiest educational institution. As you consider what is best for your child, consider his or her style of learning and your own beliefs and values; then look below the surface to determine the philosophies undergirding the schools or programs you are considering. Do some reading and visit web sites. Visit schools, learning centers, homeschooling support groups, meet teachers and administrators, talk with other parents of children attending schools or programs, and speak with the children themselves.

CHAPTER ONE

Independent schools and programs do not have a monopoly on innovative and successful educational opportunities. There are people working for true alternatives within public education, in order to enable all families to have meaningful choices regardless of their financial situations. Public schools, especially in urban areas, are increasingly creating truly alternative options within their structures, and new experiments within the charter school movement have produced some interesting options.

These reources are also included in the appendix.

Resources for those interested in publicly funded alternatives

- National Coalition of Education Activists, PO Box 679, Rhinebeck, NY 12572-0679; 914-876-4580.

- *Rethinking Schools: An Urban Educational Journal*, 1001 East Keefe Ave., Milwaukee, WI 53212

- National Coalition of Alternative Community Schools (NCACS—address below)

- Charter Schools Development Corporation, 1725 K. St. NW, Suite 700, Washington, DC 20006; 202-739-9629

- Some publicly funded alternatives may be found in the two directories: *The Almanac of Education Choices* and *National Directory of Alternative Schools*, listed below under "Books."

- An interesting story of an alternative school within a school is *The Learning Community: The Story of a Successful Mini-School*, by James Penah and John Azrak. For information about this book, contact Bob Knipe, 40-18 21st Ave., Astoria, NY 11105.

THE HOMESCHOOLING DECISION

Other helpful organizations and publications

- Alliance for Parental Involvement in Education (ALLPIE), PO Box 59, East Chatham, NY, 12060-0059; 518-392-6900, **allpie@taconic.net**. Mail-order lending library, resources catalog, newsletters, workshops, and conferences.

- Alternative Education Resource Organization (AERO), 417 Roslyn Road, Roslyn Heights, NY 11577; 516-621-2195. Newsletter, books, and videos.

- Association for Experiential Education, 2305 Canyon Blvd., Suite 100, Boulder, CO 80302; 303-440-8844, **www.aee.org**

- Association of Waldorf Schools of North America, **www.awsna.org**. This organization publishes *Renewal: A Journal for Waldorf Education*.

- Creating Learning Communities, an on-line publication, conversation, and resource center, **www.Creating LearningCommunities.org**

- Folk and People's Education Association of America, Goddard College, 123 Pitkin Road, Plainfield, VT 05667 or c/o Merry Ring, Women's Center, Lakeland Community College, 7700 Clocktower Dr., Kirkland, OH 44094

- Friends Council on Education has a directory of Quaker boarding schools: **http://forum.swarthmore.edu/fce/**

CHAPTER ONE

- Informed Birth and Parenting, Box 3675, Ann Arbor, MI 48106 or PO Box 1733, Fair Oaks, CA 95628. Sponsors workshops and conferences on Waldorf education and parenting.

- International Montessori Society, 912 Thayer Ave. #207, Silver Spring, MD 20910; 301-589-1127. Has listing of Montessori schools.

- Journal of Family Life, 22 Elm Street, Albany, NY 12202; 518-471-9532

- National Coalition of Alternative Community Schools, 1266 Rosewood #1, Ann Arbor, MI 48104; 734-668-9171, **www.ncacs.org**

- North American Montessori Teachers' Association, 13693 Butternut Road, Burton, OH 44021; 440-834-4011. Listing of Montessori schools.

- Paths of Learning: Options for Families and Communities, PO Box 328, Brandon, VT 05733-0328; **www.great-ideas.org**

- Paths of Learning Resource Center, **www.pathsoflearn-ing.org**

- Pendle Hill Publications, Wallingford, PA 19086 has Quaker-related publications and information; 610-566-4507, **www.pendlehill.org**

- Waldorf Early Childhood Association, 1359 Alderton Ln., Silver Spring, MD 20906; 301-460-6287

THE HOMESCHOOLING DECISION

Books

- *The Almanac of Education Choices: Public and Private Learning Alternatives and Homeschooling*, Jerry Mintz, ed. (Macmillan, 1995)

- *Creating a Cooperative Learning Center: An Idea-Book for Homeschooling Families*, Katharine Houk (Longview, 2000)

- *Creating Learning Communities: Models, Resources, and New Ways of Thinking About Teaching and Learning*, Ron Miller, ed. (Solomon Press, 2000)

- *Deschooling Our Lives*, Matt Hern, ed. (New Society Publishers, 1996)

- *National Directory of Alternative Schools*, National Coalition of Alternative Community Schools (NCACS, 2001)

Other alternative educators / authors to look up on the web or at the library: Stephen Arons, Riane Eisler, John Taylor Gatto, John Holt, Ivan Illich, Herbert Kohl, Alfie Kohn, Jonathan Kozol, Krishnamurti, Mary Leue, Chris Mercogliano, James Moffett, Maria Montessori, A.S. Neill, Parker Palmer, Rudolf Steiner, Lynn Stoddard.

Even if you decide to engage in home education with your children, somewhere along the way, you may wish to consider another alternative. The resources mentioned above will provide many avenues of exploration for you and your children. Happy learning!

CHAPTER ONE

Just The Facts

- Homeschooling has been around for centuries but reemerged as a "new" educational movement in the early 1960s.

- The number of homeschooled students in the United States is difficult to determine. However, estimates range between 700,000 and 1.7 million.

- Homeschooling is growing at a national average rate of 21%, but again actual numbers are difficult to verify.

- Parents choose homeschooling for a number of reasons, including: dissatisfaction with the public school system, a child in trouble, religious principles, safety, family closeness, and overall improved education.

- Many myths surround homeschooling.

- Minorities make up approximately 25% of the total homeschoolers.

- Several other countries homeschool including: Australia, Israel, Japan, Canada, and France.

- There are many famous homeschoolers throughout history.

- Homeschooling's biggest advocates include: John Holt, Dr. Raymond and Dorothy Moore, Charlotte Mason, John Taylor Gatto, and Grace Llewellyn.

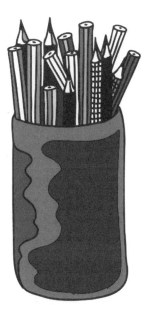

CHAPTER TWO

Is Homeschooling the Right Choice for Our Family?

"It is, in fact, nothing short of a miracle that the modern methods of instruction have not yet entirely strangled the holy curiosity of inquiry."
—*Albert Einstein*

The concepts discussed in this chapter will help you to decide if homeschooling is something that may or may not work in your family. Remember that the core of homeschooling is flexibility, so take this information and bend it to what works for you before you make a decision. Homeschooling is almost always an option if you learn to ignore your self-imposed limitations.

CHAPTER TWO

What qualifications do I need to homeschool?

You will need dedication, confidence, enthusiasm, compassion, caring, and a strong belief in the natural curiosity of your children and their drive to learn. Is that it? Basically. It's normal for you to ask yourself if you need some kind of special teacher training, but the answer from almost all homeschooling parents is a resounding NO. Perhaps John Taylor Gatto, former Teacher of the Year, puts it best when he writes in *The Homeschooling Book of Answers* (Linda Dobson, Prima Publishing, 1998), "Let me reverse that question. Can you teach your children if you *do* have teaching training, did well in it, and believe its precepts of scientific pedagogy, its psychological principles of child development, its habits of the time management, behavioral control, text selection, sequencing, assessment, and guidance? I don't think so."

Teacher training only takes a parent's natural instincts and tries to alter them to fit the public school model of how children should learn. Parents that have had this training often cite it as one of the biggest obstacles they had to get over before they could homeschool their children properly. The key to it all is to remember this: Homeschooling is not about teaching—it's about learning.

THE RIGHT CHOICE FOR OUR FAMILY?

How much time does homeschooling take? (Will I still have time to do other things than homeschool?)

At the risk of sounding like a broken record, this depends on you. There is no right or wrong amount of time to spend on homeschooling. Most of it will depend on how you decide to structure your teaching, how old your children are, and the individual personalities in the mixture. Unschoolers may tell you that they don't spend any amount of time on actual teaching a day, while structured homeschoolers may estimate three to four hours a day on the average.

Why do public school students spend six or more hours a day in the classroom? Much of their time is spent in unnecessary busy work, walking to and from classes, and other activities that don't involve learning. They also are sharing the classroom with 20 to 30 other students, rather than one or two, so they have to wait to ask questions or get help. At home, as with a personal tutor, a child can learn faster and easier. Experts estimate that what takes two weeks to learn in a public school class, takes two to three days in a one-on-one environment.

In homeschooling, you also have great flexibility with your time. If your child is a late or slow riser, why teach in the morning? Wait until the afternoon when he or she is more alert. If you work in the afternoon, homeschool in the evening. Teach on the weekends instead of the weekdays—it is all up to you and your personal schedule.

Keep your expectations of yourself and your children somewhat realistic. Don't try to be super-parent every day and accomplish so much that each night you are exhausted. Take it easy; enjoy the time, instead of feeling rushed to do more than is reasonable.

CHAPTER TWO

Lastly, it is vital that you recognize that children are learning all the time. They do not need to have a workbook in their hands to be learning. They do not need you to be talking to them or explaining something to them to be learning. They can be outside playing in mud puddles and watching earthworms; they can be talking to the grandparents on the phone; they can be figuring out a thousand-piece puzzle. All of these are learning activities. When you realize this, you can see that homeschooling doesn't have to take up all your time at all.

How much does homeschooling cost?

It sounds vague, but the answer is—as much as you want it to. You can go to a teacher's store and spend hundreds of dollars on materials, or you can hit the library and the local garage sales and spend a few dollars. Most parents do a combination, depending on their style of teaching and their budget.

According to recent research, the average private school costs almost $10,000 per year, while public school costs about $7,000, depending on where you live and what activities your children are involved in. Compared to this, homeschooling rarely costs much at all. The average homeschooling family spends less than $1,000 on each child a year, and often much less than that. Much depends, again, on what style of teaching you are following. The more structured, the higher the cost usually. The main things that you will spend money on for homeschooling are:

- Textbooks
- Workbooks
- Packaged curricula
- Field trips
- Magazine and newsletter subscriptions
- Memberships
- Private lessons
- Homeschooling conferences
- Dues
- Equipment
- Computers
- Manipulatives
- Art supplies
- Videos
- Tutors or mentors
- Games

THE RIGHT CHOICE FOR OUR FAMILY?

Again, not all of these things are necessary. Too often, new homeschoolers are tempted into spending hundreds of dollars on materials that end up sitting on a shelf unused because as colorful and wonderful as they looked, they didn't appeal to their children. Restrain yourself from going overboard on materials and wait to see what your kids enjoy—and what they don't.

How can you keep the cost of homeschooling down? Avoid those teacher supply stores that sell the new, expensive stuff and instead check out these possibilities for supplies:

- Libraries
- Garage sales
- Thrift stores
- Homeschooling curricula fairs
- Homeschooling swaps

- Schools
- Used bookstores
- Flea markets
- Other home-schoolers

Ask relatives to pay for your memberships or dues for your birthday; ask for gift certificates to your favorite suppliers for Christmas. Many families make their own manipulatives (hands on materials like fake coins, counting beads, etc.) and write their own lessons to save money. Also remember that by homeschooling, you don't have to pay for school lunches, new wardrobes, book rental fees, or transportation costs to and from school. If you really work on it, you may well find that homeschooling saves you money!

CHAPTER TWO

What about socialization?

Without doubt, this seems to be the main question that homeschoolers hear, and almost all of them shake their heads and wonder why. Of all the concerns that one can come up with regarding homeschooling, the issue of socialization is among the smallest to worry about.

First, ask yourself just what your personal definition of socialization is. What most people mean is, will my children know how to get along with other people if they don't go to school? Will they know how to communicate and be polite? The answer is, unless you lock them in a closet and refuse to have any communication, of course they will. To think otherwise means that you may well have a skewed perspective on the socializing that goes on in public schools and in home schools.

The ability to socialize well with others implies that you know how to talk with people of all ages, types, and backgrounds; how to convey your thoughts clearly; how to have your own individual thoughts and opinions that you can comfortably share with others; and how to listen to the thoughts of others in turn. Most of this does not happen in public schools.

Instead of being surrounded by people of all different makeups, children spend almost all their time with kids their same age. This is certainly unnatural and nothing like the "real world" where adults commonly interact with people younger and older than themselves. Instead of being able to talk freely, children in class are usually told to stay quiet and quit talking. How many teachers have stated, "Quiet! School is not a place to socialize!"

By spending almost all their school hours with children of the same age, kids find themselves becoming peer dependent (I need Susan to tell me if this outfit looks okay; Jamie told me to stop acting so stupid at lunch), competitive (I have to do better than them or I won't make the team), and pressured (everyone else is trying cigarettes; if I don't, they will think I am weird and won't like me anymore). They may find themselves labeled (nerd, queer, jock, etc.) and if they are unfortunate enough not to be among the elite group that is deemed popular, they may suffer from self-image and

THE RIGHT CHOICE FOR OUR FAMILY?

self-esteem problems. Is this the socialization that parents truly want for their children? Is it a positive experience? Or, as John Holt writes in his book, *Teach Your Own*, "If there was no other reason for wanting to keep kids out of school, the social life would be reason enough."

On the other hand, in homeschooling, children are truly out in that "real world" they hear about in school. They run on errands with their parents, go to church, join 4H, Boy Scouts, Girl Scouts, the YM/YWCA, interact with other homeschoolers in support groups, play and talk with neighborhood children, take volunteer jobs, play on a community sports team, visit neighbors and relatives, and enroll in any variety of classes. They meet with people of all ages and types, and even a trip to the grocery store can turn into a social event. "We never go anywhere that my children aren't talking to other people," says one mother. "They talk to people in line, they ask questions of the clerk in the produce department, they chat with the check out girl and help the bagger put away the groceries. Anyone who thinks that homeschooled children aren't social have never seen my kids!"

If you are asking if homeschooled children get the same socialization that public schooled children do, the answer is a resounding no, they certainly do not. And it is for this reason alone that many families choose the homeschooling option in the first place.

What do I do if my child is already in school?

To withdraw your child from school is usually a simple process. Often it will depend on what state you live in. In some of the more lenient states, you do nothing. Other states require specific notifications. For the most part, even if you are in a state that doesn't require notification, it is a good idea to contact your local school so that they know that your child is not truant, and so that your child's teachers can know not to expect him/her back in class. You can send a letter, call them, or stop in and tell them in person. Remember that no one knows your child or what is best for him/her better than you. Occasionally, you will encounter the public school official who smiles and wishes you all the best. Appreciate it.

CHAPTER TWO

One step to take before you contact the school, however, is to talk long and deep with your child and spouse about this decision. Make sure that what you are doing is a unanimous decision. It doesn't look good to withdraw a child from school just to have Dad bring him back the next day, and it certainly doesn't make for harmonious family relationships!

What if both of us work full time?

No matter what kind of homeschooling philosophy you choose to follow, it is going to necessitate some lifestyle changes. While the actual cost of homeschooling can be kept to a minimum, and time requirements are extremely variable, the daily routine of your household is going to be altered. If both you and your partner have full time jobs, this is especially true. Homeschooling is still possible, but it will mean you need to get creative. You won't be the only one out there looking for alternatives either. According to recent studies, more than 90% of working adults say they want to spend more time with their families, and over 60% stated they would give up some of their pay for more time at home.

Here are some possibilities to consider:

- *One of you quits your job*: Don't skip over this option until you give it a few minutes of thought. How much is it costing you to work, for instance? What bills would disappear if you quit? Would it make that much of a difference if you quit? If it does, is there a way to decrease other optional expenses like extra car payments, eating out, etc.? Homeschooling may indeed entail a financial sacrifice for your family, but consider the blessings and treasures that may come out of that sacrifice. Your children will only be young once; this might be the time to focus on being with them and leaving the pursuit of a career for later. How you decide which person is going to quit is up to you. Many parents base this decision on which person is making the best income and has the most optimal benefits.

THE RIGHT CHOICE FOR OUR FAMILY?

- *Consider different working options.* Perhaps you can job share with another parent or alternate schedules with your partner. Some flexible employers will allow you to work your job flextime, meaning you have a different schedule than the traditional nine to five, but you still work a full 40-hour week. Other jobs offer the possibility of a compressed work week, where you still work full time but do it in less than five days. You might also explore whether or not you and your partner can stagger your schedules so one of you is home most of the time.

- *Downsize your job to part time.* See if you can keep the job you have or something similar, but go part time so that you can be home more often, or switch home times with your partner. Check also to see if you are eligible for early or gradual retirement from your company.

- *Develop a home business.* Do you have a skill, talent, or hobby that can be profitable? Perhaps you're great with a hammer and a screwdriver; maybe you have a real knack for telling funny stories. Take a close look at what you are good at and what you enjoy and brainstorm to see if there are ways you can turn it into an income.

CHAPTER TWO

- *Take a telecommuting job.* Experts state that there are over 15 million people with telecommuting jobs today, and they estimate that number to be 50 million by the year 2030. There are several possibilities here, but watch out for scams because they are out there too. Before you make a commitment of time or money, check with your local Better Business Bureau or the Federal Trade Commission to see what they have to say about the company/job. Some of the more known and trusted telecommuting businesses include: medical or legal transcriptionist, telemarketing, website designer, or in-home sales like Avon, Tupperware, Pampered Chef, Discovery Toys, Usborne Books, or World Book.

Remember that homeschooling can also be done on the days and times that you prefer, so you can often arrange it around most job schedules. Homeschooling takes a commitment from parents that entails more time than anything else. Working parents can do it if they remain flexible and open to a myriad of working alternatives.

THE RIGHT CHOICE FOR OUR FAMILY?

Can I homeschool some of my children and have others in public school?

Yes, you can. However, it can create complications. Your children may resent that you are handling their education in different manners (especially if they are teenagers who seem to be able to feel resentful if you say hello in the wrong tone of voice!) Give a lot of thought to why you have chosen these different options for your children. If you chose homeschooling for its flexibility and freedom, why wouldn't you want that for each child? Don't be surprised if the child who is in public school starts to envy their siblings who aren't getting up, rushing for the bus, and facing pop quizzes each day. If you choose this option, you will need to keep an open line of communication between you and your children, as well as help them to keep one between each other. Handle conflicts as they come up, and be prepared for either one to want to try out what the other is doing.

Can my child go to homeschool part time and public school part time too?

Yes, most public school systems will allow your homeschooled child to attend part time. This may be called shared schooling, independent study, distance learning, or dual enrollment. Check out the "climate" of your local school system; some are quite open to the homeschooling world and others are not. Ask at your support group for recommendations.

Before you make this decision, however, take a careful look at why you want them to go to public school part time. Perhaps they just want to see what public school is like. In this case, it might be better to let them shadow a friend or visit classrooms for a few days before making any kind of commitment. Sometimes school can look exciting, fun, and alluring to a homeschooler, but once they see the reality of hall passes, limited bathroom trips, peer pressure, and busy-work, they may quickly change their minds.

CHAPTER TWO

You might be considering this option because schools can offer some opportunities that are otherwise hard to come by, such as choir, orchestra, drama, sports, or driver's education. Keep in mind that almost all of these opportunities can be found elsewhere also. Look into your community for local organizations that would allow your child to explore these same options without having to become involved with school. Community choirs, sports teams, theatres, and orchestras are available in most mid- to large-sized cities, so ask around. If you can't find one, consider starting your own.

As for driver's education, there are a number of options from online and correspondence courses, hiring a private company, or just teaching your children yourselves. In some states, this may mean they have to wait longer to get their driver's licenses, but that is not necessarily a bad thing. Some insurance companies offer discounts for kids who have taken driver's education and gotten a good grade; check with yours to see if that still applies to homeschoolers.

Letting your homeschooler go to public school is an option that is open to you but shouldn't be entered into lightly. It can interrupt and complicate the flow of your homeschooling routine, and it can involve your child in situations and behaviors that you have tried to avoid by homeschooling in the first place. It can undermine your confidence as he/she becomes involved in this different perspective on education—so think about it, talk about it with other homeschooling parents and with your children before you make any kind of commitment.

THE RIGHT CHOICE FOR OUR FAMILY?

What if my child is doing well in public school?

Just because some children are successful in public school doesn't mean that it is a good or positive experience for them. There is, of course, the concept of 'if it ain't broke, don't fix it.' However, good grades shouldn't be the only standard by which you measure if your children are doing well in school. While they have obviously learned to adapt to the inherent stresses and strains of traditional education, they can still be struggling in some areas. Perhaps they get straight As, but have few friends; perhaps they are excelling in sports, but feel bored in class.

If you are considering homeschooling any of your children, please consider homeschooling all of your children. At the very least, offer each one the opportunity to try it. While children may seem completely satisfied in school, they may be even happier and more successful at home.

What if I am a single parent?

You can still homeschool, but like the couple that work full time, it may mean some lifestyle changes or flexibility. The primary complication for you will be what to do with your children when you are at work. How challenging this is depends greatly on their age and maturity. Older children can be left at home to take care of themselves and do independent work, while younger children obviously cannot. You might check to see if you can bring them to work with you (nice—but rare); otherwise you will need to arrange some kind of childcare. Choices here include family, friends, and neighbors, as well as other homeschooling families. You might think about bartering childcare services or, if you aren't the babysitter type, barter a service that you could do in return. In other words, they watch your kids daily and you fix their car, clean their house, do their taxes, etc.

A support group may be especially essential for you. It can be your link to good sources of childcare, including a "mother's helper" type teen who loves kids and could use some extra income. Without a partner to discuss ideas, concerns, and questions, the support group becomes even more important.

CHAPTER TWO

Homeschooling can be a real issue in a divorce situation. If one spouse is opposed to it and decides to make it a problem that reflects custody rights and/or child support, you may well have a real battle on your hands. If this is true for you and it is heading to the court's arena, experts recommend that you make sure you are complying with all the homeschooling laws in your state and that you provide high quality information about homeschooling's benefits to your attorney so that he/she is able to go to battle for you armed with accurate material.

What are BAD reasons for homeschooling?

Homeschoolers almost always decide to homeschool because they want the best possible education for their children. However, now and then, a family comes along that is home educating for harmful or negative reasons. If you are considering this option for any of the following reasons, stop and rethink your decision.

- Homeschooling as a punishment for a child who has angered you.

- Homeschooling so that your children can work free for you all day.

- Homeschooling to get back at the school for something they did.

- Homeschooling to upset a spouse or ex-spouse.

- Homeschooling to keep your child completely shut off from the world.

THE RIGHT CHOICE FOR OUR FAMILY?

Won't the kids and I get sick of each other?

Without a doubt, one requirement of successful homeschooling is that you like spending time with your children. If you can't wait for them to get on the bus in the morning and dread the end of the school day when they return, homeschooling probably isn't the best option for you. On the other hand, if you love the look on their faces when they find out something new or figure out how to do something; if their questions amaze and delight you; if you enjoy finding out how their minds work and what is most important to them; then you are an excellent homeschooling candidate.

If you're worried that homeschooling means you will never, ever get away from your children, don't. Parents and children alike need breaks from each other occasionally, and it's not difficult to find those breaks when homeschooling.

Here are some examples of when you will get your much-needed space:

- Time the children spend with your partner/spouse.

- Errand running.

- Naps—yours or theirs.

- When they are with their friends.

- When they are off learning something on their own.

- Long, luxurious baths—yours or theirs.

CHAPTER TWO

If you find yourself wishing the kids would all go away, make time for yourself one way or another so that you can relax and come back refreshed. Take a drive, read a book, meet a friend—do something that is just for you.

Bear in mind also that if your child has been in public school, he/she may undergo some real transformation after they have been home for a while. You may not enjoy the company of your children as they are behaving now; but much of the anger, frustration, and fatigue you are seeing in them because of school is likely to disappear at home. You may indeed rediscover what delightful and enjoyable creatures they really are.

Do moms do all the teaching or do dads have a role in this too?

The honest truth is that moms do the majority of the homeschooling simply because they are at home, on the average, for more hours than fathers. This is even truer in families that choose the more structured or traditional way of schooling. However, this doesn't mean that dad doesn't have a role in the process. On the contrary, dads are often a very integral factor in whether homeschooling works for a family or not.

Most often, dad's major role is as *support person*. Besides the financial support that he brings to the family, he can be a major support for his wife as she homeschools. He can listen to her concerns, help her make decisions, and figure out what directions to go and not go. He can support her in other ways, also, like helping with the household cleaning and cooking so that her time is freer to spend with the kids. In addition to this, he can be a support to his children, listening to what they've learned, looking at their latest masterpieces, and sharing his time and attention.

THE RIGHT CHOICE FOR OUR FAMILY?

Along with this, there are a number of other ways dad can help. Here are a few ways dads can be a part of the whole picture:

- Leading/teaching hands-on experiments (science, math, etc.).

- Doing household chores (gardening, yard work, mechanical work, etc.).

- Reading aloud.

- Playing games.

- Taking on field trips.

- Sharing hobbies, skills, and personal interests with the kids.

- Transporting to and from classes and activities.

- Discussing what his kids are learning with them, and then contributing new ideas, thoughts, and perspectives on the subject.

- Taking children to work with him to show them what he does.

Many dads may think they are too busy to do much of this, but dads who want to be involved make the time, one way or another. Another influence on what role fathers play in homeschooling is the slowly growing number of stay-at-home dads across the country. According to the latest research, there are about two million fathers staying at home with their kids while mom goes to work; approximately eight percent of all dads! For these men, their role in homeschooling will be far higher as they find themselves with the time and opportunity to do what they want.

CHAPTER TWO

In the Trenches

On Being a Homeschooling Dad
~ various fathers

The first and foremost part of successful homeschooling is a positive attitude. Teaching is something that everybody does. Understanding the subject is crucial, but being able to reduce complicated factual relationships to the level of the student is the essence of teaching. Because parents are potentially capable of understanding their children like no one else on the planet, their ability to teach can easily surpass anything found in a public school.

Realize that your perspective is unique, and therefore is necessarily different, than a mother's. This means that when you cover the same subject, your child has an entirely different teacher: a kind of two for the price of one package. Blending these two perspectives makes for a truly superior academic approach. You will have areas of expertise, and you need to stand ready to add it when your wife's level of understanding tapers off.

Don't be intimidated by professionals who suggest that a child's learning progresses at a steady rate. Understanding and learning comes in leaps, jumps, hops, steps, and the occasional stumble and fall. The child's effort to learn is much more important than actual measured achievement. This is true throughout a human's entire life.

A father forms the primary emotional cushion for the mother who may sometimes feel as if the entire educational process is her personal sentence for crimes not understood. He is there when she feels that if the multiplication tables, or the recognition of nouns, is not accomplished this day at this hour, her child will undoubtedly fail at life, causing her to be ridiculed on national television. Intimate and personal communication between you and your wife is imperative—as are strategically planned meals out, and a backrub now and then. Homeschooling can be a hard row to hoe, but the rewards are many and so significant.

—*Gary, father of four, Indiana*

THE RIGHT CHOICE FOR OUR FAMILY?

My wife and I had our child late in life so we had the advantage (as well as the obvious disadvantages) of experience that young parents don't have. I also tend to research my opinions thoroughly when a big decision is coming up. The educational choices one makes for one's child is certainly among the most important decisions there are.

As soon as we knew our boy was on the way, I started reading: the history of homeschooling, policy papers and books by people like John Holt, John Taylor Gatto, Andrew Coulson, Alfie Cohn, Myron Leiberman, and many others. I read papers on the Internet from the Cato Institute, Separation of School and State Alliance, and Andrew Coulson's site. After all this reading, it was clear that public education was a broken institution and that it was not going to be fixed by any reform.

This jived with my own personal experience. My schooling was a mix of parochial and public schools 40 years ago; even at that time, it was clear public schools were substandard. Things have only gotten worse since then; the trends are obvious to anyone who has been watching for a while. For these and other reasons, public schools were never seriously an option for my wife and I. (I more often express this as "No way in Hell!")

Even though both of us have some confidence in parochial schools from our own schooling, all of my reading convinced me that homeschooling was still clearly superior. The results of testing (whatever useful information can be had from it) strongly confirm this. Since we want the best for our child, this is the way we must go.

Fortunately, the homeschooling community is so interesting and positive in outlook that it has turned out to be a pleasant choice as well. Homeschooling gives our family a lot more freedom than any other option provides—and our boy loves it! We are happy and we won't look back.

—Paul, father of one, Oregon

CHAPTER TWO

My wife and I have four children, and they have always been homeschooled. I have to say that the experience has taught me far more lessons than I could have ever imagined.

Lesson #1: Homeschooling allows me to be with my children far more than I would ever have been if they were in public school. I believe that giving my kids this time and attention will, at some level, help them to recognize that they are worthwhile people. Also, by being with them and listening to their responses and reactions, I learn more about their thoughts, concerns, desires, and how they each process their world and its information.

Lesson #2: I am currently a househusband and I am learning more about running a house and the time it takes. I have a new understanding of how homeschooling can sometimes take the time that might have been spent on chores. Since I started staying at home, I have wondered what our culture thinks of men like myself at home while their wives earn the family income. The women I have spoken to are usually positive; the men I'm not so sure about.

I am slowly learning to take care of things like the laundry, meals, shopping, and getting the kids to Girl Scouts, Boy Scouts, chess club, field trips, etc. Yet I am still aware that despite this role reversal, my wife is still doing more housework than I was when I was the primary income earner, and she was home with the kids.

Lesson #3: I am learning about myself through my children. I often see and hear myself within their childlike, innocent questions. As I struggle with them on something, I become more aware of my own ability—or lack of it—to be patient, or my own habits and irritations. I flashback to the feeling of being in school and the frustrations it brought to me, and once again, I realize how much of what I had to learn in school was pretty damn stupid. For instance, why in the world should anyone learn to diagram sentences? Isn't it better if they just learn how to write, talk, and communicate? Why do they need to know the parts are called nouns and verbs if they're already using them daily—on a brilliant level?

Lesson #4: Homeschooling has shown me that there comes a time where you, as the parent, have to know when to stop. When I am working with my 11-year-old daughter, for example, and I see the interest fade away, I often have to battle my own inner tapes on what to do next. Should I just let it go and start again later? This conflicts with the tapes in my head that tell me we should just finish what we started. However, I am coming to recognize that when the light goes out of my children's faces, it's time to go and do something else, like go shoot some hoops, walk the dog, mow the lawn, or weed the garden. Those are only other possibilities for learning, of course.

Lesson #5: I have come to recognize, through the time I spend with each child, that they each have tremendous differences. My five-year-old son, for example, shows great interest in reading and math, while his eight-year-old brother shows very little. His inter-

THE RIGHT CHOICE FOR OUR FAMILY?

est is in the physical world, not the abstract. He wants to punch, kick, climb, jump, and put things together, and then tear them apart again. Our two daughters are simply oil and water; they certainly learn in different manners, style, and pace.

Lesson #6: One of the most surprising lessons that I have had is that children are learning all the time, not just when you think they are. My eight-year-old son listens to my wife read each night and to all appearances, he doesn't hear a word she says. He is coloring, building with Legos, moving his toys around. However, she and I have both been amazed to find out that he absorbs as much, if not more, than the others who are sitting still. His learning obviously is tied into motion itself. In school, could this mean ADD/ADHD . . .? At home, it's just his way of learning.

Lesson #7: Relatives can certainly give you their opinions of homeschooling when they really know nothing about it. Are they truly concerned about the education and well being of our children or are they angry because they had to go to school? Maybe they are just thinking that since we chose to homeschool, we are indirectly stating that they made the wrong decision with their children for putting them in public school? Perhaps the negativity comes from their own secret wish that they too had been homeschooled.

Lesson #8: I have come to wonder if perhaps the process of having and raising children is actually a natural part of our own personal maturation. I know it has been a large part of mine. If we, as a society, abdicate a large part of raising children to others, don't we also stand a chance of stunting ourselves as adults?

Lesson #9: When my children are all grown up and have moved away, I am sure that I will wish that I could have them back for a little while. Without a doubt, I know that I will be glad that they spent much of their days at home with me and my wife, rather than sitting in school, away from us.

Lesson #10: I have come to believe that one of the greatest ways to protect a child for the future is through homeschooling. I know that there is little research available on how homeschoolers fare in society (emotional problems, violent crime, drug and alcohol abuse, divorce, etc.), but I have to wonder, if it was done, what it would show.

Lesson #11: I have learned that the public school system teaches all of us that we cannot trust or have faith in ourselves and our children to have the internal, inborn wisdom to make the right choices or to learn what is important on our own. They are wrong.

Lesson #12: Lastly, as I spend time talking and being with my children, I am often completely amazed at the knowledge they have that comes from I do not know where!

—Joseph, father of four, Oregon

CHAPTER TWO

One American stereotype of fatherhood assumes that the father is remote from his children and distanced from their day-to-day lives because he is away at work. He is expected to impart lessons in morality and character building by sober example, somber lectures, and perhaps punishments. He might teach his children physical skills through sports, hunting, fishing, or other outdoor activities. There might be a gesture towards the transmission of a trade or craft tradition such as woodworking or auto mechanics. "Book learning" is left to mothers and teachers (often other women) in schools and religious institutions.

This stereotype has been under attack from many directions for a while. Some popular history speculates that the "remote father" is only as old as the Industrial Revolution when paid work moved from home and field to office and factory. Whatever its origin, I have always found this view of fatherhood limiting, and I am on the side of those trying to change it.

As a homeschooling parent, I try to lead a life of engagement with my children not confined to the limits of this stereotype. We talk about astronomy as well as baseball. We work on both carpentry and fine arts. We study American history as well as animal tracks. There are lectures aplenty, but I hope there is also mutual problem solving and respect for debate. There are also failures. I hope my children will see me as a human being with a variety of passions, challenges, and responsibilities rather than a dictator who can only display his humanity on a camping trip.

Does one need to homeschool to attempt to be this kind of father? I don't believe so. Yet if my children were in school every day, it might be tempting to surrender this challenging engagement to paid professionals. Homeschooling gives me the opportunity to be a teacher as well as a breadwinner, an enthusiast as well as an authoritarian, and a fellow human being to my children as well as a father.

—*Will, father of two, Oregon*

THE RIGHT CHOICE FOR OUR FAMILY?

In the Trenches

Socialization—Our Biggest Gripe with Homeschooling
~ John Andersen

Yes, socialization has been a huge problem for our children, but with experience, we have learned to bring it largely under control.

You see, we live in Portland, Oregon. Before we moved here, we suspected it was a good place to homeschool. Talk about an understatement! Everywhere we go, we run into homeschoolers. We have associations with dozens of homeschooling families. Without exception, they are all involved in a variety of activities. There are homeschooling roller skating parties, archery classes, a homeschooling basketball group, access to high school band, community college courses, co-op language classes, volunteer opportunities, daytime art classes, music classes, singing groups, theatre productions, science labs at a local museum, organized field trips daily, Girl and Boy Scouts—the list goes on and on.

And that is the core of our children's socialization problem: too many activities and too little time.

Homeschoolers, without the constraints of a six hour a day school schedule, are extremely vulnerable to falling into the trap of too many outside activities and too much social interaction. This can be dangerous, especially if we hope to teach our children to appreciate and enjoy the quiet, reflective life.

So, my wife Mandy and I are learning to apply the brakes, to slow things down a bit. One step we've taken is to develop a weekly schedule of sorts. We don't hold hard and fast to it, but rather use it as a guide. It looks something like this:

Monday: At home academically-oriented day; also clean the house day. Our children usually spend the late afternoon and early evening outside playing with the neighborhood children.

Tuesday: Co-op learning with other homeschoolers, also some academics and afternoon outside play with neighborhood children.

Wednesday: Mandy and children volunteer at the library. At the moment, they shelve books, label items, and help with other projects. We try to do some academics as well and, of course, there is time for afternoon play outside with neighborhood children.

Thursday: Slow day (intentionally); sometimes co-op classes, evening achievement group for our daughter, and soon, Cub Scouts for our son.

Friday: Family outing day; this can be a volunteer project which we do as a family or going to the beach, visiting historic sites, the zoo, public gardens, museums, etc.

CHAPTER TWO

This general plan helps us to pace ourselves throughout the week and provides a "first line defense" against the constant barrage of social activities. It gives us a sensible framework and enables us to enjoy unhurried time together on a daily basis.

So, if you're thinking about homeschooling and you live in a city with tons of homeschoolers or lots of interesting things to do, you will definitely need to come up with a strategy to keep the socialization problem under control!

In the Trenches

Homeschooling and the Single Parent

~ Leanne Coffman

Being a single parent for the past three years has been a process of adaptation for me in many ways, especially with homeschooling. The demand on time and the individual attention both to academics and personality, can be somewhat overwhelming even in a two-parent household, but for a single parent like myself, the process can seem truly daunting. I have found that flexibility and a less structured environment are vital to success. As a mother of three homeschooled children, I struggled initially with the pressure of being the sole breadwinner as well as with the responsibility for the upkeep of a home, the maintenance on the vehicle, the grocery shopping, the cooking, and the myriad other things that required my attention, in addition to the education of my children. At first, my thought was to succumb to the pleas of so many well meaning family members and friends who implored me to place them in public school. However, one of the greatest joys in my life has always been to teach my kids, to watch their eyes light up as they discovered the love of reading, or mastered some concept that they previously couldn't grasp. Additionally, my children had undergone much transition in their lives through our divorce, and I felt that they needed as much security and consistency as possible. One of the best ways that I felt I could provide that was to continue to homeschool.

A typical day though, was now less than typical, due to errands, doctor's visits, my career, and my own continuing college education. I began reevaluating what my goals were with each child and what their specific, individual needs were. Prior to my divorce, I was extremely structured, using a grade-based system, and a certain amount of time per day deemed as "school time." As I reflected on what I was trying to achieve with my children and the lack of a consistent block of time for schooling purposes, I began to realize that education need not be appropriated to set periods of the day. Learning could instead be incorporated into our lives throughout the day. So using this approach, I began what I call "learning-as-we-go-lifestyle teaching." When we go to the grocery store, my children mentally add up the purchases, and we play estimating games to see who can come the closest to the actual price. When my early bird child comes to

THE RIGHT CHOICE FOR OUR FAMILY?

snuggle with me in the morning, often we spend our "cuddle time" reading a book. My older child and her sister take turns quizzing each other with math flash cards; the eleven-year-old learns her multiplication and division and the younger masters addition and subtraction. This is a good review for previously mastered concepts with the older child, and somewhat paves the way for the younger one to grasp math concepts that she hasn't technically learned yet. The baby of the family, currently age six, picks up on this and is frequently part of the action, surprising us with her unexpected ability to know the correct answer to math facts that many six-year-olds do not.

In finding an art teacher for my children, I was able to schedule some much-needed time for myself. Often I use this hour of free time to have lunch with a friend or to catch up on a project that I need quiet time for. When we take trips, (the most recent, a camping trip out West), we use the time to learn about nature and geology and American history. My children came home from vacation with priceless journals replete with drawings and stories of much learning and family times. Doctor's visits, errands, and car time find us using this approach as we cart our notebooks and flash cards and reading material with us. Audiotapes of famous people, great Americans, and sing along states and capitals play in our vehicle as we scurry from place to place. Instead of using textbooks for reading, as I previously had, I began to incorporate the whole book approach. Now my older child and I take turns reading quality literature aloud to the other two. Spelling and vocabulary words come from our reading. Handwriting has taken on the format of writing letters to family and friends that we often, in our structured lifestyle, neglected. My own love of art and music has been passed on to the children as we use some of our family time to explore art museums or listen to different types of music as we do our housework. My eleven-year-old shares my passion for classical music and opera, while my nine-year-old enjoys blues. Cooking together has provided lessons in math, economics, and the ever-important ability to follow directions. The older girls cook lunch most days, sometimes surprising me with their creations (although we have had a few inedible episodes!) Care of pets and the process of doing their own laundry has taught all of my kids valuable lessons in responsibility and has freed me up from tasks that used to require my attention.

While I still feel the demands from time to time of single parenthood, using the approach of homeschooling as a lifestyle and being flexible has given me back the joy of home teaching. When I look at my children, I feel good that the quality of their education has not suffered and perhaps has even been enhanced throughout this experience. The greatest affirmation of this came to me recently when my nine-year-old wrote a story about things that she was thankful for. The heading on the story was titled, "My Mommy and My Teacher."

CHAPTER TWO

In the Trenches

Homeschooling and the Single Parent ~
The Way That It's Done—or Not
~ Cindy Nichols

I never started out to homeschool my son. As a single parent, it's hard enough just getting through the day without adding the task of educating my child to the list. So, naturally, when my son Mike was five-years-old, he started public school like all the other kids we knew. It didn't seem to be a good fit, but we both tried as hard as we could to manage the situation. As far as I was aware, there was no choice in the matter: single moms go to work and children go to school. That's the way it is done.

The school situation got more and more miserable. Mike was acting up most afternoons, and I was constantly getting calls from the school. No one was happy. Mike moved on to first grade with a veteran teacher, and it soon became apparent that this teacher bullied the kids who would not tow the line and, of course, my son was one of those kids.

After observing Mike in class, I suggested during a conference that perhaps he was bored and needed something more interesting to do or maybe at least something more hands-on. The principal got huffy and informed me that NO child in her school of 650 kids was EVER bored! It only got worse from there.

Around that time I discovered that Mike was sensitive to certain foods, often the very ones that I was packing in his sack lunches. The foods were apparently causing some behavior issues for him, so I changed his diet. We also moved to another school district. Mike was so stressed from the situation at his first school, that he spent the last few months of what should have been his first grade year back in kindergarten. He was regressing socially and emotionally. At this school, he was blessed with a kind and understanding teacher, and I figured we had the whole thing worked out. Was I ever wrong!

When the next school year rolled around, Mike was back in first grade and the situation began to deteriorate again. His first report card wasn't too awful, so I held out hope that everything would work out. After all, single moms go to work and children go to school. That's the way it is done.

THE RIGHT CHOICE FOR OUR FAMILY?

The following report card was much worse, and I knew that I had to do something or risk losing my son to the crush of the system. I began to check around and discovered that it was possible to homeschool Mike even though I was a working mom. I held a major family conference, which consisted of my son, my mother (who was living with us at the time), and myself, and we discussed "The Plan." We were all in agreement that things could be worked out if we would all pull together, and so we began on our adventure.

It has not been easy, but it has been well worth it. A lot of my time and energy have been spent on building up Mike's self image. Even with all of my efforts, it took him about two years to get over feeling dumb and inadequate, which was how being in school had affected him. He refused to believe me when I told him his IQ testing showed him in the top two percent of children nationwide. He had no interest in reading, writing, or math, because his teachers had told him he was no good at it. He didn't even want to try.

I had been trying to figure out how to choose a curriculum, but finally decided that what Mike needed was a much more relaxed approach. That was a wise decision; we have had so much success with it that it is what we continue to use today. Mike still hates to do worksheets or any kind of written assignments, but at age 10, he is doing 6th and 7th grade work.

Mike and I are both very fortunate that we live next door to my mother. During the day while I am working, Mike stays with her. At first, I wanted him to do his schoolwork at her house, but that turned into a battle for both of them, so I looked for other options. He still stays with my mom during the day, but instead of trying to get him to do any particular assignments, we use the computer. There are dozens of excellent computer programs out there that cover subjects by grade level or by subject matter. Instead of setting up a big battle over what he should do while I am gone to work, I give him a choice of three or four online programs he may choose from and a specific length of time he should work (usually about an hour). Mike also watches a certain amount of educational television such as those found on "Discovery" or "Animal Planet," and he spends a lot of time creating things. My refrigerator is covered with artwork that has tiny doors that open and close, or mysterious plants, or cutaway views of gemstones and volcanoes. It is wonderful.

CHAPTER TWO

I do get a fair amount of well-meaning advice from a variety of sources including friends whose children attend conventional public schools. Lack of socialization is a familiar lament, but I watch my son and I can see that he is comfortable with all age groups. As far as I can tell, he seems more relaxed in groups of people than the other children his age. In fact, the only real social concern I have for him is the lack of a male/father figure in the family. We live in a very remote area and it is difficult to find any activities that include the participation of men. I want Mike to have some positive male role models in his life. My solution has been to seek out friends and neighbors who are willing to spend some time with Mike and show him what we call "guy stuff." This gives Mike a chance to interact with some caring adult males.

I know other single parents are not as lucky as I am because they do not have another caring adult willing to watch their children all day. I've asked others how they do it, and have heard an amazing variety of answers. Some have gotten together with other homeschooling parents and formed day care co-ops, some hire child care help, and others put their children in public school during the day, then homeschool at nights and on the weekends in order to provide a quality education for their children. No matter the method, all of us agree that it is up to us to provide the high quality educational experience that our children deserve, and to make sure that experience is geared to the needs of each individual child.

The bottom line is that I cannot think of anything that Mike needs from a public school that I can't provide for him at home just as well or better. I suppose it would be easier to send him off for a big chunk of every weekday, but would it really help him? I don't think so, and in the end, isn't that what this is all about?

THE RIGHT CHOICE FOR OUR FAMILY?

"We are students of words; we are shut up in schools and colleges and recitation-rooms for 10 or 15 years and come out at last with a bag of wind, a memory of words and do not know a thing."
—*Ralph Waldo Emerson*

From the Experts

School through Another Lens:
Some Implications of Homeschooling
~ Patrick Farenga, Holt Associates

When we discuss how to improve education, it is so often a discussion that takes place within the confines of our ideas about conventional schooling: school is simply a vehicle in need of a souped-up engine (higher standards), a more comfortable interior (better facilities), or better instructors and testing instruments. Many parents who home school or send their children to private school feel that they have purchased or built better cars for their children's education. However there are some, such as myself, who feel the automobile is going the way of the horse and buggy and that education is more than a race towards a degree that not everyone can win. By viewing the technology and rationale for schooling as out-dated rather than in need of an update, we can see new types of vehicles to use or create and new paths to follow to help our children learn and grow.

For instance, if you judge education by counting degrees granted by education institutions, America is more educated than ever—more people hold college degrees in the U.S. now than at any point in American history. Yet we are seeing many college graduates *not* send their children to school for their education. A study by the U.S. Dept. of Education, *Homeschooling in the United States: 1999*, notes that twenty-five percent of homeschool parents attained a bachelor's degree compared to sixteen percent of non-homeschoolers; 22% of homeschooled parents have graduate/professional school degrees compared to 16% of non-homeschooled parents. Why are increas-

CHAPTER TWO

ing numbers of people who have spent most of their youth in school, and gone on to higher education, not sending their children to school?

Researchers study the reasons why parents homeschool—quality of education, religion, and poor learning environment in school are often cited—but to my knowledge, no one has explored exactly why so many college graduates homeschool their children. Perhaps it is for the same reason my wife and I decided to homeschool: we did not want our children to waste their time in the same empty rituals of education that we did. Passing tests only to forget the subject matter

Patrick Farenga worked closely with **John Holt** for four years, until Holt's death in 1985. He is the President of Holt Associates Inc. and was the Publisher of **Growing Without Schooling** magazine (GWS) from 1985 until it stopped publishing in Nov. 2001. GWS was the nation's first periodical about homeschooling, started by Holt in 1977.

Farenga and his wife homeschool three girls, ages 15, 12, and 9. He has written more than thirty articles and book chapters for publications as diverse as **Mothering** magazine, **Paths of Learning** magazine, **Home Education Magazine**, **The Bulletin of Science, Technology, and Society**, and **The Encyclopedia of School Administration**. He has published and edited several popular books about homeschooling including his own book, **The Beginner's Guide to Homeschooling**.

Farenga has appeared on The Today Show, The Voice of America, NPR's The Merrow Report, and CNN's Parenting Today. Farenga has been quoted as an expert on homeschooling many times in the national press, and his company, Holt Associates and its magazine are also mentioned frequently in media stories about homeschooling. Farenga has addressed audiences about homeschooling throughout the United States as well as Canada, England, and Italy.

Farenga now works as a writer and education consultant. He is currently at work on **Teach Your Own; The John Holt Guide to Home Schooling** (Perseus Books, due out in Fall 2002).

when the grades were given; spending years in foreign language instruction and passing the courses yet being unable to have even a rudimentary conversation in the language outside of the classroom; struggling to learn advanced math skills that were seldom used outside of class; doing lab experiments that were more rote exercises than explorations of scientific inquiry. Time and

THE RIGHT CHOICE FOR OUR FAMILY?

youth cannot be regained, and therefore, perhaps the real crisis in education may be one of disillusionment among graduates rather than poor performance among current students.

One implication of the increase in homeschooling among college graduates is that the conventional K - 12 curricula are not considered by them to be vital to college admission or to finding work worth doing. The entire sequence of elementary, middle, and high school is turned on its head or simply sidestepped by many homeschoolers. For instance, many high school age homeschoolers I know take community college courses instead of high school courses. When I was in high school, community college was considered a next level, not a substitute for high school classes. Whether homeschoolers use the classical Trivium or Trivial Pursuit, correspondence school or home-made curricula to help their children learn, the point is that a wide variety of methods and schedules are used successfully by homeschooling families. By examining how and why homeschoolers can do things differently than schools, we can see new directions for school and our general social good.

Homeschoolers will no doubt argue with some of what follows, probably on grounds of politics, individual freedom, or ideology. But my point is, regardless of these concerns, the actions I describe in this essay are nonetheless happening and we should be exploring them rather than ignoring them. What I describe are not theoretical constructs, but actual occurrences that we can duplicate, expand, adapt, or simply catch the spirit of.

CHAPTER TWO

Smaller Class Sizes

The costs of training additional teachers, building new classrooms, and other expenses involved in reducing class size the way school officials want it done are immense. But there is an inexpensive baby-step that schools could take in this direction that would take very little effort on their part: encourage parents who wish to homeschool to do so. Parents help reduce public and private school class size when they decide to homeschool full-time, and there are probably other parents willing to teach their own kids just a few hours a week in certain subjects, thereby freeing the classroom teacher to work more intensively with those students who need him or her most.

Not everyone can or wants to homeschool, so there need not be worries that if schools openly view homeschooling as a complement to their efforts, rather than a threat, there will be a mass exodus from schools. There were roughly fifty million students, ages 5-17, in America in 1999; of those 850,000 were estimated to be homeschooled. This is just 1.7% of the school age population, but what other program, at so little cost, achieves this same reduction in class size so easily, and with the willing cooperation of the families involved? Rather than fighting homeschoolers and parents seeking more one-on-one attention for their children, schools should be working with both groups as one small, cost-effective step towards reducing class-size in America.

THE RIGHT CHOICE FOR OUR FAMILY?

Computers and Distance Learning

One reason why more people are homeschooling today is because more materials and opportunities are available for learning at home than ever before. Curricula, support, mentoring, courses, and texts are now as available at your average homeschooling conference as they are at a professional teacher's conference. But the Internet has added a new dimension to this, and homeschoolers have taken to it much better than schools have. Homeschooling families are among the most Internet-savvy families today, and snail-mail correspondence programs that flourished in the eighties and early nineties have readily morphed into on-line ventures. Further, families that design their own curriculum find the Internet a valuable and inexpensive research tool; for instance, there is a book entitled *Homeschool Your Child for Free* that describes over 1,200 Internet resources for homeschoolers.

I have serious reservations about dedicating your homeschooling to learning via computer, but the point I want to make is that if you want your children to learn about computers and technology, then school isn't the best place for them. Dr. Larry Cuban, author of *Oversold and Underused: Computers in the Classroom*, notes that "despite nearly $8 billion dollars spent annually on school technologies, the results get a failing grade… And when application is examined this powerful technology ends up being used in classrooms most often for word processing and low-end functions that maintain rather than alter teaching practices. The promise of a technological revolution in our schools remains largely unfulfilled."

The free form, non-linear aspects of on-line searches and communications, and the very detailed role-playing and strategy games, are particularly interesting to many of the homeschooled children I talk to who use computers as part of their schooling. I think schools and computer visionaries would be wise to study how and why computers are used in home schools instead of spending more time and money seeking ways to push conventional school content and methods over the phone lines.

CHAPTER TWO

On-line tutorials, email critiques of writing, serious research, social interactions, and the development of new teaching strategies because of the computer are flourishing in the homeschool arena. Further, this is happening among families of modest means. Homeschooling is not primarily taking place among wealthy families who can afford the best computers and expensive on-line services; the 1999 Federal study of homeschooling showed that the average household income of homeschoolers was no different than non-homeschoolers.

Other Places for Kids to Be

Sometimes neither school nor homeschool is the right place for a child to be, but where else can they go, who else can they be with, during school hours? John Holt wrote a lot about this topic, particularly in his book *Instead of Education: Ways to Help People Do Things Better*. Another visionary in the education without schools movement is Don Glines, director of Educational Futures Projects. Glines was an advisor for a lifelong learning system without schools or schooling for the proposed Minnesota Experimental City, a project that almost took flight in the seventies. There are a few alternative programs and schools that attempt to make the world more accessible for children during school hours, but homeschooling puts even more flesh to the bones of these ideas today, such as:

- *Studying or playing in other people's homes.* Homeschooling cooperatives continue to flourish as more people homeschool and pool resources.

- *Working alongside adults and professionals in safe environments.* Volunteerism, internships, apprenticeships, and helping out in family businesses are among the many ways homeschoolers create knowledge, friends, and opportunities outside of the home. Many children learn skills better in real-life situations than they do in abstract class situations. For instance, some children learn math better

THE RIGHT CHOICE FOR OUR FAMILY?

by making change at a yard sale or by building a bookcase than by doing problems in a textbook about making change or building a bookcase. Homeschoolers, and a few schools, have successfully had children of all ages spend school hours in volunteer or apprentice work situations in lieu of school attendance, not just as an after-school enrichment program.

- *Martial arts, language, cooking, hands-on science, computer, and other types of specialized schools* can be open during school hours if children were allowed to be there in lieu of public school. Homeschooling is giving many of these places new clientele during school hours, providing them with new revenue streams. Museums in Boston have set up courses and activities just for homeschoolers during times they aren't serving school groups.

- *Family resource centers.* Some are for-profit and are aimed at serving the homeschooling population during school hours, others serve any and all as afterschool programs.

- *Safe haven and financial security.* There is a need for safe places where children can go for shelter from the barrage of mass culture they encounter each day, as well as from abusive home or school situations. Areas set-aside for peaceful reflection by children during school hours, and access to people, funding, and resources to help individual children and their families during school hours could benefit not only the personal lives of children, but their academic lives as well. A recent study by the Harvard Graduate School of Education found that, "For children living in poverty, future success in social skills and school readiness can increase dramatically with just a small increase in economic resources."

CHAPTER TWO

Holt often noted that if we improve the general quality of life for people, we improve their education quality as well. These are just some of the sorts of places children can be other than home and school. Homeschoolers seek or create them out of necessity, but I think many other parents and children would welcome other safe places to go during school hours if they were allowed to use or create them.

Social Glue

We do need social glue, but I question if public school, as we have conceived it, is capable of producing this glue anymore. When Horace Mann and John Dewey put forth the concept of school as a common denominator for creating good citizens, providing a common set of civic and intellectual knowledge to a diverse, growing immigrant population, there were no radios, televisions, videotape, movies, and the Internet. These, and so many other inventions and developments over the past hundred years compete with or usurp the common denominator role of school today. Certainly it can be argued that they provide an inferior product than schools, but their seductive power, ease of use, and ubiquity make them very powerful competitors to school for creating social glue. Reevaluating how we use and perceive media and attempting to use them to help us create social glue is a discussion that only seems to happen in the realm of morality (too much sex and drugs on TV, misogynistic music, etc.), not in the realm of democracy, social integration, and education. It is time we acknowledge that we are in a new century of learning and that many other institutions, people, and influences deeply educate our children and society besides school.

THE RIGHT CHOICE FOR OUR FAMILY?

Further, school has always been less about social interaction and democracy and more about direct instruction and grades. A homeschooling mother in New York City, Rita Sherman, wrote eloquently about this dilemma in 1923 in her book *A Mother's Letters to a Schoolmaster*:

> "…We, the State, have for a hundred years, gathered our children together in school, from all classes of society, upon a common ground, for a common purpose, and then have rested our case for a democratic education upon the self-satisfied assumption that this democracy of intent is sufficient, even final. We have allowed it to presuppose a democracy applied, practiced, and produced!
>
> We must be rid of this vanity. An honest analysis will show you that the school as a democratic institution has progressed no farther than a decree of compulsory attendance."

Children are increasingly referred to by educators and politicians as resources to be exploited, whose test-scores can raise property values or cause teachers to lose their jobs, rather than as individuals with particular needs and desires. Is it so hard to imagine that the violence that has been in our public schools for decades—think of the movies *Blackboard Jungle* from the fifties and *Dangerous Minds* from the eighties—and which is now brimming over into the public's view in the nineties with Columbine and its spawn, is at least partially related to the impersonal social sorting machine school has become?

The pressure our children face today is much worse than what we faced as children in school. Doriane Lambelet Coleman, author of *Fixing Columbine: The Challenge of Liberalism*, notes, "The nation's child suicide rate increased 400 percent from 1950 to 1990. And even this extraordinary number was most recently reported to have doubled since 1990…"

A recent *Boston Globe* editorial contained this startling fact: "…According to the World Bank, which has cataloged the total number of suicides committed by children in the 25 most industrialized nations, approximately 50 percent of the total is the result of suicides among U.S. children."

CHAPTER TWO

The gross incivility schools can have towards their students has been remarked upon for years by liberal critics of schools such as Ted Sizer (*The Children Are Watching*), and by conservative critics such as Charles Silberman (*Crisis in the Classroom*), yet little has been done to make school society more civil. Pitting children against one another for the reward of grades and individual class standing, and showing how much we value this competition by continually funding it over other less "educational" areas such as athletics, art, drama, extracurricular activities, volunteerism, community activism, or clubs sends a clear message to our children about what is really important to adults and our conception of "the social good."

Feeling good about ourselves and what we can do, respecting people who are different from us, working with people from different social classes and educational backgrounds, becoming a good citizen: I just don't see how school is supposed to accomplish these things by pitting student against student, school against school, district against district, in a race for higher test scores and property values. I find it striking how in our day and age, where you went to school classifies you rather than equalizes you!

John Holt noted that "...the important question, how can people learn to feel a stronger sense of kinship or common humanity with others who are different?" can not really be addressed by talking, preaching, discussing, bribing, or threatening people in school. The answers, Holt wrote, come from people "who have enough love and respect for themselves and therefore have some left over for others."

THE RIGHT CHOICE FOR OUR FAMILY?

I believe that integrating different people into a social whole is achieved best through group activities, teamwork, cooperative efforts and projects, games, conversation, and sharing common goals, not by separating out the economic winners and losers of society based on tests taken in their youth and where their parents can afford to live. Homeschooling shows that many parents support and create group activities, such as prayer groups, play groups, Ultimate Frisbee, film and drama clubs (to name just a few that occur in my neighborhood), as an integral part of their children's school day, not as extra-curricular activities. Often, as many classroom teachers as well as homeschoolers have written, the needs of children have little to do with the needs of the school curriculum.

These are but a few of the areas where I think homeschooling can shine new light on old assumptions about children and learning, and show by its spirit and practical application new ways of integrating children and adults for society's greater good.

CHAPTER TWO

Just the Facts

- The qualifications to homeschool include a strong belief in your children's natural drive to learn, along with some enthusiasm and confidence—not teacher training.

- Homeschooling takes as much time and costs as much as you want it to. It all depends on the approach you choose to follow.

- Socialization is not a problem with homeschooling; it is an advantage.

- Pulling a child out of school is usually a simple process.

- Homeschooling is possible for single parents and for those who both work full time.

- You can homeschool some of your children and put others in public school—but it's not necessarily a good idea.

- A child can often go to public school part-time, but it's also not always a good idea.

- Even children doing well in public school can benefit from homeschooling.

- Dads play a large role in homeschooling from support person to substitute teacher and house cleaner.

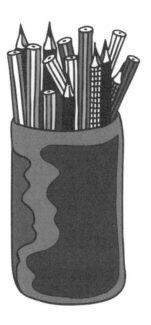

CHAPTER THREE

How Do I Get Started?

*"Education would be much more effective if its
purpose was to ensure that by the time they leave
school every boy and girl should know how much they
do not know and be imbued with a lifelong desire to know it."*
—William Haley

Once the decision is made that homeschooling is the right route to go, or at least try out, the next question is "What now?" This chapter gives you the information you need to know to start the journey. It won't list page after page of companies and catalogs, but it will tell you where to find them!

CHAPTER THREE

Where can I get curricula?

Many new homeschoolers believe that they cannot begin until their desks are overflowing with textbooks and workbooks. While finding the right curriculum is an important step for some; it is not necessarily the first step. To start, just sit back and watch your children; learn about them. What are their strengths? Weaknesses? What does he hate to do? What does she love? It is from these answers that parents can begin to choose the best curriculum.

Places to start looking include:

- *Parenting magazines* – check out the classifieds.

- *Homeschooling magazines* – ignore the articles and check out the ads.

- *Library* – what does your library have to offer?

- *Library book sales.*

- *Catalogs* – child development and educational catalogs will all offer wonderful things. Don't overlook toy catalogs too – they can be educational if used right.

- *Newspapers* – your local newspaper can have lots of helpful homeschooling material from learning to read with the comics, doing the crossword puzzles, or just reading and discussing the articles.

- *Other homeschoolers* – ask them for what materials they did and did not like and why. See if you can look at what they have or even borrow if possible.

HOW DO I GET STARTED?

- *Your own home* – your own house already contains many of the things you need to get started. Younger children can learn lessons for months just based on measuring cups, paper plates, glue, crayons, scissors, paint, cards, and dominos. Check out your own bookshelves for good books to use too.

- *Thrift stores.*

- *Garage sales.*

- *Teacher supply stores.*

- *Curricula fairs.*

Keep in mind when choosing any kind of curriculum that it is a trial and error process. You may try one company's workbooks and your son hates them, while the one you got for a quarter at your neighbor's garage sale is his favorite. Before you invest a lot of money, get a good handle on what kind of materials your children relate to. Some kids love workbooks, and others run screaming into the night when they see one. Some kids love hands-on experiments and manipulatives, while others would be more content reading about them. Also consider what you like to work with; your opinion counts too.

CHAPTER THREE

Do I have to teach the same thing the schools are teaching?

Absolutely not. You may have some basic subjects that you have to cover in your state, but how you do it is up to you, and you are only limited by your imagination. Who is to say that sock sorting isn't elementary math; that a bike ride over the mountain trails isn't physical education, and that cooking dinner for friends isn't home economics (not to mention some math and nutrition in the process?)

If you plan to homeschool a short time, for whatever reason, then place your child back into public school, you might want to use the same textbooks and materials the school is using so that he/she can merge back in easily. However, other than that, there is little reason to limit yourself to whatever your school utilizes.

Can I create my own curricula?

Yes—and please consider doing so. While your state may have rigid requirements on what has to be taught, there are limitless ways to fulfill those requirements, and many of them can be created at home by you or by mixing and matching a wide variety of materials. Packaged curricula are often attractive to homeschoolers; they are convenient and they are easy. Here, they say in their siren's song, just buy me and you won't have to give another moment's thought to any other materials you need for this entire grade/subject. However, more than a few of them will end up sitting unused and collecting dust when they don't fit the learning style, interest, or grade level of the child you bought them for. A packaged curriculum is geared for the masses, not for the individual. As John Taylor Gatto bluntly puts it, "Nobody can develop a curriculum for you that isn't, at the very best, second best and, at the very worst, a rather diabolical exercise in mind control—even if its intentions are honorable."

HOW DO I GET STARTED?

How do I know which grade my child is in?

Does it truly matter? Grades are something that school assigns to keep children the same age herded together like sheep. Your child, being the human that he/she is, cannot possibly be at the same level in all subjects. Are you? Are you as good in reading as you are in math? How well do you cook? How quickly can you convert Fahrenheit to Celsius? How are you at running laps, speaking a foreign language, or knowing the major imports and exports of Uganda? What grade level do you think you are in social studies, math, science, P.E., English, French, and home economics?

The fact is that people all have strengths and weaknesses and that is how it should be. Perhaps your child is at the 8th grade level in age but reads at a 5th grade level and does college level trigonometry, or the other way around. Toss out the concept of grades and just watch your children and see what ability they have in each subject area. If they are reading at 10th grade level, the fact that they are only nine doesn't matter. Buy reading material at the 10th grade level or above. Conversely, if they are doing 5th grade math and they're 18, so be it. If they find themselves in a position where they need to know more math, they will learn it then.

Don't let yourself get stuck in the mindset of public school. Grade levels are just arbitrary levels that mean nothing to your developing, discovering child. Real life means you do well in some areas, not so well in others. That's why you're an accountant instead of a plumber, or a sales clerk instead of an attorney. Interests and abilities are what lead each person in the direction they want to go; grade levels have no relevance whatsoever. Toss that worry out the window now.

CHAPTER THREE

What does "deschooling" mean?

You know how deep sea divers have to spend time decompressing before they can come up to the surface or risk injury? Kids who have been brought home from school often have to spend time deschooling or they may risk emotional damage. When you bring a child home after they have been in school for any time, he/she needs time to adjust, to get used to this all-new lifestyle. One child may sleep 14 hours a day; others may veg out in front of the television for their conscious hours. Some children may follow you around like an extra shadow, while others may lock themselves in their rooms and not come out for quite a while. Let them! They need this time to acclimate, and pushing them to do anything educational can often result in anger, unhappiness, or plain rebellion. Think of an animal that has been caged up for a long time. When they are suddenly set free, they often freeze in one position until they know it is truly safe to move again. Your child may freeze in front of the computer, out on the back porch, or right next to you. Forget launching into any kind of curriculum for a while and let your child just "be" for a bit, especially if their experience in school has been a traumatic one. Spend this time doing fun things together instead.

A number of homeschooling authors, parents and advocates believe that children need between six weeks and six months to decompress for every year they spent in public school. Be patient; your child is like a caterpillar going into a cocoon. Just think what may come out when he/she is ready!

HOW DO I GET STARTED?

What are learning styles?

Have you ever noticed that your child seems to process things in a totally different way than you do? Does she learn a song the first time she hears it, or does he seem to ignore what you are explaining to him and then come back later, knowing it perfectly? Dr. Howard Gardner, a psychologist at Harvard may have the explanation for this. Gardner did a great deal of research about how people think and process information, and he came up with the concept of multiple intelligences. Explained in detail in his book, *Frames of Mind*, Gardner's philosophy is that people—including children—learn in eight distinct and different ways. How does this affect you as a homeschooler? Knowing what type of style works best for your children will help you immensely in selecting curriculum and planning activities, plus it will give you a better look at why some teaching methods work great and some are flops. As the Lepperts write in *Homeschooling Almanac 2002-2003*, "Learning styles is a philosophy that recognizes that we all perceive and process information in unique ways."

Look at the descriptions of each type of intelligence listed below and see which ones seem to fit your children—or yourself—the best:

- *Linguistic*: These people love words and love using them in all of their forms. They love to read, spell well, and are often terrific storytellers. To learn best, they read the material or listen and take detailed notes. Fun activities for these learners are crossword puzzles and word searches.

- *Logical/mathematical*: These people see patterns in things; they love problem solving and can often take the abstract and turn it into reality. They enjoy doing logic puzzles, sequencing and reasoning things out. Logical learners often turn out to be computer programmers, inventors, or accountants.

CHAPTER THREE

- *Spatial/visual*: These people think and see things in images or pictures. They need to actually see what you are trying to tell them and do best with charts, graphs, and maps. They make wonderful architects.

- *Musical*: These people are almost always humming, singing, tapping, or dancing. They express themselves best through music and are often aware of a sound's pitch and rhythm. They learn best if they hear the information put to music and may request a music tutor to teach them a variety of different instruments.

- *Bodily/kinesthetic*: These people have just got to move to make life tolerable. They seem to be in constant motion, and they learn best from activities that are hands-on. They want to touch the materials and move them around. They may memorize facts while doing jumping jacks or running laps because it is through movement that they are able to process information the best. Yes, these are usually the children who are labeled ADD or ADHD (attention deficit, hyperactivity disorder). Instead of a having a learning disability, many children may just have a learning difference, and since schools aren't able to cope with teaching in a kinesthetic manner, the style becomes a problem—a problem that far too often results in a mind numbing drug that shuts down any of the normal learning processes for that child.

- *Interpersonal*: These outgoing people have the ability to bring people together. They enjoy other people and work best if they are with a partner or a group. They are sensitive to how individuals around them are feeling and often act as the peacemaker. Some may perceive them as too talkative, but these are the people who are never friendless and make fabulous leaders.

HOW DO I GET STARTED?

- *Intrapersonal*: These learners are often loners; preferring to spend a lot of their time in the complex workings of their own inner minds. They are introspective, with a very high self-awareness. They tend to be rather bookish and independent; what some may take as aloofness is really just their style of relating to the rest of the world.

- *Naturalist*: These types are keenly aware of their environment. They enjoy spending time outside communing with and studying nature. They usually enjoy working with animals or plants and make terrific gardeners.

How do you know where your children fit into these different intelligences? Watch them closely. Where are their interests? What do they do when you give them new information? When they are deeply interested in something, how do they seem to take in the material? The answers to these questions will give you clues to what blend of learning styles they use. Remember, of course, that just because one of your children happens to be a spatial learner, that certainly doesn't mean any of your other children will be. Just like one loves bananas and other can't stand them, children's tastes and learning styles are unique and personal. One of the biggest perks of homeschooling is that you can support and adapt to each one of those specific learning styles, as you need to. Instead of being in a situation where they are forced to learn in ways that feel difficult and frustrating, your children can learn in ways that are comfortable and natural. As the Lepperts write, "Imagine putting 30 different people in one room and then wondering why they don't do things the same way, see things the same way, agree on everything and desire the same things. Yet this is exactly what is expected in mass schooling today."

CHAPTER THREE

What is the homeschooling continuum?

There are many different philosophies within homeschooling and they range from one extreme to another, thus making a sort of continuum. Where you and your family will fall on this line is up to you and your attitudes about children and learning. Your memories of your own education will often send you in one direction, while watching your children on a daily basis may well send you the other. Virtually no parent chooses a philosophy and sticks with it as time goes on. It is very much a trial and error process that will shift with time, experience, children, successes, and failures. What works for you might not work for your children; what works with the first child may not work for the others; what works the first year may feel wrong the next. This is an area that calls for true flexibility and open mindedness.

As you read over the styles listed here, you may find one that sounds best to you overall, and that is most likely where you will start your homeschooling venture. As time passes, you are likely to shift one direction or another as you listen to your inner feedback and the feedback of your children. Remember that if anyone in the homeschooling picture is feeling miserable, something is wrong and needs to be altered. For instance, if you are trying to teach your child to read and they are ending up in tears as you mutter under your breath, there's a problem that needs to be explored before you go any further.

On the (arbitrary) far left of the continuum is simply *traditional homeschooling*, also known as *school at home*. This philosophy is based on teaching the same material and using the same methods as the public school system. It can even go so far as to utilize report cards, tests, school desks, recess periods, and bells. Families often choose this philosophy when they first start homeschooling because it feels the most familiar to them. This method usually utilizes a packaged curriculum based on those old three R's: readin', writin' and 'rithmatic. It is very structured with certain times of each day allotted for specific subjects. It is a parent-centered method as

HOW DO I GET STARTED?

they are the ones in control of what will be learned, as well as when and how. Parents are seen as authorities, just like teachers. While this method can work very well for some families, it also tends to be tiring and can cause a lot of burn out for both parents and kids.

Next along the line is the *principle method*. This philosophy is based on learning moral character through a Biblical worldview. It tends to be quite structured also, but differs from school at home by the fact that all materials and subjects are related to Christian principles.

Classical home education is next and its focus in on developing critical thinking skills in children through a combination of teaching classic languages (Latin and Greek) and using a curriculum based on the "great books"of the Western civilization. The foundation for this method is the Trivium. Parents who follow this philosophy believe that children's cognitive development comes in three stages and that each one requires different materials. The first stage is *grammar* (up to age 12), and this is when reading and writing are taught, as well as the skills of listening and observation. The second stage is *logic* (middle grades), and it brings in the abilities of in-depth and abstract thought. The last stage is *rhetoric* or wisdom (later teens), and this is where the child should be able to express his knowledge eloquently. This philosophy is not a common one and the heavy emphasis on reading classics often makes it difficult for children to stick with.

Following this is Dr. Raymond and Dorothy Moore's philosophy of *delayed academics*. After years of research, this husband and wife team determined that most academics should not be taught to a child until at least age 8 to 10, or even 12, because they are not truly able to competently understand and perform them before then. They also advocate strict schedules using a three-pronged approach to a balanced education: study on a daily basis, spend equal time in manual work of some kind, and spend at least an hour a day doing some sort of home or community service. Much of what they base their recommendations on is Biblically based. Some parents find that the strict routines this philosophy calls for is too difficult for them to maintain.

CHAPTER THREE

Next is a homeschooling style based on the tenets of Charlotte Mason, an early 19th century British educator. It is often called the *Living Books* method as it places a very strong emphasis on having children read books that are lively and relevant to them rather than textbooks. She recommended a minimum of one hour a day on structured academics, followed by time out in nature exploring and observing. One of her biggest concepts was the importance of reading out loud to a child and having him/her repeat the information back to you in a narrative style. She felt this helped them to play an active part in learning information, as well as helping comprehension and listening skills.

As you approach the middle of the continuum, you arrive at the teaching philosophy of *unit studies*. Utilizing unit studies in your homeschooling plan means that you or your child (depending on where you fit between parent-centered and child-centered schooling) selects a subject of interest, and you immerse yourselves in it for a month or more. The topic is looked at as a whole, not just as a history assignment or a science assignment. For instance, if you wanted to do a unit study on Egypt, you might go to the museum and talk about the mummifying process (science), look up some Egyptian recipes and try them at home (home economics), learn how to write your names in hieroglyphs (penmanship), get some books on Egypt from the library (reading), build a pyramid out of paper and glue (arts and crafts), write a skit about King Tut and perform it (English/Drama), and go out to an Egyptian restaurant and talk to the people there (field trip). Unit studies are quite flexible and can be made part of the structured homeschooling schedule or all the way to the other end in the unschooling department. Since so much time is spent on one subject, kids can weary of it; letting them make some of the choices can make a real difference in keeping their interest.

The *eclectic approach* is probably the most popular method with veteran homeschoolers. Here you will find families using a little of everything in their homeschooling plans. They mix their packaged curriculum with what they have made themselves; they each select different topics to study; they

HOW DO I GET STARTED?

spend time on the basic academics and a lot of time studying other things entirely. As Kathy Ishizuka writes in *The Unofficial Guide to Homeschooling*, ". . .eclectics truly expound the smorgasbord approach to homeschooling. They pick and choose from the array of philosophies, teaching methods and curricula, employing whatever happens to work in their home at a particular time. . . eclectics make deliberate choices according to their children's nature and abilities." With this method, there is a great deal of flexibility, substantially decreasing the risk of burnout for both parents and children.

Finally, on that arbitrary far right of the continuum, there is the concept of *unschooling*, a term originally coined by educator, author, and homeschooling forefather, John Holt over 40 years ago. Also known as natural learning or the discovery method, this philosophy is as opposite of school as it can get. Instead of emulating or imitating the traditional method, it sheds those concepts and wants little to do with them at all.

In unschooling, the child is the one in control of what is learned when and how. Parents are not so much teachers as they are guides and mentors. They closely watch their children and help them to explore and learn about what they are already curious about. Unschoolers rarely utilize any kind of formal curriculum; they don't expect a child to follow a set timetable for when he/she learns something. Instead, these parents have a deep trust and respect in a child's inherent drive to learn, explore, and discover. In return, they make sure to provide a very rich environment to learn in, with many materials and opportunities available to use on a daily basis. With unschooling there is no coercion to learn because the child is at the helm of the direction his/her education is going. A child is allowed to learn in his/her style and at his/her pace rather than trying to match the style and pace of a teacher.

This method is very difficult for some people—even some other homeschoolers—to accept. It appears too easy, even negligent to some, yet it is the same method that was used to teach children how to walk, talk, get dressed, etc. Those lessons weren't taught or graded; they were modeled, and assisted, and they happened. Unschoolers believe this is true in all

CHAPTER THREE

aspects of education. For those children who have been in school for a year or more, this method may be difficult since they are used to being told what to do, when to do it, and how to do it. That will improve, but it can be frustrating for parents and kids before it does. If you live in a state that requires documentation for what your children are doing, this method can be challenging since much of your children's activities will not clearly fall into one subject area or another. Mary Griffith writes in her book, *The Unschooling Handbook*, "Unschooling parents who live where they must document their children's learning to comply with their state's legal requirements often devote considerable time and ingenuity to translating what their children do into terms that make sense for reports designed for a more conventional approach to education."

Whatever method you end up choosing to use with your children, be flexible. Homeschooling is a trial and error process as you discover what works and doesn't work for you and your children. Try it one way, and if people aren't happy, change it. Experiment and find the right niche on the continuum; just don't be surprised if you're changing it again in the months to come.

HOW DO I GET STARTED?

What if tests are required?

If taking tests is part of your state's homeschooling requirements, prepare your child for taking them. You can do some practice tests, often found in test preparation books or on various Internet sites as noted in the resources section. Community colleges also often offer test prep classes so call them and see what they have going currently. Make sure you have covered all of the material that needs to be covered before taking the test and that you review it with your child. By taking a few trial tests, you can also pinpoint your child's weaker areas and spend some extra time on those before the test.

Make sure that you know all the rules of the test; how and when it will be administered, who has the right to administer it, what will be done with the results and so on. One mother who had to have her child tested stated with a chuckle, "He has to take the test—but the results don't have to be mailed in or reviewed by anyone. So, we just take it for fun and to fulfill the silly requirement."Check to see who has to administer the test. In some larger areas, there are homeschooled parents who are former teachers who qualify to do this and are easier to work with since they understand your perspective and feelings. In other areas, the test can also be done in your home where your child is more comfortable

Don't let yourself be fooled either—some public school administrators may try to tell you that you have to test your child when the law does not require it at all. Learn your state law (noted in detail in Chapter Eight), and then don't let anyone sway you on what has to be done.

CHAPTER THREE

How early or late can I start to homeschool?

The question of how early is simple; you began when your child was born. Every single day of your new child's life was a lesson in a myriad of different things. There was no set time when you said to yourself, "I am going to start teaching my baby how to talk now, or I am going to start teaching my infant how to walk." They were genetically driven to do so and you were a terrific role model. Homeschooling starts at birth.

How late? There have been parents who have pulled their children out of school in their senior year of high school. There is no such thing as a time that is too late to homeschool. You do it when you perceive the need to be there. All else doesn't matter.

Should I go year round or take the summers off?

Like so many other decisions, this is up to you. If you are following the same basic pattern as the public school, you may want to stop lessons for the summer. Others who unschool go all year round since they never actually have set class times and schedules. Many families opt for a mixture of philosophies; they teach formally during the typical school year and let up during the summer, focusing on more fun and relaxed lessons like field trips, vacations, experiments, etc.

Do I need to keep records/report cards/documentation on what we do?

How much you do in this department will depend primarily on what style of homeschooling you follow and what your state regulations mandate. Some parents never write a single thing down while others maintain accurate and precise records on every child.

HOW DO I GET STARTED?

Here are the main types of record keeping that homeschoolers tend to use:

- *Journal.* This is written by the parents and/or the homeschooler and acts as a log, which lists the projects done, books read, field trips taken, etc. It can be divided in any way the writer sees fit from separate sections for each child, day, subject, event and so on. This is probably the most casual, relaxed approach to record keeping.

- *Portfolio.* Compiled by either/both the parents and kids, this is a multi media record of what the homeschool year has encompassed. It can contain:

Poetry	Ticket stubs
Stories	Test results
Projects	Attendance records
Letters	Drawings/art work
Certificates	Photographs
Rewards	

A portfolio can be as casual or formal as you want it to be, and it is a great way to reflect the many different results your kids produce during their homeschooling adventure. Author Loretta Heuer, M.Ed., writes in her book, *The Homeschooler's Guide to Portfolios and Transcripts*, "A portfolio is a collection of artifacts that has been selected from a larger body of work—a carefully designed sampler that is created for a specific reason. In essence, it is a portrait of you in a particular setting."

CHAPTER THREE

- *Schedule and subject log*: Modeled after public school teacher's daily logs, this has places to show what each child does each day, attendance, grades, and other typical school information. These logs can be created at home, or you can buy them at teacher's supply stores.

- *Transcripts*: These papers will list the titles of the courses your children take, as well as the credit hours and grades, just as public school transcripts do. These are certainly the most formal way of recording what you do, and some families like them because they are easy to show to school officials, college interviewers, and other people involved in education. Heuer writes, "A transcript... is like a snapshot. It gives the reviewer a quick look at you, your skills, and your knowledge."

Whatever type of records you keep, remember that you will need to know how to take your children's daily activities and figure out how to label them in educational-ese. Was the trip to grandma's house physical education (you took a long hike in the woods there), history (she told you all about her experience with rationing during World War II), or home economics (you helped her can her summer green beans)? If you look carefully enough, you will see lessons in almost everything your children do, and all you need to do is log them in the appropriate places.

If you are required to keep records for state regulations, be sure to follow their exact outline of what they expect and NOTHING more. Extra information will only complicate issues and open the door for interference. A number of companies offer packaged record keeping systems and computer programs that can make it easier for you also.

HOW DO I GET STARTED?

A last note—don't let the prospect of having to keep records be so daunting that it discourages you from homeschooling in the first place. As Larry and Susan Kaseman write in their book, *Taking Charge Through Homeschooling: Personal and Political Empowerment*, "Valuable as records may be, they need to be kept in perspective. It does not make sense to spend so much time keeping records that there is not enough time for activities a family wants to do. Also, home schooling should not be abandoned just because record keeping does not work well; another can be tried."

How do I homeschool children of different ages and levels?

With a lot of love and patience! Homeschooling children of multiple interests, ages, and levels can be challenging, but also wonderful. Depending on the age of your kids, you can often cover the same topic for all of them in different ways. For instance, a lesson on how magnetism works might mean reading an essay on it for your high schooler, while your elementary school child goes around the house checking to see what things a magnet sticks to and what it doesn't, and your toddler is in the kitchen taking magnetic letters off the refrigerator and creating an art form. Older children sometimes find themselves helping younger ones, and younger ones find themselves trying to imitate their elder siblings. Connections are made between your children that are profound. Of course, there are also days where all they do is bicker and squabble—which is just as natural. Those are the days when you will need to schedule some one-on-one time with each child in order to keep peace in the household. That time may be hard to find sometimes, but Mary Griffith reassures everyone when she writes, "If you worry you won't be able to give each child enough time and attention, keep the problem in perspective: even if you can't give each of your children all the time they want with you, they're undoubtedly getting far more individual attention that they'd get in a school classroom."

CHAPTER THREE

What role do television and the Internet play in homeschooling?

Television seems to be both a blessing and a curse. On the positive side, it can introduce new and exciting ideas to your children; take them on journeys to faraway lands; show them interesting concepts; present different perspectives. On the negative side, it can numb their brains; teach them unwanted lessons; be used as a convenient babysitter and turn them into couch potatoes. Studies have shown that most homeschooling children spend far less time watching television overall than their public school counterparts, despite the fact that they are in the house more hours. Many homeschooling parents limit their time in front of the television, and more than a few of them do not own a television at all. How you choose to use it is up to you entirely; however, here are a few helpful ideas:

- Don't use television as a reward or a punishment; it gives it too much importance.

- Consider putting the television in a little used room; children are less apt to ask for it if they don't see it.

- Practice what you preach; don't watch an excessive amount of television yourself and then tell the children they cannot.

- Tape the shows they like the best and save them for days when a field trip is cancelled, the weather is lousy, etc.

- Make television watching a family affair; watch the shows with them and discuss what you see.

- Limit what shows they can see to ones you know and approve of; consider using it only for public television and other educational shows that tie in with what they are learning at present.

HOW DO I GET STARTED?

Another common question is whether you need a computer and the Internet to homeschool your children. The Internet is to successful homeschooling like a set of encyclopedias is to being a successful writer. In other words, it's a great tool to have at hand, full of important and useful information, but it has little whatsoever to do with success.

Homeschooling families can certainly make the most of the Internet; it has great lessons, virtual field trips, and scads of long distance learning for the educational department; and fun, friends and games over in the entertainment department. Trouble only comes along when the Net turns into something that a family either unwisely completely avoids or completely depends on. Each perspective has its own set of problems.

The family that avoids computers and/or the Internet is denying their children access to skills and information they will most likely need for the rest of their lives. Whether people like the idea or not, today's culture is definitely computer-oriented and there are very few jobs or directions in life a person can take that won't include the need for some element of computer savvy. Learning how to operate a computer, log on to the Net, and use its almost limitless resources will not only enhance a child's education, but also make him/her more employable. For those parents who are reluctant to bring the Internet into their children's lives, here are some suggestions:

- Learn about how to access the Internet yourself and how it can help.

- Limit the amount of time your kids can be on the Internet.

- Only allow access to the Internet if you are sitting with your kids.

- Don't purchase a computer for your home and use the ones in your local library or a friend's home instead.

More on the Internet from Parent's Guide Press

- **A Parent's Guide to the Internet**, the project oriented non-technical guide to family Internet use. Dozens of hands-on projects for parents and children help de-mystify the Internet.

- E-mail, Discussion Groups, FTP, IRC Chat: the Internet that isn't the Web and the opportunities for enlightenment—and abuse—they offer.

- Written by **Ilene Raymond**, an award winning writer, essayist and educator. Her interviews with child psychology experts, homeschooling parents, academics, involved educators, and many others confirm a simple truth; parents need to be involved with their children's Internet activity. The Internet is not a teacher, parent, sibling, babysitter or friend, though it is a powerful communication medium that can help children, grow, learn, meet, and explore.

CHAPTER THREE

On the opposite end, there are families who come to depend on the Internet for their children's education, and this is a mistake too. No matter how high-tech and well-designed a web site is, it doesn't take the place of a real person. Lessons taught by parents can certainly be supplemented by the Net, but rarely replaced. Time spent staring at a computer monitor, regardless of the interactiveness of some sites, means a child isn't out exploring, moving, and being in the "real" world. It also means that a child is learning only one way of researching or hunting down information—the Net—and that is far too limiting. Children need to know that they can also find information in books, by talking to various people, and by their own observations and investigations.

If your child only wants to sit in front of a computer screen when it comes time to learn, here are some suggestions:

- Put a firm time limit on time spent on the Net.

- Organize outside activities like trips to the library, field trips, etc.

- Give them assignments to do and specifically state that a computer cannot be used to find out the answers.

- Wait until your unit study is over before you introduce the relevant web sites. This way the material is learned before the computer is turned on.

The Internet often plays a very important role for homeschoolers, and that is understandable. The key to seeing it as a tool and not a threat or a crutch is, like most things in parenting, moderation. As Mary Griffith puts it in her book, *The Unschooling Handbook*, "It's best to think of the Internet not as a single, unitary resource but as what it really is: a vast collection of wildly disparate items, some valuable and some worthless, some harmless and some potentially dangerous."

HOW DO I GET STARTED?

How do I teach a subject I dislike or don't know?

There are several different options in this case. First of all, ask yourself if this is something your children really have to know and have to learn about right now. Just because you learned this particular subject matter in 7th grade doesn't mean they need to. Maybe you can wait until they develop their own interest in it, and when that happens, you won't have to teach so much as guide them to good resources and information.

Secondly, you can choose to learn the subject right along with your children. Now that you are older and not being forced to learn it, you may be pleasantly surprised to find that you like the subject after all. Learning material together can also strengthen the bond between you and your children, especially if they actually learn it faster than you do, and you switch roles for a while—a real possibility with homeschooling.

Thirdly, you can seek outside help with this subject. Can your spouse cover this one? How about a friend, neighbor, or relative? You might hire a tutor for just this course or find a local mentor that can help out. Find outside materials from the library or teacher's supply store and see if your children can teach themselves this subject. They may find that they love it as much as you don't.

Also remember that it's okay to show your children that you don't like a subject and are going to tackle it nonetheless or find someone more qualified to help you do so. It's like admitting that you honestly don't like cucumbers. It makes it easier for them to admit that they don't like beets; they see it's just part of being human.

CHAPTER THREE

How do I know if my child is learning what he/she is "supposed" to?

Start by asking yourself why you think your child is "supposed"to know anything. That may sound strange, but think about it for a minute. While there is some information that a child will need to know to keep safe and function in this world, there is also a lot of information that isn't necessary. For instance, knowing your name, address, and phone number is important; knowing the main export of Bolivia isn't (unless you're looking to move and get a job there!). Knowing how to add, subtract, multiply, and divide is pretty important—they are vital to writing checks, earning money, getting a job, and so on, but is geometry necessary? It may be fun, it may be interesting, and you may indeed find yourself using it in some future job or project, but does every person need to know it? No.

Homeschooling can often be difficult for some parents because its tenets and possibilities sometimes run in opposition to what is "right" and what is "supposed to be." Questioning these things can feel wrong or be very upsetting, but when it comes to homeschooling, it is almost inevitable. By recognizing that perhaps public school isn't the best way to educate your child, you are opening up the door to asking a lot of other questions, and some of them can make you uncomfortable. If you can, push past the discomfort and look seriously at the question. What do your children really need to know? When do they need to know it? What are they "supposed"to be taught? Why?

Because parents do worry about whether their children are learning what they are supposed to, whatever that might mean to them, they may decide to have their children tested now and then. Some states even require it. While the drive to do this is understandable, it is equally important that you realize that these national standardized tests are, in no way, an accurate measure of how your children are doing. They simply show how he/she is doing at that moment, on that subject, compared to public schoolers who may be covering the material completely differently. The results can

HOW DO I GET STARTED?

be interesting, but they aren't reliable and taking them only helps to perpetuate the concept that standardized tests are accurate summaries of how your child is doing. One mother whose six year old was tested recalls her response to the results. "They didn't know how to score her,"she says. "She couldn't tell you the days of the week ('Daddy goes to work days and Daddy stays home days') or the names of the months ('Spring, Fall, Winter and Summer'), but she had off the chart responses to real life questions like what would you do if your house was on fire or if you found a wallet laying on the floor of a big store. The tester was especially confused,"continues the mother, "when she would finish her answer and then ask the tester what she would do in that same situation."

More importantly, these tests are not able to measure some of the most important things you will be teaching your children; things like compassion, responsibility, love, and curiosity. How do these measure up next to knowing all the state's capitals?

Take time to ask yourself too—what is your personal underlying reason for wanting to test your children? Is it to evaluate how they are doing? It won't be accurate. Is it because it's what you did in school? Is it to prove to others that your child is learning, that he is intelligent? There are much better—and more effective and meaningful ways. Is it to find the areas where they are strongest and weakest? It won't likely let you know; however it might give you some information on how well they can take a test. Is it to help prepare them for the future when they might have to take tests (SATs, college exams, etc.)? That has validity, but it doesn't merit giving them more than a couple of tests and some basic instruction. There are too many test prep web sites and books available that you can use that are far preferable to actually putting your child through a test. Perhaps you are worried that welfare or a divorce and/or custody issue will put you under fire sometime in the future? If that's a true possibility, then it's an option to consider.

CHAPTER THREE

Instead, decide if your children are learning by observing them. Are they asking questions? Are they keeping busy? Are they happy? Have they learned things that they didn't know before? Have they improved in something or some area? Examine the projects they have done; the awards and certificates they have earned; the journals or logs they have kept. Do you see progress and development there?

Don't expect them to be learning every single minute either; learning is sporadic. They may go through a period of soaking things up like a sponge and then seem to be doing nothing. That "nothing" time is when their brains are processing what they have learned. Think of the child learning to ride a bike. He takes several trips up and down the sidewalk with Dad or Mom hanging on for dear life, then they don't touch the bike for days. Suddenly, the next time out, before you can grab that shirt, they are off! Speeding down the sidewalk, hair blowing in the wind, and screaming in delight (or is that you?). Those days of nothing were the ones where the brain laid down the pathways to know how to ride that bike. They are using the information that they have learned, and there is little better measure of success than that!

When asked the question of how a parent can measure how their children are doing in relation to their peers, Mary McCarthy, writer and homeschooling mom, wrote (Dobson, Prima Publishing, *Homeschooling Book of Answers*): "Why would you want to? Your child is an individual. Celebrate the individual. No one is good at everything; no one is going to be perfect in every subject, so why would you want to compare your child to someone else's? Diversity is the blessing of humanity; individually, we lack in certain skills, but put together, we make a whole. If your child is learning—and enjoying it—that's success." Mary and Michael Lepert agree when they write in their book *The Homeschooling Almanac 2002-2003*, "homeschooling affords the student the opportunity to soar ahead in favored topics of study while spending more time on less popular academic areas. Keep in mind, grades are used in school settings mainly to keep children at one place and move others along."

HOW DO I GET STARTED?

How do I keep my children and myself motivated?

In other words, how do I prevent homeschool burnout? The best way to do this is to identify why it is happening in the first place and then fixing that element. Just like the old saying advises you to not throw out the baby with the bath water, don't throw out homeschooling altogether because one aspect of it isn't working for you.

Burnout, no matter where it occurs, is due to stress; find the source of your stress and see what can be done about it. The number one reason for burnout in homeschooling is trying to do too much. This can come from several different directions. Perhaps you are trying to do too much within your homeschooling. Burnout is definitely higher in families that are trying to school at home in a very structured manner. It can be exhausting for parents and for kids, as each one of them struggle to meet standards and requirements they simply may not be up to—and don't need to be either. Lillian Jones, homeschooling mom and advocate, writes in Linda Dobson's *Homeschooling Book of Answers*, "The best homeschooling experience comes with no attempt to re-create school at home, and re-creating school at home is the single most stressful force against successful homeschooling. This message is hard to grasp sometimes, but it is a vital one. Pay heed."

Consider relaxing your approach to homeschooling so that scheduling and routine aren't as strict and inflexible. If you're in the middle of a unit on frogs, for example, and you're on the way to the bookstore to find a book on them, be willing to stop and watch a telephone pole going up, talk to a friend you haven't seen for awhile, or stop by the library and see what they have to offer. Interrupt your typical lessons with a field trip or by visiting an area expert on the your topic and asking questions.

A majority of the parents who seem to experience burnout are also people who place great value in the ability to control things in life. In homeschooling, this can lead to trouble; give deep thought to whether you really need to exert so much control here, or if you can relax and let go a little

CHAPTER THREE

more. Give your children the opportunity to learn some self-control and influence the direction of their own educations; lighten up on some of your expectations and requirements and see where it may lead you.

The pressure you are feeling may also be coming from trying to homeschool your kids and still do everything you did before. If you try to do all the cooking, cleaning, running errands, and all the many other responsibilities of being an adult in a household, you will wear out quickly. This is the time to get help where you can. Have your partner either help with housework or take over some of the homeschooling. Make chores part of your children's daily curriculum. Hire a friend to come in and clean for you on a regular basis. Don't try to take on too much, or it can all come crumbling down, and you will be miserable.

If you start feeling burnout creeping into the homeschooling picture, talk it out! Talk to your partner about it. Get his/her feedback and thoughts. Talk to your kids; where do they think the problem is stemming from? Their insights can be incredible. Talk to a friend, a neighbor, a relative. Pick someone who is supportive of homeschooling, however; else you are apt to get the unwanted advice of "Just put them all in school!" Talk to others in your support group and complain a little; they have all been there, and they can often either just empathize so you don't feel so alone, and/or give you some useful ideas to try to help. If you can't see them in person, call or email them.

Sometimes you are feeling stressed out simply because you are generically stressed. Look at the rest of your life: are you sleeping well and long enough each night? How is your diet? Are you eating nutritional foods and enough of them? Are you getting any regular type of exercise? Have you had any time for just you lately? Time to read, relax, watch a movie, chat with a friend? If not, do so. You need that time to rejuvenate and refresh. Go to the mall alone. Meet a friend in a coffeehouse. Take a walk through the park. Even doing errands alone can help. Remember, you certainly cannot homeschool well if you aren't taking care of the basics.

HOW DO I GET STARTED?

Life isn't always smooth and easy; there are bad days whether you homeschool or not. When those lousy days happen, have back up plans. Toss out the schoolwork and go to the library, the zoo, the museum, a friend's house; anywhere that is fun for all of you. Spend the day reading and coloring and building and dreaming. Enjoy your kids: their sense of humor, their joy in discovery, their unique perspectives on life. Have faith in yourself, in your children, and in homeschooling, and that will carry you through to the next day, which is a completely new start.

In the Trenches

Homeschooling All Ages

~ Patty Kurdi

In my opinion, there are no right or wrong ways to homeschool multiple age groups; every family finds what works well for them. It has taken some time, but this is how I have finally coped with it.

My first goal is to get my children to develop a love of learning. I do this by example; I show how I can learn also from all the materials being taught. Secondly, once they are readers, I teach them to develop independent learning styles. I think that is especially important for children who want to continue their education. Colleges have been known to recruit homeschoolers because they believe they have stronger independent learning abilities.

The following is what a typical day is like in my home. My 12th grader has come to the conclusion that she needs more than one teacher so we decided to incorporate Internet Homeschooling. We have all courses available to us, including teachers and counselors to assist as needed. She gets up in the morning just as though she is about to attend outside school. She checks in at 7 a.m. and independently studies the necessary subjects. If need be, she contacts the teachers for online conferences. I do all the grading and testing, and I work hand-in-hand with her Web teachers to assist my daughter in gaining as much as possible from the course work.

My 3rd grader is a different story. Each week, I prepare the necessary coursework for the upcoming week. We begin the day with a mile run, breakfast, clean up, and then the books. Because he can read on his own, he goes over his instructions and then follows through on them. This is probably one of my most successful teachings. You can teach a child the basics like reading and counting, but if you can teach him to be an independent learner, you've accomplished something wonderful. I am always there to answer questions, give tests, and assist him in his experiments.

CHAPTER THREE

Then there are my preschoolers. I run a small business and have preschool hour twice a day. On one hand, it is the hardest age to teach, but on the other, it is the most exciting. We use arts and crafts to teach almost everything. My third grader loves to take breaks from his work and assist in teaching the other kids. Sometimes, the craft requires more than one adult, and this is where my own children help me out. The preschoolers look up to my kids like they were their own brother and sister. They are fine role models for the younger students.

We do more than course work. We attend Park Day twice a week for three hours with children ranging from eight months to 16 years old. Twice a month we go to Kid's Club for workshops, and we love incorporating field trips to zoos, museums, plays, farms, beaches, and local companies who are willing to teach our children about our community.

When teaching several age groups, I have used separate course work for each grade, but still try to bring the children together as much as possible. This has helped me to develop a love for learning, and it has reinforced my children's love and respect for each other. This is not something taught in your local public or private school. I allow for age appropriate course work, but always find a way to integrate the different ages together. After all, the world is full of different ages, colors, and beliefs. This is just a part of learning to be together and have mutual respect regardless of those differences.

In the Trenches

A Charlotte Mason Education in Our Home

~ Lisa Donnelly

After seven years of homeschooling, my style is an eclectic blend of methods and ideas gleaned, borrowed, and plundered from many sources, yet the writings of Charlotte Mason have been one of the biggest influences on my educational journey. Books describing her methods and the schools she founded left me wishing my own child-hood education had been at such schools. Many of her ideas work for both my oldest, who, like me, is an avid reader and responds well to Miss Mason's emphasis on litera-ture and history, and for my middle son, who isn't much of a reader but appreciates facts and information given to him en toto, from real books, not doled out in tiny bits and pieces from a textbook or dumbed-down children's book.

Our homeschool day runs according to a schedule modeled closely after Charlotte Mason's original school program, though nothing is ever written in stone. Real life can and does take precedence over the written plan. But the schedule keeps us focused, helps me be certain that essential subjects such as math, reading, and other language

HOW DO I GET STARTED?

arts are being covered. The nine-year-old, Daniel, is given short lessons on a variety of subjects, as Charlotte recommended, while Michael, the twelve-year-old, is ready for more challenges academically—and longer lessons. At five, James participates only when he wants to. Because of my husband's and my belief that boys need time to develop and that a late, relaxed start on academics is better than an early, rushed beginning, we're not always "on track" with traditional grade levels. However, like many other homeschoolers, the boys are constantly learning, and know a great deal about a wide variety of subjects that have captured their interests.

Depending on our activity schedule for the day (which can range from a museum visit or a game day at a local store to just getting together with friends after our twice-weekly fencing lessons), we start about nine in the morning. On days we don't have to be anywhere, we'll gather about ten or ten-thirty to start scheduled lessons. Because Miss Mason believed so firmly that much of a child's learning takes place during play and free time, we've always tried to be done with our structured lessons in as short a time frame as possible. Daniel spends perhaps an hour and a half a day in traditional schoolwork; this includes his oral reading and my reading of books and literature out loud to him. Michael spends more time, but that is in part because we have introduced Latin at his request and also because he appreciates being able to work in his room, taking as much time (with as many breaks!) as he wants.

Miss Mason emphasized introducing children to poetry as well as good literature from an early age. While my husband reads aloud books such as *The Hobbit* to the boys, my choice has often been to read poetry. This year our gathering time, also known as the "settle-down-and-get-ready-for-study" time, is poetry reading. Currently we're reading through Scholastic's "Poetry for Young People" series, enjoying both the poetry and learning about the individual poets' lives. Some days we simply pick up a collection of poems and read several randomly from its pages. We've covered poets from A.A. Milne and Edgar Allen Poe, to Shakespeare and Walt Whitman.

After poetry reading the older boys start on subjects such as math and their critical thinking projects. This is my time to focus on James. Some days we do puzzles, sometimes I read to him. Other times he chooses to get out his math or other workbooks. And there are mornings he'd rather go play with Legos or his myriad stuffed animals. Lately, James has wanted to learn to read, so we're following Charlotte Mason's ideas and playing with word families and learning the sounds various letters can make.

CHAPTER THREE

After this individual time, we all get together and go through our history studies. Miss Mason has heavily influenced my approach to this subject. The history curriculum we use was chosen because of its chronological approach and its use of living books and historical fiction to convey the information—all ideas directly from her. I read aloud to the boys from the various books, and have them narrate back to me what we've read. Michael does written narration one or two days a week. We fill events in on a time line, and look up answers to any questions that might have come up. When we've finished with a subject or time period, we spend a day discussing the civilization or person we've read about. As Charlotte Mason recommended, instead of a test on facts and dates, the boys tell me everything they remember about our studies. Then we talk about how the material is interconnected and related to other subjects or people or places we've already studied, and trace any modern connections. Miss Mason believed firmly that we should not separate subjects artificially, and no one "subject"such as history exists in a vacuum. We are constantly interrelating our studies in this manner.

Charlotte Mason's teaching methods for language arts are where I do have some differences of opinion with her. I cannot see waiting until 15 for formal composition instruction, nor am I comfortable trusting just narration for giving my child the skills to convey his ideas effectively to another person. Yet at the same time, I have seen her ideas borne out in my own experiences with my sons. This year we've started Daniel in a book written directly for a Charlotte Mason style of education. It's a very gentle beginning to language arts; the student works through short, simple lessons on the mechanics of language, with an emphasis on the verbal retelling of stories and information, and memorization of poetry and fables. However, Miss Mason's theories are borne out with this child, since narration is a very natural process for him. He is always ready to share what he knows, and he generally is very clear about whatever idea he is communicating. The trick is for me to be willing to listen when he starts talking!

Michael just began a formal study of composition and grammar this year, at the age of 12—still early for a true Charlotte Mason follower. While I do see the need for instruction and practice in his efforts, I also see him expressing his ideas clearly and naturally using complex sentence constructions I know he has never been taught. It is obvious that he's read, and read widely; again, Miss Mason's beliefs bearing fruit. So my approach to Language Arts with both boys is a balancing act, between their natural desires and abilities to share information, as Charlotte Mason thought best, and what I believe is necessary instruction in those skills that will allow them to do so in a clear and concise manner.

HOW DO I GET STARTED?

For science we've moved away from the straight nature/observational approach Charlotte Mason advocated. His interests lying mostly in other areas, Michael is getting some simple physics instruction, while both quirky modern animals and dinosaurs fascinate Daniel. He doesn't appreciate the detailed study of the natural world Miss Mason recommended for his age, but still, her ideas about teaching children in general have been a big influence here. Not a strong reader yet, Daniel avidly watches any science videos provided, eagerly listens to any such book read to him, and always remembers far more than I give him credit for. He's never seen a science textbook; all his experience with written science has been with "whole" books, as Miss Mason termed them, an entire book giving complete information and not just "sound bytes" on a subject. As a result, he is thinking for himself, putting together his own theories of science, and asking to write experts in the field for their opinions of his ideas.

Fine arts and music appreciation are one area where Charlotte Mason truly shines. For us, implementing her methods can be as simple as playing classical music for the boys during the day or finding and reading biographies of musicians and artists. We spend time every two weeks or so looking at collections of famous paintings, and study of the art of a culture is always part of our history lessons. Again, it's not assuming children are incapable of appreciating the fine arts because they are "too young;" it's making the material and the information available to the child and allowing his or her natural interest to take over. My sons are not "art experts" by any means, but due to Miss Mason's ideas, they are familiar with a wide variety of art periods and styles.

Our homeschooling journey has never followed the Charlotte Mason model completely; my three boys don't respond well to the genteel, moralistic approach to home education that many Charlotte Mason devotees seem to adopt. Yet her theories and ideas on educating children have greatly influenced my thinking on my own homeschooling. Because of her, I have eschewed textbooks in most subjects, and I have been very careful with what curriculum I do use, choosing it for the complete information given and the respect shown for a child's native intelligence. No twaddle, and nothing dumbed down. She's given me a way to keep the fine arts and literature involved in our homeschool, while honoring my boys' natural, more active learning styles. I truly believe Charlotte Mason's basic ideas combine the best of both worlds, the unschooling, child-directed approach, and the more structured methods of homeschooling.

CHAPTER THREE

"Children who are forced to eat acquire a loathing for food and children who are forced to learn acquire a loathing for knowledge."
—*Bertrand Russell*

From the Experts

What is an Unschooler: A Little History
~ Nancy Plent

The term "unschooler" began as a shortcut word in the 1970s. Author John Holt suggested that families use it to refer to parents who were teaching their kids at home—so we wouldn't have to keep saying parents who are teaching their kids at home. It wasn't until later that it acquired other connotations.

> **Nancy Plent** has edited **The Unschoolers Network**, a New Jersey homeschool newsletter since 1977. She and her husband, Mac, co-authored **An 'A' in Life: Famous Home Schoolers**, a book of mini-profiles of 150-plus successful people who had little, if any, formal education. This essay is an excerpt from her forthcoming book, **The 25 Year Phone Call: A Personal History of Home Schooling in NJ**.

The "un" part was probably why the term caught on. Like UnCola drinkers who want a beverage as different from cola as possible, early homeschoolers seemed to want their children's education to be as unlike public school as they could make it. Being an "unschooler" sounded very liberating. Our family was open to starting from scratch and inventing something new, but we soon discovered that not everyone wanted to be liberated. Some families had no quarrel with public school concepts of education; they just had their own ideas about how these concepts should be carried out.

One of the first families I met, for example, had a perfect replica of a public school classroom in their basement. The mother and my friend, Meg, had a green alphabet chart over the chalkboard and a brass teacher's bell on her desk at the front of the classroom. Her four children began lessons promptly at 9 a.m., sitting on real school furniture purchased from the attic

HOW DO I GET STARTED?

of a local elementary school. They had tests and recitations and homework and textbooks. I couldn't understand why they had bothered to leave school!

They, in turn, were startled by our notion that our son Eric would learn math by managing his allowance, or helping us with baking and carpentry, or working with the family business. We were sure that if our lives were busy and absorbing enough, we wouldn't have to sit him down to scribble in workbooks and do formal lessons.

Meg's family, on the other hand, was sure that their kids wouldn't be educated without those very same workbooks and formal lessons. We studied each other with interest. We each thought our own plans made so much sense, but here we were, taking opposite roads to the same goal.

These opposite roads were eventually named. "Homeschoolers" were the ones who, like Meg with the basement classroom, created a miniature public school at home. Those of us eager to chuck everything about school and try what Holt wrote about in his books were tagged with the word he had coined, "Unschoolers."

Differences in the Homeschooling/ Unschooling Day

Meg described what she wanted for her children as a classical education. Their days as homeschoolers looked like a scene from a small private school, though she imprinted a lot of her own style on it. She knew, for example, that with only four students and a concerned mom for a teacher, her children got plenty of individual attention by lunchtime. When the kids left their Latin and grammar lessons and trooped upstairs to eat, the formal part of the school day was over. Their afternoons were filled with hobbies, household chores, and playing with the neighborhood friends.

Every few weeks, they would all pile into their station wagon and make a two-hour trip to spend the day at our house. When I asked Meg how they got their schoolwork done on those days, she replied with a twinkle, "Well, today is different. Today is just a fun day."

CHAPTER THREE

Our own days as unschoolers looked pretty chaotic by contrast. There wasn't much of a routine at our house, even in the mornings. We didn't necessarily scorn routine, but we weren't in charge. Each day made its own demands, and we decided to use that instead of fight it.

My husband Mac had a small plumbing repair business, so sometimes he went off in his truck right after breakfast; sometimes, he was home all day with us. When there was a simple local call, Eric often went along. He learned the names of the tools, how to fix things, and he met all the guys at the supply house. It was a kick to see Mac and Eric go off together in coveralls with lunch boxes in hand. Other times, if Mac's ulcer was acting up, we hung around home to make soup and read and play quiet games. We made the best of whatever each day presented to us.

Eric was four when my Dad died. It seemed like a good idea to try and keep Dad's plant nursery business going; a way to add some income to the family without having to leave Eric with a sitter. The nursery was on seven acres, and any time we went there to work, we were sure to have some neighborhood kids tag along. They played in the woods, explored the nearly abandoned orchard, and helped water plants. The high point, of course, was eating at McDonald's on the way home, or romping at a local park we passed along the way.

Either of the two scenarios by itself would have made a good life for us, filled with learning experiences. But, as complications piled on us from Mac's uncertain health, we found ourselves selling plants at a weekend flea market, opening a health food store, and taking part time jobs like delivering phone books. Eric jumped into each project with gusto. He chimed in on discussions when he had a business decision to make, learned to wait on customers, and make change, and one year, he even started a little flea market business of his own. We did our best to let him take part in ways that interested him the most.

Every week, every month, was a little different from the past. We knew he was learning a lot from all of this, but it wasn't due to any smart plan on our part. When he was old enough to be fascinated by computers, we were gratified to see that he did well on the SAT software tests. Maybe we hadn't been exactly methodical in our approach, but something was going right.

HOW DO I GET STARTED?

So which way works best?

Over the years, I have been able to talk with hundreds of homeschooling families—some like Meg's, and some like mine. When they shared the details of their schooling plans, it was easy to see that the two modes described above (homeschooling and unschooling), had dozens of variations, and that they were all successful.

In time, I would find myself explaining to reporters that they could line up 100 homeschoolers and ask how they educated their children, and they would get about 99 different answers, and I could truthfully say that any of those methods appeared to work. You just had to pick one that fit your family.

Drawbacks and Pluses in a Nutshell

Homeschoolers I watched over the years who followed the traditional model often seemed to move seamlessly from being successful achievers in grade school to being successful in high school, college, and jobs. If being organized, methodical, and structured fit their outlook and family style, the results were impressive.

Sometimes though, I met a family that insisted on the homeschool mode for a child who would have been happier without having Latin forced on him, would have done as well or better without a college education, or would have achieved more personal satisfaction in his/her life if allowed to live in a looser framework.

Unschoolers I talked to, if they were encouraged by their family to plunge into a beloved hobby and forget about learning geometry if they hated it, often became accomplished professionals in their field at an early age. Other unschoolers confused letting kids choose their own path with just watching them choose no path at all. If the kids were offered no guidance in their unschooling, sometimes the family wasn't happy with the outcome.

CHAPTER THREE

Shopping for the Right Fit

If both ways work and both have pitfalls, how do you know if you are making the right choice? Here's a simple analogy. Essentially, the home-schooler sees education as a complete grocery list of needs, and they set out to efficiently and methodically acquire everything on that list. The danger here is that sometimes it can make the shopper miserable in the process and unable to enjoy the full basket at the end.

The unschooler might agree with much of the list, but their tactic is to set a kind of natural shopping process in motion. If an unschooler is allowed the time and freedom to acquire the important things from that grocery list, according to their inborn talents and hungers, their education pantry will be stocked with what is most nourishing to him/her.

An unschooler who finds him/herself content and successful with only part of the list in their shopping basket might well ask, "Do I really need to get the rest of that stuff?" The danger here is in whether the answer to that question is accurate.

I am betting that some part of the above analogy gave you a gut feeling that one way was right for you, and the other would make you crazy. Knowing that is a good place to start.

Parting Thoughts

It is a shame that the division of homeschooling and unschooling ever happened. I believe that John Holt was right from the beginning—we are all unschoolers. School insists that children have a one-size-fits-all experience, an approved curriculum, and a list of studies that fit some national goal. Unschooling means we don't buy that; it means that we forget all of those ideals and terms and methods and philosophies and instead, teach our children in whatever mixed, blended, hybrid way that works for their unique needs.

HOW DO I GET STARTED?

From the Experts

Unschooling Adventures
~ Nancy and Billy Greer

Billy, Nancy, Glen, and **Lane Greer** have run FUN Books in Pasadena, Maryland since 1994. They are now the proud owners of the John Holt's Bookstore and are helping to keep alive the spirit of **Growing Without Schooling** magazine as the exclusive source of almost 25 years worth of back issues. You can find them on-line at **www.unschooling.org** and **www.FUN-Books.com**, contact them by e-mail at **fun@FUN-Books.com**, or write to them at 1688 Belhaven Woods Ct., Pasadena, MD 21122.

The decision to homeschool is very personal. Our culture makes it easy to send children to school, so parents must have a strong motivation to defy the norm and keep their children home. While I can't tell you why every parent decides to homeschool, I can tell you about our family and how we became unschoolers.

Nancy is a person who likes to plan ahead. Before our first child was born, she started making plans for their education. We discussed the pro's and con's of public schools versus private schools. Nancy lived practically all her life in the same house in Northern Virginia and attended public school where she was subjected to an "experimental program of the month" education during the 1960s and 1970s. She remembers starting school as an outgoing child who enjoyed reading to her classmates, but somewhere along the way becoming shyer and developing a fear of speaking in public. She did well academically, but just didn't enjoy going to school. Some of her strongest memories include the year that "mainstreaming" put older kids with developmental and behavioral problems in her class, and one boy held her by the wrists over a stairwell and threatened to drop her. She also remembers the morning she felt sick and wanted to leave, but by the time the teacher finally acknowledged her raised hand and called her to the front of the room, it was too late and she threw-up on the teacher's desk. Nancy just didn't think much of her public school experience!

CHAPTER THREE

I grew up as a Navy brat and attended about a dozen different schools. Like Nancy, I also did well academically, but unlike Nancy, I viewed my public school experience fairly positively, and wasn't as inclined to opt for private school for our children. Besides, I figured we were going to be such supportive parents that the actual school environment wasn't very important. Our involvement could make up for any of the shortcomings of the school.

We started out evaluating and visiting lots of private schools and public schools. As we checked out the public schools, we found they weren't the same as when we attended. Classes were larger, students did more poorly, and weapons and drugs were much more commonplace. My frugal (okay, cheap) nature rebelled against the idea of stretching our finances to pay thousands of dollars for a private school, but I was beginning to think it might be our only option, and so we visited several private schools. We liked many of the philosophies and approaches we came across, but we ended up feeling that there were major shortcomings at each school. For us, the perfect program would involve combining the best ideas from two or three different schools. We also realized that most private schools were based on the same model of the public schools, only "more" and "better." They had more computers, more hands-on activities, better student/teacher ratios, better discipline, etc. We slowly came to realize that we didn't just want a better version of a public school education; we wanted something completely different.

We had heard about homeschooling from various sources and decided we wanted to read more about it. We checked out a handful of books from the public library, including ones written by John Holt and the Colfax family. In defending sending our kids to public school, I had argued that parental involvement was more important than the actual school they went to. How could you have more parental involvement than homeschooling? With the private schools, we had wished for one that combined the best of the different philosophies and techniques we saw at the various schools we visited. With homeschooling, we could pick and choose the best methods for our family. We were even more convinced when a careful self-evalua-

HOW DO I GET STARTED?

tion made us realize that our important life skills, the activities we enjoyed doing for fun or as hobbies, and most of our job skills had all been learned outside of school! By the time our firstborn was a year old, we had decided to continue educating him at home.

During those early years of child rearing, we got to experience the wonders of learning new things through the eyes of a child. We saw how children are the ultimate scientists, exploring and experimenting with everything. They learn by trial and error and are able to master difficult tasks such as walking and talking with virtually no instruction. Despite these observations, I still wasn't likely to be a natural unschooler. I tend to be a "here, let me show you how to do that" type of person. Fortunately, our son Glen was able to teach me to be an unschooler pretty quickly. He wanted to do things himself, and if I tried to help him, he got mad! I discovered that whenever I offered unasked for help, it was almost guaranteed that Glen would not only ignore my offered advice, he would stop trying completely.

Nancy likes to research anything she gets involved with and was more widely read than I was when it came to homeschooling. She directed me to some good books and articles that soon made me an unschooling convert. I love to tinker and experiment to figure things out for myself and often disliked it when someone would take away that pleasure of learning by telling me what to do without checking to see if I wanted any help. Unschooling started to really make sense to me! Someone once told me that in a conversation with John Holt, Ivan Illich compared education to eating an orange. I can imagine him describing the whole process—the feel of the orange against your fingers as you peel it, the sharp citric smell and the sticky juice that might squirt when you bite into a section of the orange, the seeds you have to spit out. The modern education establishment would declare such a process too messy and inefficient. It would be distilled to a few essentials with the result that a vitamin C tablet would be considered a superior substitute. How could anyone compare the sensual pleasure of eating an orange to swallowing a vitamin tablet?

CHAPTER THREE

With the fervor of any new convert, we were eager to share our ideas and to discuss unschooling with others. We decided to start the Family Unschoolers Network and use a newsletter to help unschoolers support each other. That was the start of FUN News. We also were involved with starting a local support group. With her love for researching her interests, Nancy began to build an extensive collection of resources. She carted a file box of articles, newspaper clippings, and books to our meetings. She wrote a resource column in FUN News to share much of the information she came across.

Many of the books we liked were not easily available. To satisfy our own voracious appetite for new books and to help the many homeschoolers who asked us where they could find the resources we recommended, Nancy decided we should start a bookstore. FUN Books was born with a handful of titles and a handful of customers. From the beginning, it was important to us to show homeschoolers that there was an alternative to pre-packaged curriculum materials and that learning really can be a fun process for the whole family.

Over the years, we have seen that new homeschoolers have a tendency to want to start off with a prepared curriculum, but the longer they continue, the more they are likely to relax and feel comfortable choosing individual materials to use in a personalized program. Unschooling becomes an even more important learning approach as our world is becoming a place of more rapid changes. For unschoolers, learning is a continuous process and that makes them more adaptable to change. When learning comes from a sense of purpose and a high degree of self-motivation, it is more likely to be an enjoyable process that is embraced rather than a process that is viewed as drudgery to be avoided if possible. Learning how to learn is perhaps the most important lesson of unschooling, and keeping the experience enjoyable and rewarding helps ensure that unschoolers can learn what they need to know when they need to know it. It's just-in-time learning for our fast changing world.

HOW DO I GET STARTED?

As homeschooling grows and becomes more mainstream, there are more people who recognize that an advantage of homeschooling is the freedom to throw out traditional educational approaches and to try alternative approaches that can work better for your family. Unfortunately, there are also more companies marketing to homeschoolers and promoting the idea that homeschooling means bringing the school process home or that homeschooling is just a less expensive private school. They are happy to sell you curriculum materials or sign you up for their programs. These companies have their place, but it is important that they not drown out the voices of the alternatives. If homeschooling becomes too regulated and too standardized, it runs the risk of becoming just another form of public education and will lose many of its benefits. If we're lucky, the opposite will happen and public education will become more like unschooling!

CHAPTER THREE

From the Experts

Homeschooling and the Internet
~ Beverly Hernandez

The Internet has forever changed the homeschooling world. It has changed how individual families homeschool, and has also changed the network as a whole. I use the Internet in my homeschooling quite extensively, but I'm nearing the end of my homeschooling years. I would have loved to have the World Wide Web available during the early years because there are many resources available for

> **Beverly Hernandez** is the homeschooling guide at the popular About.com web site **http://homeschooling.about.com**. To contact her, check out the About.com site, or email her at **homeschooling.guide@about.com**

the beginner. In fact, there is so much available right at our fingertips, that it is amazing and sometimes somewhat overwhelming. The Internet features resources to use in daily homeschooling, free worksheets and unit studies, instant support, the means to buy and sell curriculum year round, and much more!

Beginners

For the beginner, the tips on getting started are plentiful. Nearly every homeschooling site has a "getting started page" that outlines the steps to take.

Many new homeschoolers want to start by checking the laws in their particular state and that information is readily available online. It is important to read up on this information and make sure that all regulations and requirements are met.

Two popular web sites to check out are:
- About Legal Information by State – **http://homeschooling.about.com/library/bllegal.htm**
- HSLDA Legal Information by State –
  www.hslda.org/hs/state/default.asp

HOW DO I GET STARTED?

The next thing to consider is joining a support group. Support groups come in all shapes and sizes, and the trick is finding one that meets your needs. Support group information is available online, but there are many small groups that aren't on the Web yet. Contact your state association for a more complete list of groups, or check with your local church or library.

Curriculum is the next big decision, and for some, it is the most difficult one to make. You can do a lot of curriculum research online by visiting publishers' websites, reading curriculum related articles, and talking to others in forums or email lists. You'll want to read up on different learning styles and homeschooling methods before making your curriculum choice. Many beginners choose to stick with one publisher at first. After gaining experience in homeschooling and finding out what works, it gets easier to mix and match.

The Homeschoolers Trading Zone is a new forum at About Homeschooling for buying, selling, and trading your homeschooling materials. There are many sites that offer a similar service allowing you to list the books you want to sell. You can also list what you are looking for, and the books will come to you. I have found that it is a great way to try out a curriculum. You can purchase books cheaper used and resell them if they don't meet your needs.

Explore your options at these web sites:
- Homeschoolers Trading Zone – **http://forums.about.com/ab-homeschool2/start**
- VegSource – **www.vegsource.com/homeschool**
- Ebay – **www.ebay.com**
- Half.com – **www.half.com**

CHAPTER THREE

Online Support

One of the best advantages that the Internet offers to the homeschooling world is instant access to support and help when it is needed. In the wee hours of the night, when you're all alone and having doubts that you're doing the right thing, you can turn to homeschooling sites and forums and be uplifted and encouraged—ready to go on another day. There are many online forums, chats, and email lists that keep you connected to the homeschooling world, and many homeschoolers will respond in your time of need.

Homeschoolers are being united by means of the Internet. There are local and national groups arising, and many different support groups are making their newsletters available online. The instant notification by email is making last minute changes easier to handle in support groups. Groups are making their record keeping forms available over the Internet, and leaders are beginning to work together and share resources.

To find out more, click on:
- About Support Groups & Associations –
  http://homeschooling.about.com/library/weekly/aa072999.htm
- National Home Education Network –
  www.nhen.org/support/index.htm

There are online support groups for different homeschooling methods, religious affiliations, geographical locations, etc. A homeschooler can find support online from others who also practice their methods, even though they might not have support in their immediate area. People who live far from other homeschoolers are no longer as isolated as they used to be.

HOW DO I GET STARTED?

Online Studies

The online world also offers many studies and worksheets to add to your homeschooling curriculum. The resources are endless and sometimes overwhelming. When I first began using the Internet with my homeschooling, I was lost in a sea of sites and URLs and struggled to get them organized. Now that I do the homeschooling site at About.com, I am slowly organizing the best sites for each subject and topic to make it easier for homeschoolers worldwide. Now when I need something, more often than not, I can get the information at my own site.

For more information on this option, check out:
- Online Unit Study Directory – **http://homeschooling.about.com/cs/unitonline/**
- Distance Learning – **http://homeschooling.about.com/cs/distancelearning/**

The Internet also offers online schools and classes that can meet the requirements for your homeschooling. Basically, they offer curriculum and teachers to make the assignments. Your role is more of a facilitator than a teacher, and you help your student when it is needed. There is controversy as to whether this is considered homeschooling. As one who has participated in such a school, I can assure you that you'll still be doing the bulk of the teaching and the work. I never felt that it wasn't homeschooling, but after many years of homeschooling on my own, it was frustrating to not have full control.

News and Information

Another important advantage the Internet offers is the ability to stay informed of the news and changes in the homeschooling laws. With this information at your fingertips, you can act in a more timely manner when issues arise by writing the appropriate people. It is important to keep on top of these matters to help protect your right to homeschool.

Keep up to date by accessing these web sites:
- Homeschooling in the News – **http://homeschooling.about.com/cs/homeschoolnews/**
- NHEN-Announce – **http://groups.yahoo.com/group/NHEN-Announce**

CHAPTER THREE

Internet Safety

The Internet is a great learning tool and an excellent resource for finding information, but there is also a lot of harmful material readily available. In my searching for educational material for my site, I've been subjected to more than I bargained for many times. Don't let this happen to your children. The Internet can be an enjoyable addition to your children's education; just be wise and supervise.

Follow these simple steps to help prevent your children from stumbling across objectionable sites:

- Warn your children of the dangers.

- Install a filtering or blocking program on your computer or activate the feature provided on your browser or ISP.

- Keep the computer screen in plain view.

- Keep the logs available; don't allow them to be erased.

- If the logs are erased, investigate why.

- Keep your children accountable to you or someone else.

- Be careful of using chat rooms.

- Don't allow personal information to be given out.

Any time I talk about the Internet and homeschooling, I include warnings and information about Internet safety because I feel it is very important and should not be put off until later. At the same time though, don't be afraid of the Internet; get acquainted with it. If you take the necessary precautions, the Internet can be very useful in your homeschooling. It is what you make of it. You can use it for an occasional resource, or base most of your homeschooling on it. The Internet can be a tool that enriches your homeschooling experience for years to come!

HOW DO I GET STARTED?

Just the Facts

- Homeschooling curriculum can be found a many different places and does not need to cost a fortune.

- You do not need to use the same curriculum as your school system.

- You can create your own unique curriculum or purchase packaged sets.

- Grade levels are irrelevant in homeschooling.

- "Deschooling"is a process that most homeschooling children will need to go through when they have been removed from public school.

- The eight different learning styles are important to know so that you can better understand how your child processes and understands material/information.

- The homeschooling continuum ranges from bringing school home to unschooling. Most families fall somewhere in the middle through a trial and error process.

- Standardized tests are required in some states, and kids need to be adequately prepared for them. They are rarely, if ever, an accurate assessment of how your child is actually doing.

- You can begin homeschooling any time you choose.

CHAPTER THREE

- You can homeschool year round, take the summers off, or devise your own personal schedule for what works best for your family.

- Some states require homeschooling documentation. There are several different kinds you can use including: journals, subject logs, portfolios, and transcripts.

- It is possible to homeschool different ages and levels at the same time.

- Television and Internet can play important roles in homeschooling; the key is moderation.

- You can teach a subject that you don't know or like either by learning it along with your children or by getting outside help.

- What children are "supposed" to know is very arbitrary and requires some real thought.

- Avoiding burnout isn't difficult if you are able to relax, consider changing your approach, take time out, vary your routine, share household responsibilities, talk it out, and take care of yourself.

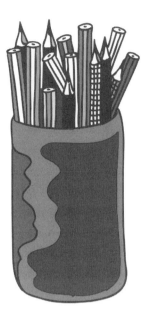

CHAPTER FOUR
Where Can I Find Help?

"Much education today is monumentally ineffective.
All too often we are giving young people cut flowers when
we should be teaching them to grow their own plants."
—*John W. Gardner*

As truly wonderful as homeschooling is, having strong internal and external support is essential. This chapter will show you where to get it, how to get it, and how to make the connections you will need to succeed.

CHAPTER FOUR

How do I find a local support group?

Finding a local support group is usually not a difficult process, depending on how large the city is that you are living in.

Some of the most helpful places to ask are:
- Libraries
- Bookstores
- Children's stores
- Churches

Check your local newspaper for announcements of group meetings and calendars. If you run into another homeschooler, ask them for assistance. Many of the homeschooling magazines will list state-by-state contacts as well, so find a recent issue and see what is listed under your state. If you have access to the web, check there for state web sites, or go to national web sites and see if they list regional representatives. These support groups will be your key to keeping up-to-date about homeschooling activities/events/conferences, legislation and current court cases. They are a key to your networking with others in all realms of homeschooling, from the next-door neighbor to your Congressman.

How do I find a state support group?

Your best sources are homeschooling books, magazines, local support groups, the Internet, and perhaps, your state Department of Education, if you have made the choice to be in contact with them. Sometimes schools will have this information also. See Appendix B for a list of state homeschooling organizations.

How do I find a national support group?

Once again, look in homeschooling books and magazines and on the Internet. Often in searching for one of these groups, you are going to run into information about the others also. Before joining one, check out what is available so that you can compare. Pay close attention to the group's mission statement for their organization to make sure it is in line with your homeschooling beliefs and foundations.

WHERE CAN I FIND HELP?

How do I start my own support group?

Sometimes the group in your area isn't meeting your needs or perhaps it is too far away to get to on a regular basis. In this case, you might want to start your own. Here are some guidelines on how to do it:

I. **Set your mission or goal.**
    In other words, what are you looking for in this group? List what you hope to achieve and ask the following questions of both yourself and anyone else who is interested in forming this new group:

    A. **Will this group be a casual, informal group or more structured?**
        Is everyone going to be friends and socialize together, or will the group be primarily for setting up field trips and events?

    B. **Will the group be religious based, secular, or a mixture?**
        Some groups require members to sign a Statement of Faith to belong. Is this something you want to do? Do you want to welcome all faiths to your group? How about atheists?

    C. **How large should the group be?**
        The larger it is, the more structure will be needed. All sizes have their benefits: large groups can organize better events while smaller ones get to know each other better. Do you want to set a limit?

CHAPTER FOUR

D. **Where should the group meet?**
Most start out in churches or at each other's houses. This can work well, or it can become a nightmare if the group gets too large. Libraries and other public buildings often have meeting rooms available at no charge, so check around your area and make a list of possibilities.

E. **How often should the group meet?**
It usually varies from once a week to once a month. What day and time is best?

F. **Do you want officers?**
Membership dues? A newsletter?

G. **Do you want children to come to the meetings?**
If so, remember the facility will have to be big enough to accomodate everyone.

H. **What will you name the group?**
The name will probably be used in promotion so think about it for a while.

I. **Look at other homeschooling groups in your area.**
See what you do and do not like about them. Use these ideas in forming your own group.

WHERE CAN I FIND HELP?

II. Promote your group. The primary ways to get word out about your new group are:

A. **Regular announcements.**
Place them in newspapers, including what you did at the last meeting and the agenda for the next one. Make these sound exciting and always include an invitation for other families to come.

B. **Advertise on TV.**
If your local cable company has a channel for local advertising, ask if your non-profit group can advertise for no charge.

C. **Advertise on the Radio.**
Put public service announcements on radio stations in your area.

D. **Create flyers.**
Hand them out at church, the library, etc.

E. **List your group in homeschooling publications.**
There are places for this in several publications, like *Home Education Magazine*.

F. **Names and Numbers.**
Leave your name and number at the most common places people will ask for homeschooling information (bookstore, libraries, etc.) If you're called, invite the caller to the next meeting. Take his/her name and address for your files and send them notices of upcoming meetings or events.

CHAPTER FOUR

G. **Hold Open Houses.**
Host this event regularly for new families to come and ask questions.

H. **Speaking Engagements.**
Offer to speak at your local library about home-schooling and hand out flyers then.

I. **Talk to everyone.**
Word of mouth is always the best advertising.

III. **Maintain your group. To keep growing strong, be sure to:**

A. **Organize a telephone chain.**
This way each member is responsible to call the next to remind them of upcoming meetings and events.

B. **Plan a number of different activities.**
This will help to meet the needs of all the families in your group.

C. **Check with other members often.**
See if there are improvements, changes, or problems that need to be discussed.

D. **Set up an Internet chat room or mailing list.**
This way members can keep in contact at all times.

Lastly, be patient. Creating a support group that is strong and growing is a gradual process and not likely to happen overnight. It can take some groups a year to feel they are on track and getting what they need. It is definitely worth the work, however, to have a place you can go to and people you can be with that make you feel welcome and encouraged.

WHERE CAN I FIND HELP?

What kinds of field trips are available?

This is a little like asking where can I go for vacation? The possibilities are virtually endless; the only boundaries are your time, money, and imagination.

Here are just a few of the gazillion places you can choose from:

- Factories
- Theatres
- Restaurants
- Churches
- Museums
- Universities
- Stores of all kinds
- Doctors/hospitals/medical centers
- Government buildings
- Libraries
- Historic sites
- Rivers/mountains/caves/forests – whatever your area has
- YMCA/YWCA
- Experts and their businesses – from the beekeeper to the barber, fireman to photographer, and everything in between.

Many organized homeschooling groups will have field trips set up for a month or more at a time, and you can participate in them. However, many times the field trips your children will like the best are the ones you set up for them.

If you keep your eyes open at all times, you will be astonished at all the places and people there are out there who would make terrific field trips for your family.

Once you have targeted one, contact the place and ask to talk to the person who is responsible for setting up field trips. Arrange the day and time that is convenient, and be sure to ask how many children can comfortably come (you can invite friends!), what ages are welcome, and if you should bring money for any reason (i.e. buying donuts to take home after the trip to the bakery). Get any directions you might need, and prepare your list of questions before you go so that you are prepared.

You can follow up your field trips with various crafts to make, books to read, and discussions to have. Don't focus too hard on making the field trip a lesson, however. Instead, make it a fun time where children also happen to learn things, albeit not always the things you think they are going to learn. One mother, for example, was on the way to a museum

CHAPTER FOUR

field trip in a town she wasn't familiar with, and she was soon lost. Instead of giving up, she stopped at a nearby bagel shop for a snack, and her three children ended up following the business complex's window washer around and finding out all about his work.

Virtual field trips, taken through the Internet, can be fun for your kids too. They aren't as wonderful as the real thing, but on days when money is short, the weather is rotten, or the energy is in short supply, they are a nice alternative.

Why should I to go to a homeschool conference?

Homeschooling conferences are like that first cup of coffee in the morning; they wake you up, rev you up, and get you going with more energy and enthusiasm than you had before (and they are all decaf!) There are two main reasons that you will want to attend a homeschooling conference: to take the classes and to network with the other people there. The classes offered at most home education conferences often supply the answers to your questions and provide information that you can take home and apply immediately (perhaps even in the car on the way home). Just as importantly, however, these conferences allow you to be immersed and surrounded by people who think a lot like you do—they share the same worries and wonders, dilemmas and delights. Just sitting around talking with all of them can be enough to send you home brimming with confidence. One mother, after attending her first conference was heard to exclaim, "This is better than Christmas! I've never felt so comfortable and accepted anywhere else in my life!"

An additional perk to these gatherings are the vendors that line the hallways. All of them have a service or product to offer homeschoolers, and they are great fun to look at, ponder, and sometimes purchase. You might find just the book you needed for your history unit, a complete curriculum that fits one of your children, or just a nifty toy for your preschooler to play with while you are in class. Many conferences also have a book-

WHERE CAN I FIND HELP?

store set up for you to wander through. The materials here are frequently enough to make the trip worthwhile. If you're on a strict budget, make sure you leave those credit cards at home and only take as much money with you as you can afford. The temptation can be overwhelming.

Homeschooling conferences are often held on different levels. If you live in a sizable city, there may be some offered locally. Most states have their own conferences, and some groups, like the Clonlara Home Based Education program, hold an annual conference for families, enrolled or not. They can be found on the different homeschooling websites and magazines and are frequently listed in local homeschooling newsletters and announcements. Before you pay your money and pack your bags, however, request a conference brochure, which tells you all the particulars of the conference: keynote speakers, activities, accommodations, costs, food, and so on. Once you have this, look through it carefully so that you can mark which classes and speakers you want to attend the most, as well as look at classes for your partner and children. You will also want to make sure that the theme or philosophy of the group meshes with yours. If this is a Christian based conference, for example, you may not want to attend if you're a secular homeschooler and vice versa. Also check to see what the conference's policies are regarding children. Some welcome them and even offer special programming just for them, while others prefer you don't bring any children other than nursing babies. If children aren't welcome in classes, you will need to make some alternative childcare arrangements. Older children can be left at home but younger children rarely can, unless dad or grandparents are going to be around. Consider bringing a homeschooled teen to the conference with you to watch the kids, or maybe a parent, partner, or friend.

Whether you are a novice or a veteran, a good homeschooling conference can be a real blessing. Try to find a space in your budget to fit in at least one a year.

CHAPTER FOUR

The expenses you will need to cover include:

- *Cost of the actual conference itself.* Many offer family rates to make it more affordable).

- *Cost of transportation* How much will you spend getting to and from the conference (car, bus, plane, train, etc.)?

- *Cost of food.* Many conferences offer reduced meal prices at the place they are based; check and see. If they don't or if those prices are still too expensive, you can hit the less costly restaurants or bring your own food in a cooler.

- *Cost of lodging.* Hotels usually have discounted rates for groups, so be sure to ask. If there is only one or two of you, consider sharing the room with another small family and split the cost.

- *Cost of child care.* Will you arrange this yourself or bring your kids along and use that provided by the conference?

Homeschooling conferences can cost several hundred dollars before all is said and done, but many families feel it is more than worth it. "We consider this our annual vacation," says one mother of four who attends the Clonlara conference each year. "We wouldn't miss it for anything."

WHERE CAN I FIND HELP?

How do I talk with school officials?

Carefully. There are some wonderful school officials out there who only want the best for your child, and so they will support you in your decision to homeschool as much as possible. Unfortunately, this isn't always the case.

When you are in contact with school personnel, do as little talking as possible. Find out exactly what they want to know as well as what they legally have a right to know, and then provide only that information. Stop there. As much as you might want to share the miracle of your non-reader sitting up in bed until 2 a.m. because he was reading a book, it's unlikely they will share your joy. Instead, you may find yourself labeled as negligent for obviously not caring enough about your child to make sure he gets adequate rest.

Will the State Department of Education help me?

Unlikely. The vast majority of homeschoolers that do not have to contact their State Department of Education chose not to simply because they see no reason for it. They don't want their input or their interference. If you live in a state that requires registration and contact with your DOE, then only provide what they legally can ask for and nothing else. If you don't have to be in contact with them, don't. Too many times they will give you misinformation; telling you that you need to turn in material or information that you do not have to, scaring you into thinking you are not capable of educating your own children, and as a number of families can attest, trying to convince you that you have bitten off far more than you can chew. While there are certainly DOEs that are informed, supportive, and understanding, they are the exception to the rule.

CHAPTER FOUR

What if there aren't any homeschoolers close to us?

If you live in an area that is remote, and you have little access to local homeschoolers, you will have to depend on regional, state, and national support groups and organizations for your advice, encouragement, and assistance. Check out the pen-palling/networking section of magazines like *Home Education Magazine*, which list parents and children looking for others to correspond with.

Make sure there really aren't any homeschoolers in your area. There may be some that you aren't aware of simply because they have kept it quiet. Ask permission to post something in your church, library, or grocery store and list your phone number or email address so others can get in touch with you.

This is one situation where a computer in the house would most likely be very helpful also. There are chat rooms for homeschoolers of all ages, and they can be wonderful outlets when you or your children need to rant, spout, or brag, or just remember that there are a lot of others just like you out there.

WHERE CAN I FIND HELP?

In the Trenches

Why a Former School Teacher Chose to Homeschool

~ Francy Stillwell

This afternoon after lunch, I had the privilege of snuggling with my kids on the sofa and watching an old episode of "Perry Mason." I fully appreciate how lucky I am to get to do this with them. We almost led a different life until I decided one day that society had a warped idea of how we are supposed to live and I didn't have to comply.

I worked as a public school teacher for 10 years. While I started out very idealistic and enthusiastic about it, over the years, I became increasingly disheartened about the whole public school system. It felt like my students came in the door hating school and me before I had even been given a chance. As hard as I tried to be "up" on the current information about learning, I found no support about applying that knowledge from my administrator or very many fellow teachers. Worse, some of the students were becoming alarmingly violent at younger and younger ages. Finally, during my seventh year, I realized just how incredibly dysfunctional the public school system was and that the way to change things was not from within. I was tired—tired of being constantly exposed to viruses and stress; tired of having to teach developmentally inappropriate, irrelevant content, tired of seeing violent kids being kept in school and jeopardizing everyone's safety just to keep their dropout rates low. I was weary of hearing the excuse, "This is/isn't what is best for kids," when I knew that what was good for one kid isn't necessarily good for another. It was a one-size-fits-all system, and if it failed to work, the child was viewed as the problem, not the system.

I came to see schools as a factory processing children as its main product—and not very successfully at that. Over the years, I watched as more and more students and teachers became angry, disaffected, burned out, broken, and violent. I am not ashamed to say I felt some of this, too.

Then, I had my own two children, one 21 months after the other. It was killing me to have to drop my babies off at daycare each day. We had a wonderful daycare provider, but my children were spending the day with someone other than me, and it felt wrong. In my heart I knew they would not be children for long, and I wanted to be a part of as much of their lives as possible.

CHAPTER FOUR

Four years ago, after surviving my 10th year as a public school teacher, I quit. Somehow, we made it work financially—just. There have been a few times when I have had my doubts about whether we're doing the right thing or not. My husband certainly had his doubts too, but time has shown us both some outstanding results. Our kids are filled with a growing creative spirit that isn't being squelched in the name of institutional socialization. On the contrary, I get to see their creative processes grow on a daily basis. They are getting firsthand experience at being valuable citizens in our society—they get to be kids. All life experiences create potential for learning, and we feel good that we are preparing them for life in this world, the way it really is—you know—LIFE, mixed with real people of all ages, shapes, colors, and cultures. LIFE—something to survive and thrive in. That just doesn't happen in schools.

There is always a concern from others that my children may not be "getting enough socialization." I guess these folks think I keep them locked up all day. Quite the contrary; we are out in the world on a daily basis. We take part in a variety of groups and classes. We go to museums and parks; we know our neighbors. In school, children are learning about the world from each other—equally inexperienced peers. The result is not acceptable.

People seem relieved that I am a teacher when they discover we are homeschooling, and I just have to laugh when they say this. To be honest, there isn't much about my teaching experience that is helpful except as a model of what not to do.

I now find joy in every day. I feel so grateful to have this time with our children. Both of them are curious, and we can pursue things while they are still feeling curious. I endeavor to expose them to all kinds of things so that they will have something new all the time. I try hard to listen to them so I can be an effective guide, and if I listen carefully enough, they are guides for me as well. And sometimes, we have lunch, snuggle on the sofa—and watch an old episode of "Perry Mason."

WHERE CAN I FIND HELP?

In the Trenches
Encouraging Learning Passion in Children
~ John Andersen

Wise parents expose their children to the community, to complex issues, to a broad spectrum of people, to the greatest minds, and so forth. There is a variety of ways they might do this and here are a few examples:

- **Take your children to the art museum**. Interpret a painting for them, then ask for their interpretations of that one or another painting. Go home and create your own paintings.

- **Attend public meetings.** Arrange for your children to meet the mayor, senator, or congressman. Take your children to a street demonstration and discuss why people are participating in it.

- **Go to the zoo**. Sit on a bench and watch a particular animal. Take about what you see and let your children tell you what they see. Check out some library books about their favorite animals.

- **Take walks together through nature preserves**. Intentionally slow down and truly notice the plants and wildlife. Talk about and record your impressions when you get home.

- **Seek out interesting and creative people in the community** such as inventors, authors, scientists, and poets. Arrange to visit with these people in their homes, attend their lectures, write letters to them, or become their apprentice.

- **Read books together everyday**. Talk about ideas and philosophies while eating dinner. Be a passionate scholar yourself.

CHAPTER FOUR

- **Visit historical sites**. View films together about historic events. Write letters to grandparents and other people who are much older. Nurture strong connections with the past.

- **Make it a point to talk with people on the street and in the shops, when appropriate**. Ask them questions and listen carefully; be endlessly curious.

- **Taste the joy of many diverse interests**. Be actors in a local play. Join a gymnastics club. Take fencing lessons as a family. Learn to play a musical instrument.

The list goes on and on. We don't have to do all of that at once. Rather, the idea is to be active learners, to create your own intellectual stimulation, to sincerely believe you can actually learn something without tests, tuition payments, classroom time, or grades.

This method is anything but passive and directionless. On the contrary, it's arguably the most demanding of all learning methods and potentially, the most stimulating as well. For it to succeed, parents need to be their children's facilitators, constantly finding ways to harness the endless learning resources of their local communities, and ultimately, the world around them. Essentially, it's about lighting a fire within yourself and letting it burn brightly enough that your children naturally desire to become engulfed as well.

WHERE CAN I FIND HELP?

In the Trenches
Homeschooling from the Jewish Perspective

~ Melisa Crosby

I homeschool my children and I am a practicing Jew. As time goes on, I find that these two elements of my life become more intertwined. In the beginning, I never thought that my Judaism had much to do with my decision to homeschool, but over time I have come to believe that Judaism positively influences my homeschooling endeavors, and homeschooling certainly enhances my family's ability to live 'Jewishly' every day.

Converts to Judaism have traditionally been referred to in English as "Jews by Choice," but many people now believe that the term has come to be an appropriate label for all practicing Jews, regardless of affiliation. While it isn't at all difficult to walk away from Judaism in contemporary secular America, many of us choose to embrace Judaism and live by its wisdom and ethics on a daily basis. I made a conscious decision to live by the teachings of my heritage at about the same time I began looking into homeschooling my two sons. Perhaps the clearest parallel between the two choices has to do with stepping outside the mainstream. Just as stepping outside mainstream secular American culture may seem like a leap, so too might the choice to opt out of the public school system. Jews have nearly always been outsiders in any culture in which they might live, and homeschoolers, until recently, were outsiders as well.

There are many wonderful reasons for Jews to consider homeschooling, including control over the family calendar. Homeschooling families tend to spend far more time together than those involved in school. American public school schedules are built around the Christian calendar. Even if the subject matter isn't explicitly Christian, the timing of events and activities generally fails to take the Jewish calendar into consideration.

Both in-class and extracurricular activities frequently conflict with holidays and/or Shabbat. Most schools allow children to miss class for holidays, but these absences put the Jewish child at a disadvantage both educationally and socially as they are forced to make up missed work. Homeschooling empowers families by enabling them to take control of their schedules.

Another advantage of homeschooling is that it allows us to live our lives more easily in Jewish time. My family's weekly rhythm includes preparing for Shabbat and studying the weekly Torah portion. As holidays approach, we might put other studies aside to focus on holiday preparations and observance. Many of the synagogue holiday observances take place in the evening. Because my boys don't have to get up early for school, they can enjoy festivities at Purim and Simchat Torah wholeheartedly. Many Jewish families make daily prayer a part of daily life, and homeschooling allows time for contemplative worship without hurry.

Homeschooling can be an ideal option for families who wish to make Jewish teachings the core of their educational pursuits. Torah study, Hebrew skills, and Jewish ethics can all be included in the curriculum along with secular studies. Some families choose to tackle these subjects on their own, while many others incorporate synagogue religious school into

CHAPTER FOUR

their education. Most of the homeschooling children I know are happy to attend religious education programs. Because they don't spend all week in school, homeschooled children may be particularly engaged and attentive during their hours in religious school. Most Jewish educators are happy to assist homeschoolers, and numerous Jewish publishers will make their educational materials available for individuals as well as institutions.

Jewish children who are homeschooled are not constantly bombarded by messages that conflict with the values of their families and their faith. Public school classes often focus on themes that many Jewish parents consider inappropriate for their children. In addition, I feel that the majority of schools are overrun by consumerism, racism, violence, stereotyping, cliquishness, and numerous other elements that I feel are inappropriate for my children. Homeschooling drastically reduces the conflicting messages that children receive when moving between home and school. Certainly, the world is full of unpleasant things, and it is essential that children learn to be discriminating in their choices. Homeschooling allows children to build these skills from a solid foundation of moral teaching.

Tikkun Olam (repairing the world) is a central value in Judaism. While the average schooled child may have very little time available for charity and social action, many homeschooled families include these as part of their educational plan. When we talk about feeding the hungry and clothing the naked, we can reinforce the importance of these goals by volunteering at the food bank or collecting clothes for a homeless shelter. Sometimes it takes some work, but one can generally find volunteer opportunities for even young children. I find it particularly advantageous that my children usually accompany me when I help out at our synagogue, giving them both a sense of ownership and firsthand knowledge of how much effort is involved in running a synagogue.

Because many Jewish families feel very strongly about Jewish education, there are private day schools in nearly all American cities with sizeable Jewish populations. These schools can offer high quality Jewish and secular education but, like public schools, may not meet the needs of everyone. Private tuition, even with scholarships, is prohibitive for many Jewish families, especially those blessed with several children. Because of the additional subject matters taught, school days are even longer than those of most public school children. Not all children thrive in the social environment of the day school, and the chosen educational philosophy is unlikely to work well for all children. While day schools are a central part of American Jewish communities, more and more families are finding that homeschooling is a preferable educational option.

Education is valued highly in Judaism and is considered a lifelong goal. There is no end to learning from our sacred texts. I love studying and learning with my children, and I am grateful that I am able to model lifelong learning for them. The time I have with my children under my roof is limited, and I feel extremely blessed that we get to spend the majority of our time together, learning and growing as a family.

WHERE CAN I FIND HELP?

"Too often we give children answers to remember rather than problems to solve."
—Roger Lewin

From the Experts

Dealing with the Rest of the World
~ Pat Montgomery

Pat Montgomery is President and Founder of Clonlara Home-Based Education, Ann Arbor, Michigan.

As founder and director of Clonlara School, I bring to this essay my experiences in advocating for families who enroll in our home based education program. I have taught in public, parochial, and alternative schools for my entire career—all 47 years of it. The following is advice that we regularly prescribe. It can be applied to any home educating family, I believe.

The whole idea behind Clonlara School's philosophy is "do it yourself," seize the power, take control. But early on in the home education movement, it became abundantly clear to me that parents were on the low rung of the power structure when dealing with public school officials. Only students were lower on the ladder. In the late seventies/early eighties, most local school officials took grave issue with the notion of home education. Some scoffed; others threatened.

A father in northern Ohio was arrested and jailed in 1980 for teaching his seven year old at home. Another in Michigan was jailed for two weeks for home educating his eight youngsters. These are but two examples of the animosity that existed. Parents justifiably felt that they were on the opposite side of the trenches in a war. They were, after all, denying the public schools coveted tax monies by removing or not sending their children to be counted on the school rolls.

It was clear to me that parents could not face this foe alone, so one of the first things Clonlara School established in its array of services was to

CHAPTER FOUR

become a team with parents. As a credentialed school official myself, I was able to interact with, and for, parents when they dealt with school authorities, prosecuting attorneys, judges, social services workers, social security authorities, college admissions officers, and others. The result of this unified approach was that outside officials were persuaded to deal in a respectful manner with parents.

Clonlara School filed suit in federal court against school superintendents, truant officers (a.k.a. pupil personnel directors), boards of education, and the Michigan Department of Education for denying the rights of parents to educate their own children. We lost that suit, but another that we filed simultaneously in Circuit Court in 1985, *Clonlara* v. *Michigan Board of Education*, was a major success. The Michigan Board of Education was ultimately restricted to treating home educating parents exactly the way it treated nonpublic schools.

So much for early history! Has the scene changed? Are today's public school officials dealing fairly with parents? Yes and no. More of them are, but far too many are not. These latter take a proprietary stand. They resent having non-professionals (parents) insert themselves into the sacrosanct arena of schooling. They deal with students similarly. It is not uncommon to hear of boards of education that forbid public school students to invite home educated students to a school dance, for example. When students transfer from home to their local public high school, it is not unusual for them to be threatened with denial of credits earned through home schooling.

So, what's a parent to do? How can they deal with hostile officials?

The most successful step they can take, in my albeit slightly biased opinion, is to enroll in Clonlara School. We attend to all of the administrative duties associated with their home education, chief among which is dealing with all contacts with officials. For over 20 years, I have witnessed the substantial difference that this makes in parents' and students' lives. Clonlara stands alone in providing this service. It makes a great deal of difference to school officials and to other outside officials when they learn that the family is willing to receive guidance and counseling from a school.

WHERE CAN I FIND HELP?

Having school people dealing with other school people puts the issues on a different level entirely.

A parent does well to learn what the regulations are. Knowledge of the law on compulsory school attendance and on home education is essential, first off. Librarians have this information. State senators and representatives can supply it. Local home school support groups have it. It is spelled out clearly in the volumes of education law for each state. Knowing the regulations is a must. Knowing one's rights is the corollary.

Perhaps the most devastating thing that I have observed amongst parents is that they lack self-confidence when dealing with authorities. They are, in this sense, victims of an upbringing and/or schooling that renders them virtually powerless. These are capable people who can run a successful household, fix appliances, operate costly equipment, diagnose illnesses, and so on… yet they cower before the school principal. It puts them at a decided disadvantage. We are, after all, just humans. We deserve respect and dignity. We are equals. That fact seems to have gotten lost.

When contacted by school people, parents do well to act in a respectful, dignified way. They also do well to get everything in writing. It is far too easy, when talking informally to a principal, teacher, or school clerk, for example, to omit or to gloss over important pieces of information. School (and other officials) are themselves sticklers for getting things in writing; so ought parents to be. It is perfectly reasonable to respond to a telephone call by stating, "I don't want to discuss matters by phone; please put whatever it is you wish to tell me into writing; I will respond with more intelligence then." Spoken firmly and politely, that is a professional approach.

Clonlara recommends to its families when they are withdrawing children from public or private schools, for instance, to do it in writing. A courtesy note simply stating that the child "is no longer enrolled" in that public (or private) school can be slipped into a cumulative file folder. This assures a parent that the message was received and understood.

A telephone conversation is not as effective, and it leaves the parent open to all manner of prying. Acting with dignity invites the same treatment from the school officials.

CHAPTER FOUR

Many parents assume that they must give lengthy explanations about what they intend to do, why they arrived at the decision, and the like. This is simply not so. A parent's decision is his own; he needs explain it to no one.

Relatives of a family that chooses to home educate are, sad to say, often the violators of parents' rights. Those who disagree with a parent's decision to home educate have been known to make anonymous reports to social services agencies accusing the parents of child abuse or neglect. Of course, social workers are not at liberty to divulge the name(s) of the complaining party, and they are responsible to check out the complaint.

Should this happen, parents must be aware, once again, of their rights. They are, for example, under no obligation to answer a knock or doorbell. Clonlara recommends that they do not. The social worker will leave a business card. The parent then has a chance to assess the situation and to respond *on his/her terms* rather than being caught unawares. Make the call; arrange an appointment—this can often be in the office of the social worker—at a time when both parents can be present or when a trusted friend and advocate can come along. The parent is cooperating and can better hear and understand and respond to the allegations.

One parent reported that she was doing kitchen work when two men, one a sheriff's deputy, rang the doorbell of her rural home. She ignored the ring and went about her business despite the fact that the men could see her through the window. After trying repeatedly to get her attention, the duo left. She retrieved the card stuck into the doorframe and phoned me. I had a call in to the social worker before he returned to his desk. He was irate that she didn't answer the doorbell. How dare she? Was she deaf? I asked him whether he would recommend that a young mother with two young children ought to automatically respond to the ring when two strange men were at the door—in a rural area like her own or in an urban one. He agreed that this could be dangerous and then he calmed down enough to address the reason for his visit rationally. The public school bus driver had reported that he saw children at the home but they were not registered in school; he feared they were truant.

WHERE CAN I FIND HELP?

For those relatives who are simply ignorant of home education, one can offer them books or articles to read. If they are open minded, they may eventually support their relative's choice, or at least not actively oppose it. The same applies to neighbors who take umbrage with a family's choice.

When a person who questions home schooling is sincere in her questioning, and open to learning more about the issue, a parent does well to assist her. When the questioner is a faultfinder, lacking an open mind on the subject and only interested in discrediting it, the less said the better.

As Director of Clonlara School, I caution parents and students to make it easy for school officials. Use the words, "enrolled in a private school" first when introducing themselves. It allows the official time to get accustomed to the idea of home education. A large part of the fear that a principal, a superintendent, a counselor, or a teacher has is that a student educated primarily at home will have no records. No cumulative file folder. No test results. No student transcripts (for high schoolers). Putting the best foot forward by revealing that the student was enrolled in a private school as a supplement to home schooling puts the official's mind at ease.

What can parents do who choose not to so enroll? They can take as much hard evidence as possible with them when they seek to place a student in public school. Cartons of the educational materials used in the home, photos of a student's art accomplishments, any written product that a student may have, documentation of classes the student attended at a community college or elsewhere—these assure the official that the student was seriously pursuing an education. Many students create a portfolio of their work and add to it during each of the high school years. Explanations about apprenticeships or mentorships—anything that a student did ought all to be there.

When dealing with college admissions officers, students and parents do well to submit a listing of all classes completed and an evaluation of the student's work in the classes. This is called a student transcript. The portfolio (if any) can also be submitted. It need contain only samples of what the student actually did, lest it become too large and unwieldy. Having letters of recommendation from respected community members (a teacher friend, a pastor, etc.) is, yet again, a reassurance to the official that the student is a serious scholar.

CHAPTER FOUR

One thing that a family ought to do early on in their home educating is to introduce themselves to their state and federal senators and representatives. These individuals usually have local teas or other occasions to meet their constituents. Letting them know that you reside in the district and are active in the political process (if you are) allows them to get the correct impression of home educators: They are reasonably intelligent parents who opt to teach their own youngsters at home in favor of sending them to an institution. This goes a long way toward educating the politicians, and it may help that person make good choices when legislation is introduced that could impact on home education. These are people who are very familiar with institutional schools, most of which have state and national lobbyists. Home educators are themselves walking, talking advocates of parental choice at its best (and of education at its best, most would agree).

As I see it, parents who are respectful, who act from a position of equality when dealing with any outside officials, are helping both the officials and themselves. It is the children who benefit most, all told.

Just the Facts

- There are local, state and national homeschool support groups and organizations available to help you in your home educating.

- You can start your own homeschooling group.

- Homeschooling field trip possibilities are endless.

- Homeschool conferences are usually a source of education, encouragement, and great fun.

- Talking with school officials requires care and conciseness.

- State Departments of Education are rarely helpful or supportive to homeschoolers.

- There are ways to connect with other homeschoolers even if not nearby, including Internet, pen palling, and persistence.

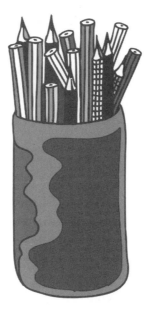

CHAPTER FIVE
How Do I Cope with the Rest of the World?

"I am always ready to learn but I do not always like being taught."
—Winston Churchill

What happens when someone else in your world doesn't support your homeschooling? What if they think you are crazy, delusional, neglectful, or just plain wrong? There are ways to cope based on who it is that's making life difficult. Remember, however, that no matter if you are dealing with a grumpy spouse, or an intrusive neighbor, the one element that will help convince all of them that homeschooling is the right decision for your family is your overall attitude of confidence and conviction. If you remain strong and sure in what you think is best for your children, you are almost assuredly going to rub off onto others and help the entire process.

CHAPTER FIVE

What if my spouse doesn't want to homeschool?

This will be the biggest problem of the bunch. Let's face it, if your third cousin twice removed doesn't want you to homeschool, you can blow it off and walk away. But if your partner, your spouse, doesn't want to do it, there could be some trouble straight ahead. Can you homeschool without their support or blessing? It's possible, but it isn't probable, and it certainly won't be pleasurable for anyone.

The key to solving this dilemma is to find out exactly what it is that your partner is objecting to. It's not the entire concept of homeschooling; that's too broad and too vague. Talk with each other and find out the precise reason he/she is reluctant. Perhaps your wife doesn't want to homeschool because she doesn't feel capable of the job or because she is afraid it will take up so much time that she will have to sacrifice other aspects of her life to do it. Maybe your husband doesn't want to homeschool because he thinks it is an inferior education or that it will cost too much. No matter what the specific issue is, the first step to resolving it is pinpointing it; then you can work together to see if it can be resolved.

How do you handle the other conflicts that come up within your relationship? Do you talk things over, make lists, get quiet and think, do some research, talk to others? Whatever method has worked best for you in the past is most likely going to be the one that will work for you both now.

No matter what your partner's main objection to home education is, there are ways to learn more about it that can lead to a resolution. If money is the concern, for example, spend some time talking to homeschoolers, looking through catalogs, and coming up with a basic figure of what you think it will all cost. (Most likely, your estimate will be high, since beginning homeschoolers often think they need more than they actually do.) Show your partner this figure and talk about how it can be figured into the budget. Putting real numbers to worries can frequently dispel the fear. The same will work if the concern is time; talk to others, read some books,

HOW DO I COPE WITH THE REST OF THE WORLD?

and figure out how much time you think homeschooling will take each day (once again, your estimate is probably going to be way too high). Then, together, look at how that amount of time can be handled on a daily basis. Many times it won't entail huge lifestyle changes but perhaps just getting up a little earlier, spending a little less time on other things, and sharing chores and other responsibilities.

As a team, write down what elements within homeschooling are causing one of you difficulty and then list the ways each one can be addressed. Often the answer lies in just doing a little reading and a little research.

Here are some other ways to help:

- Read a wide variety of books about homeschooling.

- Attend local homeschool meetings together and meet other homeschoolers. (This is a great way to meet new friends and dispel a lot of negative notions one or both of you might have about what homeschoolers are like.)

- Attend a homeschooling conference together.

- Agree to homeschool on a temporary or trial basis, and then evaluate it to see how each person is doing or feeling.

Like any other difficult issue that comes up in a relationship, the key to working this problem out lies in keeping communication between both of you open and friendly. Work hard to understand each other's viewpoints; listen to each other's opinions; be willing to discuss the same things again and again until you start to make some progress; be flexible enough to do some compromising if it means you come closer to an agreement. Homeschooling is a family project; it takes cooperation, encouragement, and support from everyone. Without your spouse's approval, you are in an uphill race that just might take too much effort for you to finish. If you remember that both of you really do have the same goal—the best possible education and life for your child(ren)—then you can come closer to sharing the same pathway to that goal.

CHAPTER FIVE

What about unhappy grandparents and other relatives?

Perhaps the best way to keep your cool when your parents or other relatives start to express their unhappiness over your homeschooling decision (sometimes loudly and repeatedly; sometimes subtly and annoyingly) is to remember their true motivation. It isn't to make you gray before your time; it's not to make you dread their visits or phone calls—it's because they also love your children very much, and they are concerned that perhaps your decision isn't in their grandchildren's (or nephew's/niece's/cousin's) best interests.

Once more, the key to solving this problem is in finding out precisely what it is about homeschooling that worries your relatives, and then addressing that particular concern in much the same ways you would with a negative spouse. Many times, the entire conflict can be solved through two simple steps: communication and involvement. Welcome their questions (if they're asked nicely; you should insist on no hostility) and hopefully, they will then welcome your answers.

Involve them in your children's education if you can. Invite them to a homeschool meeting; take them along on a field trip; have them come and visit and teach a class or two to your kids. Often just seeing what you are doing with your children, seeing that you are actively involved and that you are not letting their minds rot in front of the television for 14 hours a day, can allay many of their fears. Show them the story your son wrote, or the model your daughter put together. By giving them this glimpse into what your family's homeschooling truly is, many of their concerns about socialization and/or academics will lessen, if not disappear altogether.

Many times, once a dialogue is started, you may well discover that the main reason they are upset about your homeschooling decision is that they perceive it as an implied criticism of their long ago choice of public education for you or your spouse. While you are actually rejecting public education, they may feel you are rejecting *them* for choosing that very same public education. They may see your decision as a judgment on them. While you may fervently wish that you too had been given the chance to be homeschooled, most of us recognize that our parents did the best they could for us and that home education was simply unknown when we were children. There is no blame there—something grandparents should be told in case this is what they are feeling.

If, however, no matter what you say or try to do, you find that these relatives are not coming around and are, in fact, undermining your position with your children by asking questions like, "Don't you wish mommy and daddy would let you go to school?"or "It's a shame for you to miss all the fun of school,"then it's time to take off the nice hat and put on the protective one. Insist that they not make comments like that to your children. If they have an issue, they can take it up with you or stay quiet. If they refuse, consider limiting their access to your children.

What about nosey neighbors and other nuisances?

Sometimes the majority of the unpleasant comments and questions you and your children encounter will come from people that aren't close to you, or even complete strangers, like store clerks or co-workers. How much you choose to tell them or how you choose to respond to their words is up to you. How important is this person to you? Is it someone you and/or the kids will have to deal with on a somewhat regular basis? If so, you might want to invest more time and attention to your responses than you will to the lady behind you in the grocery store. As Susan Evans writes in Linda Dobson's book, *The Homeschooling Book of Answers*, "In the end, consider where your obligations lie. Are you obliged to keep the neighbors and relatives stress-free or to raise your children the best way you know?"

Borg Hendrickson, in his book *Homeschooling: Taking the First Step* responds to the question of how to deal with disapproving people this way: "Smile. Just smile... your own homeschooled children will eventually be your live evidence." Believe it or not, you will find that many of your most harsh critics, if enough time and information is involved, will become your strongest supporters of all. It isn't uncommon for grandparents who once despaired at the idea of their grandkids being homeschooled to regale their friends and neighbors with how smart, kind, mature, and wonderful these children are now, and isn't homeschooling just terrific?

CHAPTER FIVE

What happens when my child doesn't want to homeschool?

While many children love the idea of homeschooling, especially if they have been in a stressful or negative school situation already, there are some that may object to your decision. Don't ignore this, and don't think it will just go away. If your child isn't behind this decision, there is going to be a lot of stress and unhappiness for everyone in the family.

Once again, the key to this dilemma is in finding out exactly what your child is objecting to. Is he afraid he won't be able to play basketball anymore? Is she upset that she isn't going to be able to see her friends? Any objection your child has is bound to have some merit, and although it may seem somewhat trivial to you, it most likely is not remotely trivial to him.

Start by talking about how your child feels. List the questions, worries, concerns, and objections, and then address each one. If she is afraid that she won't be able to see her friends, show her the different ways they can still stay in contact and get together on a regular basis. If he is afraid he won't get to play ball, find other places to play, or call the school and see if he can still be part of the team (schools vary on their policies of allowing homeschooled students to be involved in extracurricular activities). Make a list of other ways to get fun and friends in (socialization is almost always a child's main objection to homeschooling) like 4H, Boy/Girl Scouts, the YMCA, church, youth groups, and of course, all the kids in the local homeschooling groups.

Involve your child in the homeschooling plan. Talk about all of the reasons why you made this decision; it's important that he understand your motives and your thoughts. Shift the focus from what she isn't going to be able to do to what she is going to be able to do as a result of homeschooling. Brainstorm on what she might want to learn and places he might want to go. Be willing to propose a compromise: if your child will try homeschooling for six months, for example, you will be open to the option of putting him back into school.

HOW DO I COPE WITH THE REST OF THE WORLD?

Point out what they won't have to cope with when homeschooling. Did he hate to ride the bus? Did she hate taking showers after P.E. with all the other girls? Did he keep falling behind in math class? Did she get threatened in the hallway? No problem anymore. No more rushing out of the house in the morning for him to catch the bus; no more dealing with the teacher that just never seemed to like her. Get excited at the possibilities that are opening up on this grand new adventure. In time, your recalcitrant child may just become your staunchest fan of homeschooling.

How do I cope with the questions everyone seems to ask?

Even though homeschooling is in the news and certainly becoming more common, it seems like people continue to ask the same questions when they meet homeschoolers. For some, especially young children, these questions are uncomfortable. Some families have been known to carry around a sheet with typical homeschooling answers on it, and when people start to question them more than usual, they hand them a copy and, with a polite smile, walk away.

Here are some of the most common questions you or your children will be asked and some of the answers you can use:

- *What grade are you in then*? For some families, this is an easy question; if they are following a more structured format, they know the answer. However, for unschoolers, or those that are close to being unschoolers, this is a toughie. A child may be in 6th grade in math, 9th in reading, and 3rd in science, or vice versa. If so, how can they answer this question? Options include saying their age instead of their grade or a simple "Depends on the subject". Older homeschoolers have been known to have more flippant answers like "I'm a student of life so I have no grade."

CHAPTER FIVE

- *Don't you miss _____ (fill in the blank)?* This can vary from the prom, to being around your peers all day, to getting out of the house everyday, to name a few. The problem with this question is that it indirectly implies that the child is missing out on something wonderful and isn't that a shame? Some homeschoolers have the wherewithal to counter the question with a list of all the amazing things they are doing so they don't have time to miss the _____, but others who have just been withdrawn from school, or who are simply shy, may find this question upsetting.

- *What school do you go to?* While many kids are used to being asked this question when they are out and about during the day, it still can present a dilemma for them. If they reply, I go to homeschool, they know that they are probably going to be asked a lot more questions which they may or may not want to take the time to answer. One solution that works for many homeschooling families is to give their home-school an actual name and then the child can answer with that. It also comes in handy for older homeschoolers who are filling out job applications and other forms. You can also use it on letterhead paper when ordering materials. You can name your school whatever you want; the more "official" it sounds, the fewer questions you are apt to be asked. You can put your name in the title, or use your address and combine it with words like "school," "academy," "institu-tion,"etc.

HOW DO I COPE WITH THE REST OF THE WORLD?

- *What curriculum do you use at home?* Again, for some, this is a no-brainer since they already use a set curriculum in their homeschooling. All they have to do, in this case, is whip out the name of it and they are set. For others, it's difficult because they use a combination of materials that are difficult to list or pinpoint. Often the actual answer to this question involves more information than the listener really wants to know. Typical answers can range from "A mixture of this and that" to "A little of everything" to the more facetious (albeit honest) "Life is my curriculum."

- *Don't you get tired of being with your kids/ parents all day?* and/or *Don't you wish you could be with friends more often?* This is a pretty intrusive question, but you may well hear it asked anyway. How you answer it depends on how involved you want to get. Some parents simply state that they love their children, so of course they do not get tired of them. They often go on to list all the many, many activities their children are involved in; rarely is there a home-schooled child who doesn't get a chance to be with friends, public or homeschooled. It can be great fun to watch someone's face when a homeschooled child handles this question and surprises others as they rattle off the different things they do in the course of any given week.

CHAPTER FIVE

How do I deal with hostile or negative school personnel?

Fortunately, encounters with truly hostile school people are not that common. For the most part, public school administrators are familiar with homeschooling and are, ever so slowly, becoming more accepting and supportive of it. However, there are always exceptions, and there are certainly teachers and principals who view homeschooling families as both a threat and an insult, and they can make life difficult.

Pat Montgomery, the founder and president of Clonlara Home Based Learning, has excellent advice for parents who are in contact with school personnel: Do your homework. Before you open your mouth or sign a paper, know EXACTLY what your legal rights and requirements are, and stick to them like super glue. Know what you have to do, say, and provide, and don't move an inch past that. Fulfill the law and then just stop. Be polite (remember—you may want to enroll your child in a class or use the school's facilities sometime in the future) but be careful. Borg Hendrickson writes, "Program yourself to be firmly, persistently, but calmly diplomatic."

If you do have to deal with the school system, do it in writing if at all possible. Avoid the phone and certainly avoid one-on-one encounters. Keep copies of any correspondence you send and any you receive. If you are required to answer questions, make sure the questions and your answers are written down. Send your mail with a Return Receipt Requested so that you know it was delivered. This may sound mistrustful, but it is the best way to protect your family in the long run.

If you aren't sure who to talk to or what to say, or you have some question about contact with the school system in your area, start by talking to other homeschoolers whom you have met and get their opinions. Often they can help you with hints and tips you might not have otherwise known and perhaps save you some grief.

HOW DO I COPE WITH THE REST OF THE WORLD?

Lastly—but certainly most importantly—do not be intimidated by public school personnel. Remember that you are not asking for their permission to homeschool your children; they are your children and this is your right. You are the one in control and with the power to make this educational decision. Even if they disagree and caution you that you are making a mistake, remember that this is your child, your right, and your decision. They cannot change that.

In the Trenches

A Difficult Decision

~ Carol Hogenkamp

Homeschooling was a very difficult decision for me to make. I didn't know if it was the right thing to do for my eight-year-old son, or if I could even teach him for that matter, but I also knew we couldn't go on with the battle we were having with the school. The struggle with the IEP process, the teacher's frustration with Jeremy's attention level, referrals for his "bad behavior," were all very overwhelming. I also had to consider the reactions of the other two boys we have living in the house. I have another son (Josh - 12), and my fiancé also has a son (Zack - 16). So many decisions to make. Where do you start? How do you start? When is the best time to pull them from public school?

I think the deciding point for me was when I got his last referral. I was told that Jeremy was no longer allowed to use the restroom without supervision because he was causing the other boys to be disruptive. I saw red. My son was NOT responsible for other children misbehaving. They knew what was right and wrong and made a choice to misbehave; Jeremy had nothing to do with it. It was at this point that I talked with Matt (my fiancé) and Jeremy about homeschooling. Matt said he would help me as much as he could. In talking with Jeremy, he asked me if he would still get to see his school friends. I assured him that he would, but he would have to wait until they were out of school. After that conversation, he seemed to be okay with homeschool, but we have had our ups and downs with that.

After withdrawing him from school, we had a short "school detoxing," which was highly recommended by members of the Oregon homeschooling support group we joined. Looking back, maybe this period should have been a little bit longer. I suppose I went through what most new homeschoolers do, which is having the feeling that their children should be learning something instead of playing and watching TV all day. It just didn't seem fair that Zack and Josh had to get up and go to school every day, while Jeremy got to stay home. So, the first day we really "homeschooled," I thought

CHAPTER FIVE

it would be fun for Jeremy to say his final goodbye to school. I gathered up all my copies of his referrals that he had received from school, gave him the referrals, and led him to the garbage can. I told him to rip them up. We were starting out new, and we didn't care about what those referrals said. He got a smile on his face and started ripping! We then went and set up the card table in the living room, got him something to drink, and started working in his spelling, phonics, and reading comprehension books.

He loved homeschooling for the first couple of weeks. He liked the fact that I would let him take more breaks and work at his own pace. Then he started thinking he needed a break every couple of minutes. He started fighting me on sitting down and doing his work. I was getting frustrated, Matt was getting frustrated, and Jeremy was getting frustrated. Then, I started listening to what Jeremy was saying. I started absorbing what other ORsig members were writing in their email loop. Jeremy needed to be stimulated more. Workbooks are fine, but it does nothing for his creativity and imagination. Workbooks don't do anything to stimulate conversation or get him thinking about what he is studying. I finally asked him what he WANTED to learn about. We went to the computer, and I asked him to give me a topic that he wanted to learn about. He said, "Hamsters." I pulled up web pages for hamsters. Well, there isn't a whole lot about hamsters that he really was interested in, so we moved on. We just surfed the web for a little while until we came across a website that had pictures of the planets. BINGO! We spent a couple hours looking at the pictures of space.

The next day we went down to the library and checked out some books. I chose some books about the solar system, and he checked out some books about sharks. He is finding the books about sharks aren't quite as interesting as he thought they would be. Yeah, okay, but he is still learning about them! We had a little power struggle about doing his solar system packet that I made up, but once I got him to sit down and actually work with me on it, we had a good time. THIS is the reward of homeschooling... YOU get to see the light come on, when they finally grasp what you are telling them. YOU get to hear their reasoning. YOU get to see them get excited and make up their own explanations of why certain things happen, and to feel pride when they answer a difficult question correctly.

When I first started homeschooling, I was more of the "school-at-home" type. Sit down, do your workbooks, correct your spelling, turn your numbers the correct way, do your math problems. Now I feel I am more "eclectic," taking a little bit of everything and throwing it together. The reading, writing, and arithmetic are still important in my eyes, but there is more to learning than sitting at a table with paper and pencil. I imagine we will shift gears a couple more times before we get it right, but that is what homeschooling is all about... finding out what works. Talking to other people who have been through it, taking the advice of others, listening to others' stories, and experimenting with all the different ways of teaching, THAT's what homeschooling is all about.

HOW DO I COPE WITH THE REST OF THE WORLD?

Now that I am finally feeling somewhat comfortable with homeschooling Jeremy, we have the other two kids to contend with. Zack was the one to start it. He started putting the school system down by saying things like, "School is boring. I don't feel I am learning anything,"and "I am never going to use any of this stuff anyway!"We explained to him that the only reason we were homeschooling Jeremy was because he was struggling in school. He was behind in his reading, and we were having trouble with the "IEP team"in getting him some help. We told him that if he REALLY wanted to homeschool he could, but he would be working on his studies and not playing and lounging around the house. We told him that if he wanted to take the G.E.D., that was a different story, but if he thought he was going to take the test, pass, and then hang around the house all day he had another think coming. If he got his G.E.D., he was either going to be working a regular job or going to college. School didn't seem so bad to him after that.

Josh is having his own little protest now. Before we started homeschooling Jeremy, he was doing excellently in school. He was getting good grades and never really minded going to school. Now he is falling behind in his schoolwork, resisting going to bed at night, and then as a result, not wanting to get up in the morning. When I ask him to bring his books home so that I can help him with whatever he is behind on, he gives me all kinds of excuses why he can't. They had two weeks off for Christmas break and already he is saying he can't wait for Spring break. We are still at a loss of what to do with his situation. Josh seems to want it both ways. He likes public school because he is with his friends all day and likes most of his teachers, but he wants to stay home too.

I don't really know what to do about our situation. It seems like most homeschool families have all their kids at home. It is all trial and error though. While Jeremy gets the advantage of staying home, the others have the advantage of school activities, being around other kids all day long, and escape from home life. Will Zack and Josh ever get over their jealousy of Jeremy not having to go to school? I don't know. Maybe eventually we will decide to homeschool Josh. Maybe we will let Zack get his G.E.D. and move on. Maybe we will just get too frustrated and put Jeremy back into the school system. I don't know all the answers right now. Does anyone? The point is, we never know if the choices we make are the right ones when we make them. We learn from our mistakes though, and this is something I am willing to deal with right now. Life's decisions are never easy.

CHAPTER FIVE

From the Experts

When Methods Collide
~ Teri Brown

I never even saw it coming. While the children and I were happily unschooling through our days, a train was coming inexorably down the pike that would change our lives forever.

> **Teri Brown** is the author of **Christian Unschooling: Raising Your Children in the Freedom of Christ.** She and her family live, play, and homeschool in Portland, Oregon.

The train was my husband, and the collision was his inability to come to terms with unschooling, his coming face-to-face with my natural learning philosophies. The wreck would leave us stunned and groping for new ways to reach out to each other. Amid the wreckage the entire family would learn what compromise, diplomacy, and love really mean.

Okay, it wasn't quite that dramatic, but it would change how school was conducted in the Brown household. My husband has always been supportive of homeschooling and very interested in the unschooling philosophy. He listened intently as I waxed poetic on the beauty of natural learning and admitted that our children were indeed learning every day. For several years things went beautifully. We were busy educating ourselves, chasing interests, and living our lives. While we were doing that, my husband was watching—both proud of our progress, and worrying about all that he felt we were missing.

Finally after dropping a few hints here and there, it all came out. He wasn't satisfied with the children's education, he felt there were gaps and strongly felt that there are things you need to learn whether you want to or not. Period.

I felt as if the wind had been knocked out of me. Not only was I a confirmed unschooler, I had even written a book on the subject! Now, here my husband was telling me that he couldn't stand behind our unschooling any longer—something had to give.

HOW DO I COPE WITH THE REST OF THE WORLD?

A word about my husband here—he is not an overbearing, over-structured fanatic. He is an organized, disciplined person who wants the very best for his children. He is almost as educated on homeschooling methods as I am. While he believes unschooling to be a fascinating philosophy with some merit, he is not prepared to "gamble" with our children's entire life. He is far more conventional than I am, and unschooling is just too radical.

So there we were. Stuck between a rock and a hard place where diverse viewpoints meet, and we were unsure of where to go next. I couldn't just ignore his concerns; he is my husband and the children's father. In this, as in most of marriage, one person cannot just toss their head and do what they want no matter what. Not and have a good marriage anyway!

So we did what most loving couples do when faced with the unknown. We argued. Now my dear husband and I love a good argument. We learned long ago how to do it without going for the jugular. Our concerns were brought out in the open and analyzed. Reasoning, logic, and tradition were all discussed. Intensely at times, but honestly.

We finally decided to have a summit meeting, a meeting where east meets west, where radical meets conventional, where—you get the idea! Off to Starbucks we went (isn't that where all important meetings take place?) We each wrote out a few sentences of our different philosophies. Why was it important to him for our children to have more structure to their education, and why was it important for me to unschool them?

Addressing these things, we began to compromise. "What is important for them to know?" I remember asking. "If you were to list three things that you feel they absolutely have to learn, what would they be?"

"Besides fishing, changing the oil in your car, and how to order a good cafe latte? I would have to say, spelling, reading comprehension, and consumer math." My husband the comedian.

"Reading comprehension can be learned by living," I argued. "Following a recipe, learning to play a game, and talking about your favorite books are all exercises in reading comprehension."

He conceded that they were.

CHAPTER FIVE

"But what about consumer math?" He countered. "Our children are good at the consuming part, not so good at the math part." He had a point.

"How much time?" I asked. "How much time constitutes being educated to you?"

> When we listed what we had in common, we chose to start with those instead of our differences.
> - Neither of us believed that the school at home method was right for our children or our family.
> - We both believed that our children and our family functioned better when our days were more structured (not our "school days" but the basic tenor of our days and weeks).
> - Both of us wanted our children to leave our home with the ability to learn whatever they needed to meet their own personal goals, and be educated enough to have a myriad of choices.

He snorted, far too wise to fall into that trap! "You know their learning styles better, what do you think?"

"A half an hour, twice a week?"I asked hopefully.

"Two hours a day, five days a week."

HA! Like that was going to happen! Little by little, bit by bit, we reached compromises and understanding. This is how we worked it out.

Since the children had already made educational goals for themselves, I would use those to make some of the changes that were important to my husband. In order to preserve their own independence, I make up books that have each day's activities in it, along with almost everything they need in order to accomplish them. I used a unit study approach using books they were interested in reading, and from that, I was able to pull together quite a bit of subject matter in a few well-chosen activities.

HOW DO I COPE WITH THE REST OF THE WORLD?

In our weekly schedule, I set aside five hours a week for "book work"(gritting my teeth a little here) and another two for educational games that are a take off on their own work. Following some of the thoughts of John Taylor Gatto, I am setting aside several hours (they don't have a full day) for volunteer work of some sort. I wish we had family closer so they could spend more time with their family as well, as I believe that is an integral part of education.

So there it is. Does that mean we are un-unschooling? I don't think so. I still consider myself and my family as being unschooler—for the most part. We all compromise, make adjustments, and otherwise adapt to the needs of those we love. When differing educational philosophies or parental styles start to create problems, a functional family finds a way to make it work. One of the beauties of educating your children at home is the time you have to find out what works best for everyone involved. And that includes the parents. That is just a part of being a family.

CHAPTER FIVE

Just the Facts

- A spouse or partner that doesn't want to homeschool can be a problem. The key to finding a solution lies in open communication, compromise, and pinpointing the main objections.

- Relatives who don't support your homeschooling decision are almost always acting out of good intentions. Involving them in your homeschooling, being willing to listen to questions and concerns, and knowing when to draw the line are all steps that can be taken.

- Neighbors, coworkers, and others who are negative or intrusive do not have to be told much of anything at all since their roles in your life are usually minimal. Know how to handle the basic questions and how to respond when their interest becomes a problem.

- If your child doesn't want to homeschool, there are several options available. The most important key is finding out exactly what the objections are and dealing with them. Always be willing to listen to their concerns and perspectives and keep the option of staying in school open.

- Many people tend to ask the same questions of homeschoolers, so it helps to be prepared as a parent—and to prepare your children with simple answers.

- Dealing with negative/hostile school personnel requires equal parts diplomacy, patience, and confidence. Know what your law requires, be polite but firm, and always get it in writing.

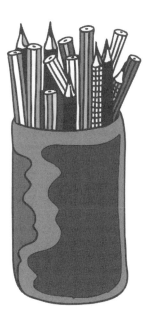

CHAPTER SIX
What about the Teen Years?

"Teach children what to think and you limit them to your ideas. Teach them how to think and their ideas are unlimited."

~ Sandra Parks

Ah, the teen years. I think that they make parents all over the world sigh a little. If there is life on other planets, I imagine that even those alien creatures must sigh when puberty hits. The teenage years can be tough for each person in the family, but how tough and how bad can vary greatly from family to family. Does homeschooling stop all that teenage angst? Do homeschooled teens stop thinking that the entire world revolves around them and that mom and dad just don't have a clue about anything? Nope. Can it make these days easier, however? Can it help put a buffer—not a shield—between teens and the dangers of drugs, alcohol, and pregnancy? Can it keep you a little closer so that this time isn't so much about breaking away,

CHAPTER SIX

as it is letting go? Yes, it can. No guarantees, of course. These teens will still waffle between child and adult; they will still struggle to find their places in the world, and they will still look at you like you are not too bright now and then. However, homeschooling can give your teens a chance to excel in the world at a time when it is most needed. It's a time when they are often so emotionally vulnerable, afraid to look to the future and equally afraid not to, when their desires outweigh their expertise, their income, and their abilities, and it's a time when your presence, whether acknowledged or not, is so vital.

Homeschooling a teen is different than the elementary years. Whatever method you have chosen to follow, this period will allow for more autonomy, as less time is needed for instruction and follow through, and more is devoted to guidance and listening. Please remember that the time you spend listening to them tell you about a best friend who has let them down, a boy around the block who might be interested, or a work situation that has proved quite challenging, is just as important—perhaps even more so—than any of the so-called curriculum you are going over together. These are the moments that sustain the bonds through the turbulent times ahead.

WHAT ABOUT THE TEEN YEARS?

How do I prepare my teen for college—and how do I teach things I don't understand myself?

Common questions—and understandable ones. Fortunately, we are living in an era where the options for education just keep increasing. The subjects typically covered in high school can be intimidating for parents; many of us don't remember how to conjugate verbs in French, or how trigonometry works. What to do? First and most importantly, stop and ask yourself *does my child really need to know this information*? Think about it. Have you ever used the information in your life? Is this information that will be needed in most work situations or in daily routines? If the answer is yes, then your kids need to know it. But, if you can't come up with any sensible reason why your child needs this specific information right now, be willing to discard it. It's important, as you approach these years, to have a rough idea of whether or not your teen is planning to pursue going to college or some other form of higher education. This can change the slant of your curriculum since most colleges (this is explained in greater detail later in this chapter) will have some basic requirements. They might, instead, be looking at going directly into a job or vocational school, or perhaps their plans are to travel awhile, or start their own business. The options are almost limitless. Don't get caught into the notion that the only way to be successful in life is to get a college degree. That isn't true; many, many people have rewarding careers and lives without such a degree. It is only one avenue of many.

So—you have determined what you think your teen needs to know at this point. Have you asked your teen about this? I encourage you to do so. Their input is invaluable; you might discover that they have some goals that you didn't know a thing about. Together, come up with a kind of curriculum, or a list of what you want to cover between now and "graduation," and then figure out how you are going to get the material for the subjects you don't feel you personally can cover.

CHAPTER SIX

Here are some of the best resources:

- Find a local tutor or mentor to teach a subject.

- Purchase a packaged curriculum for this subject.

- Attend a community college class on this subject.

- Take online classes on this subject.

- Learn the subject right along with your teen.

- Join an umbrella school (private schools that help homeschoolers).

If you decide to enroll in an umbrella school, make sure you check that their educational philosophy meshes with yours. Also ask about fees and what those fees include, how they want to contact your teen (email, mail, fax), and also ask how to contact enrollees for their opinions and thoughts about the school.

How does my child get a diploma?

The very first thing you need to do when you come up against the idea of a diploma for your child is to repeat to yourself at least 10 times: *It is just a piece of paper.* It is just a piece of paper. A diploma truly is just a piece of paper. Have you looked it up in the dictionary lately? While some might believe that its definition is "a magical piece of paper that allows all high school graduates to find worthwhile jobs and entrances to any quality college or university," what it actually means is "a paper signifying the completion of a line or course of study." A diploma is not a ticket into a better future, but simply a paper saying yep, you're done with this section of education. While it is important to have a diploma for some life journeys—the military for example—it doesn't have to be a high school diploma that came from a public high school. Job applications often ask if a person has

WHAT ABOUT THE TEEN YEARS?

one. No matter where it came from, if you have one, the answer is yes. Employers care far more about experience than GPAs. Even the military is beginning to relax its requirements on having one. As for colleges, they depend more on transcripts, test scores, letters of recommendation, resumes, and portfolios than on an actual diploma. If you are positive that you still want one, however, here are some choices you have:

- *Make your own.* You can get forms from many office supply stores or homeschool catalogs. You can also just create one on your home computer or hire a calligrapher to make a beautiful one. If your child has homeschooled through high school and completed the course of study you/they have outlined, then this diploma is completely legitimate. As homeschooling author Cafi Cohen says, "Do home-schoolers need a high school diploma? The answer is sometimes. Do they need a diploma from an accredited school? The experience of thousands of families indicate that the answer is almost never."

- *Get a GED* (General Equivalency Diploma) instead.

- *Join an umbrella school.* Many provide a diploma as part of their services.

- *Enroll in an independent study program.* Again, many of these provide a diploma as part of their services.

- *Check with your state DOE.* Find out if your state offers state approved diplomas if certain requirements are fulfilled.

CHAPTER SIX

What about graduation/the prom?

A graduation is a lot like a diploma; it doesn't have to be sponsored by the local public high school to be valid. When your teen completes his/her course of study, have a graduation ceremony. Rent a hall, open up the backyard, reserve the church, call in that favor that your Aunt Mildred owes you and use her garden. Invite friends, family, neighbors, coworkers, and anyone else you want and make it a real celebration. Take pictures, have speeches, play music, and make it clear that your child has accomplished something wonderful. That's what graduation is all about.

As for the prom... many times, we parents put more emphasis on this tradition than our teens do. For some kids, it means little to nothing. First, being in public school certainly doesn't guarantee an invitation to this dance. There are many public school students sitting at home on prom night. Second, your teen may well be dating a public school student and get invited that way. Third, think about many of the tragedies that occur after prom. In the past decades, it has frequently been a prime time for drunk driving and the accidents that accompany it, as well as the risk of teen pregnancies and drug use. Is the risk of that worth a simple dance? Fourth, (is this getting old yet?) create your own. Have your teen invite their friends from near and far and have food, music, lights, whatever they want. Let's face it—some teens would gag at the thought of the corsage, formal, and tux model of many high school proms. Each year at Grace Llewellyn's annual Not Back to School Camp in Oregon, the summer camp holds its own prom. Someone acts as D.J., often a camper who does D.J. work for real back home, CDs are gathered and played, and it goes until about 1 a.m. As one attendee put it, "People dress up for this dance, but in very individual ways. One person might have wings on; another might be wearing a 40s style swing skirt with sequins, and there are even people in drag for fun. No one has to worry about who is with who or what they are wearing or if it's in style or not. We are there with our friends to have fun and that's it."

WHAT ABOUT THE TEEN YEARS?

Prom-like dances can sometimes be organized and/or offered through some private schools, local or state homeschool groups, or at conferences. The annual Clonlara Home Based Education conference, for example, hosts a dance on the Saturday evening of the gathering. Teens come with and without dates, and it's common to spy some parents out on the dance floor, often with a young child in arms.

How does my homeschooled teen get a job?

The majority of homeschooled teens have part time jobs because they have big plans for the money they make—be it college, an expensive hobby, or perhaps some traveling around to visit friends in other states. The advantage that these teens have is that their schedules are far more flexible than those of their public school counterparts, and this availability makes it easier for them to get hired. Many teen homeschoolers have jobs within their own families' businesses or have even started businesses of their own. It's not unusual to read about homeschooling teens who have their own store, product, or service and making a decent income at a relatively early age. The entrepreneurial spirit is often alive and thriving in this group. Others may get your typical teen job: waitress, clerk, babysitter, lawn care, etc. Whatever position they get, a job can teach them all about money management, attitude, responsibility, and motivation.

As their parents, you might guide them towards choosing some kind of job that relates to their personal interests. If they are thinking about becoming a veterinarian, how about a part time job at a local pet shop? If they are into music, why not apply at the local music store? Of course, make this suggestion very subtly—even homeschooled teens tend to view their parents' recommendations as suspicious.

Before your teen goes out on that first job hunt, give them some pointers (refer to subtlety mentioned in above paragraph) about filling out an application. You might brainstorm together on who to put as references and even create a resume to take along. Many homeschooled teens have done enough interesting traveling, volunteering, and experimenting that

CHAPTER SIX

they can create a very impressive resume for potential employers. Because these teens are more used to being around adults, they often do an excellent job in interviews also, coming across as mature and confident. Of course, this isn't true of ALL teens, but quite a few.

If taking on a part time job is not what you or your teen wants at this point in time, consider volunteering on a regular basis instead. Many of the foremost leaders in the homeschool movement strongly advocate incorporating some kind of community service into a family's overall curriculum because of the important values it can teach a person. Volunteer opportunities can often be found through local nursing homes, humane shelters, community centers, YM/YWCAs, libraries, and parks and recreation departments. For other possibilities, check out **www.volunteeramerica.com**.

What about an apprenticeship or internship?

A truly wonderful idea for your teen is an apprenticeship and/or internship. It can help them discover that yes, they love this work and it is their future direction, or no, they can't stand it and it's time to look elsewhere. It gives your teen a taste of the responsibility that comes with a job, and the experience just might make them more employable down the road.

Who can you contact for this kind of arrangement? The possibilities are endless here. You can check with:

- Friends
- Relatives
- Neighbors
- Coworkers
- Other homeschoolers
- Businesses
- Trade schools
- Career centers

Other resources include the web sites:
- **www.jobshadow.org**
- **www.jobshadow.monster.com**
- **www.internshipprograms.com**
- **www.rsinternships.com**

WHAT ABOUT THE TEEN YEARS?

To give your teen some direction, refer them to **The Internship Bible** by Mark Oldman and Samer Hamadeh. According to them, the ten best internships are:

- Academy of Television Arts and Sciences
- Elite Model Management
- Ford Motor Company
- Georgetown Criminal Justice Clinic
- Hewlett-Packard
- Inroads
- Lucasfilm/Lucas Digital
- Northwestern Mutual Life
- TBWA/Chiat Day
- The Washington Post

For more ideas than you could imagine, also check out the book *The Back Door Guide to Short-Term Job Adventures* by Michael Landes (Ten Speed Press, 2000).

It includes information on internships, seasonal jobs, volunteering, working abroad, and other "extraordinary experiences."

Can my homeschooled teen get into college?

If you had asked this question a few years ago, the answer might have been a shaky "possibly." Today it is a resounding "yes," well on its way to "absolutely." With each passing year, more and more colleges and universities are opening up their doors to homeschoolers. They are finding this new breed of student to be more self-motivated and self-disciplined, with a background of rich and varied experiences.

Experts predict that more than one million homeschooled children will be enrolled in colleges and universities by the end of the decade. Approximately 1,000 colleges accept homeschoolers, but that number is climbing quickly. On the list of those taking homeschoolers are such prestigious names as Amherst, Northwestern, West Point, Yale, Oxford, and Cambridge. In Stanford University's letter that is sent to homeschoolers who apply, it reads, "Homeschooled students are no longer unusual for us and several are usually admitted and enroll at Stanford each year... We are scrupulously fair in evaluating these applicants and they are not at any disadvantage in the admissions process."

CHAPTER SIX

The application process can often be an area where homeschoolers can shine. Instead of just turning in the traditional high school transcripts, many have been known to turn in impressive portfolios full of letters of recommendation (from teachers, employers, pastors, coaches, tutors, coworkers, and other community members), resumes, test scores, writing samples, awards, certificates, projects, and essays. All of these things can help to make an excellent impression on college officials. However, a word of caution here— always make sure that you know precisely what the college your teen is applying to requires; sometimes colleges can be persnickety to the point of ridiculousness. For example, in 1999, when homeschooler Rio Benin scored a perfect 1600 on the SATs and won a $20,000 scholarship from Intel, the University of California San Diego turned Rio down because he didn't have a high school transcript. Rio ended up choosing Harvard instead.

Scholarships are just as available to homeschoolers as to those in public school also. The key to success when it comes to getting a scholarship is to make sure your child meets all the requirements before he/she applies and then, according to Cafi Cohen, the next thing to do is make a follow up call. "It's the single most important thing to do," she assures teens. "It gets you noticed."

One last note on the subject of college; keep in mind that your independent teen may decide that college is not what he/she wants to do. You may agree; you may strongly disagree. Forcing a child to go to college is rarely a good idea in any family and with children who have had the freedom of homeschooling, it can be disastrous. When they turn their noses up at your suggestions or the brochures you laid on their desks, stay cool and don't let it become an issue. If that happens, communication often stops completely, and anything you have to say is going to fall on deaf ears. They may just need some time off between high school and college. Listen to what they have in mind and remember that they might utilize this time to save money for future education, gain additional career experience, travel, volunteer, be part of a foreign exchange program, or take some local college prep classes. There are many choices out there beyond college, and perhaps

WHAT ABOUT THE TEEN YEARS?

one of those is just the right one for your teen. By giving them the freedom and trust to make decisions, you may just find that they were right—college wasn't the best option for them, or conversely, they may find that you were right and after spreading their wings for a little while, they will pick up the brochures and start asking questions.

What about playing sports, joining the drama club, being in the orchestra and taking driver's education?

Let's face it. The public school system is always going to have some kind of program that will interest your teen. You have several options here. You can contact the school and see what their policy is on allowing home-schoolers to be on the team or in the class. Some are very open to the concept, while others are reluctant or even hostile. A number of them have school policies that simply don't allow for non-students to be enrolled in any of their programs.

If this is the case, or if you simply would rather stay away from the public school system altogether, there are other places that can fulfill many of your teen's interests. If playing sports is their thing, look into activities at the YM/YWCAs. Check to see if there are local leagues through businesses or community groups. Perhaps you live in an area with enough homeschoolers in it to start your own team. Can your teen join the team of a private school in your city? How about personal lessons? Can your teen join a local martial arts studio or a dance class?

The same is true for drama and orchestra and choir and art and any of those other classes that require a group. Check with small theatre groups or the city orchestra. Arrange for private lessons. Look beyond the school as the place for this activity.

CHAPTER SIX

Driver's education is another dilemma some teens face. Again, some schools will allow them to come in and take that course only; others will not. A teen can just let mom and dad teach the class, but often this means he/she cannot get their licenses until they are 16 years and six months. (Some parents appreciate that delay.) It may also affect the discount on your car insurance. There are private businesses that teach driver's education sometimes, and you can purchase a driver's ed curriculum from some of the larger homeschooling and education companies. Check with your individual state to see what its regulations are. For example, in Texas, parents can teach their children to drive, but have to show some kind of "certificate of attendance." That certificate is often made on the home computer. Other states might require additional training like California's Drug and Alcohol Awareness course, which sometimes means an outside class and a hefty fee.

WHAT ABOUT THE TEEN YEARS?

In the Trenches
From the Mouths of Teens
~ Various Homeschooled Teenagers

A look at the contributions from **teens** below will be eye opening for anyone who thought that these teens were sheltered or bored. These stories aren't special ones; they are typical of the home-schooler that has time and freedom to explore his/her world and see what it has to offer. Enjoy the words of these teens.

I don't really think I'm missing out on anything at all by not going to school. Except perhaps I miss having to learn things that I'll never remember because they aren't important to me. And I'll miss out on the cliques and worrying about how popular I am. I'll miss out on spending all my daylight hours and then some on schoolwork, and then homework, and then do it again tomorrow.

Instead I'll just have to be content with getting up and going to work all day. I work at a veterinarian's office as an assistant. I've worked on every thing from cats and dogs, cows and horses, to tarantulas and camels, otters and eagles. Then when I get off work, I'll maybe go ride my horse and practice for all the shows that I go to in the summer. Or perhaps tonight is one of the nights when I have a TaeKwondo or dance class. Or maybe I'll go home and read.

Right now that would be reading about how to build natural energy sources such as solar power systems or hydro plants or how to build cob houses. I'm also designing a garden for our house and to go along with it, I'm reading about medicinal herbs. As long as we"re going to have a garden, we might as well grow some herbs that will do us some good. Plus it's just nice to know what's edible when I'm out in the mountains hiking or camping, which I do a lot of, and get hungry or feel like munching on something.

Perhaps I could learn some things from school, but I wouldn't learn them as well nor would they stay learned as well. One of the best things that ever happened in my life was quitting school at the age of nine or so and becoming an Unschooler. Since then I have had more practical and hands-on learning than I ever had in my first three years of school. Since rising out of school, I have moved away from the city, helped build our straw bale and timber frame house; I've worked as a dog walker for our humane society, as a grocery stocker, helped do janitorial work at a grocery store, worked on a horse ranch and learned to ride, washed dishes and been a back up cook at a small restaurant in town, and now I am working with the veterinarian.

And so I would say that for me, Unschooling is the best choice there is, although for others, school may be more their style. I think of unschooling as more of a state of mind than of a state of not going to "school." An Unschooler is someone who wants to learn: someone who will look beyond the conventional learning atmosphere and seek out people who know the things they want to learn, and to learn from those people or libraries or the nighttime sky. Unschoolers never stop learning because they realize that they learn from everything they ever do, and that they will only stop doing things, even so much as sitting and watching the birds, when they die.

—*Ruth, 17, Colorado*

CHAPTER SIX

There was a point in time when I scoffed at the idea of being homeschooled. I was nine or ten and the thought of not actually physically going to school where my teachers and friends were was somewhat heartbreaking. A year or two went past, and as I began to experience more and more of my public school system, the more the idea of homeschooling began to appeal to me. By the time I was in middle school, I was ready to be rid of the insane insomnia that plagued me weekly, brought on—I'm positive—by my intense loathing of school. This was coming from a kid who couldn't wait for September when classes would start up again. Clearly, something was wrong; and when coupled with my mom's long time interest in self-education, we all made the decision to start homeschooling both my sister and I.

I know popular belief is that homeschoolers tend to lead a somewhat sheltered lifestyle, and while this is true of a small percentage of homeschoolers, it's certainly one of the biggest urban myths around today. From the time I was 12 years old until I started college in 2000, I was homeschooled, and I led a varied and exciting existence. I was always off somewhere during what were my "high school" years. Whether it was traveling around the country with my mom and sister, volunteering at one of my many places of interest, or attending yet another meeting for a council I was part of, I was never home and never bored.

I had lots of friends. I had boyfriends. I went to regular high school sporting events. I went to regular high school dances, including yes, the senior prom. I went to plays and musicals and conferences and other social events in my area and around the country. I didn't miss out on anything during my homeschooling years except perhaps the harmful peer pressure, or pressure from adults in suits behind desks who had to pretend like they cared about where your life was going after high school when really, you were just another name in the books or more state money in their pockets. To miss out on something, you have to feel like there's a void inside you somewhere that hasn't been filled. I never had that feeling about my schooling or the experiences I had. I can honestly say that while I am sure I could have done more or done better, I never felt unfulfilled.

As I've ventured off into the wonderful world of higher education, I've come to realize that my education was far more rounded than the majority of the people I attend college with. My instructors have come to realize that I am not just another shut away, anti-social, puritanical homeschooled production, but rather an individual who has experienced enough to be able to relate to any subject with some clarity and understanding. I can hold an intelligent conversation about the Beatles, or about the pros and cons of RU486, and at the drop of a hat, I can quote you Shakespeare, Weezer, and the Rocky Horror Picture Show.

I couldn't have asked for a better education. The years I spent in public school were beneficial in their own way, and I wouldn't go back to change those if I had the chance. They led to an even greater appreciation of the chance to control my own education once it was thrust into my own two hands, and now that I've had two years to look back on it all, I realize that I had the education of a lifetime.

Now all I need to do is get through this college stuff . . .

—Cloe Rose, 19, Michigan

WHAT ABOUT THE TEEN YEARS?

My name is Thomas and I am 14. I've been homeschooled all my life. I have all sorts of interests; here are all the things that unschooling has allowed me to do. First, I work five days a week at an Internet provider in town doing tech support and creating web pages. I am working a job and I am associating with the public.

Now—for fun, I am a cadet/airman 1st class in the United States Civil Air Patrol (C.A.P.), an auxiliary of the United States Air Force. The CAP's three missions are emergency services, cadet programs, and aerospace education. They fly 90 percent of inland search and rescue missions. I have been involved with them for about six months and through them, I am able to fly a Cessna 182 sky plane and a glider.

I also participate in Tae Kwon Do, a Korean martial art. I am currently a high green belt and will soon be a blue belt. I've been involved in it for about 15 months and I have fought in one mini tournament, placing second in my age group. I am a part of the U.S. Tae Kwon Do Federation and the International Tae Kwon Do Federation.

I have also just started dancing; currently I am doing jazz, but I hope to start ballet soon. I enjoy snowboarding, reading (lots of that), drawing, hiking, building rockets, working out, washing windows, thinking, and living life to its fullest.

I recently went to a New Year's Party in Canada with 28 other kids, and it was the best 10 days of my life. One of the greatest things about this gathering was that all of the people were mature, kind, caring, and helpful. We cleaned up our messes; we cooked all of our food and cared for one another. (Yea, I know you're thinking "Wow! teenagers that clean up after themselves?" And yes, it's true!) The ages varied from 13 to 19, and everyone got along great, and I think that was because of the maturity levels. Before I left for this party, I had been pretty stubborn about not doing my chores at home, but this gathering was a real eye opener for me. I saw how responsible and helpful kids can be—and how kind.

Here is my advice to listen to and maybe even follow. If your kid is having trouble in school, stop. Sit with him or her and listen to their problems. Maybe try to homeschool or unschool them—just try. Maybe they will become the best they can be!

—Thomas, 14, Colorado

CHAPTER SIX

The decision to homeschool is one of the best things that's ever happened to me; it lets me live. I don't know what I would do otherwise. I can't imagine a life without the choices that I have, the freedom and the opportunities. I feel so lucky that I can live this way, without people telling me what and when and how to learn it. Instead my parents encourage me to follow my interests wherever they may lead. To just do it, whatever it is; just go out and live my life. That may mean working at a Montessori preschool for four years, learning how to teach kids while they teach me how to learn, or working at a living history museum where I gave tours to school kids, showing them things from the past, and telling stories about how the pioneers lived.

Community theatre is another place my interests have led me. I've worked in almost every aspect of it from backstage hand to stage manager, props, costumes, makeup, and recently, assistant director. I love the adrenaline rush of a show, and how well I handle the chaos of it all. This year I might get to be a guest director.

This past fall I was interested in history, so I got to visit some friends out of town and hear Howard Zinn, author of **A People's History of the United States**, speak. My friend and I had a great time reading out loud to each other from his book while we made apple crisp and took breaks to discuss the events of history.

Recently homeschooling gave me the freedom to take a trip down to California to visit my grandparents. My grandma, who's a writer, worked with me on a report about women photographers. My grandpa, an avid photographer, took me on long walks and taught me how to take good pictures. They shared with me their love of photography, writing, art, and their curiosity about life, all things I hope to retain and incorporate into my own life more.

Now I am hoping to take the freedom I have and use it to work on my writing, learning to finish the things I start, and perhaps even getting published occasionally. This essay seems a good beginning, as it is in itself another good example of the opportunities I am given.

When I think back to the two years that I did spend in school, I can't think of anything I miss now. I know that the first year of homeschooling was difficult. At one point I wanted to go back to school. But when my parents and I talked, I realized that the only reason I wanted to go back was for recess. Now I have found a group of friends, much more interesting and varied than I ever had at recess, and I can't think of a single thing I miss about school. In the end, I think the decision to homeschool has been one of the best things in my life. It has provided so many opportunities that I never would have had otherwise.

—Elizabeth, 15, Oregon

WHAT ABOUT THE TEEN YEARS?

When the word "homeschooling" entered my vocabulary, my life began again. Like any new project you start, the beginning is shaky, nervous, and unsure. At the beginning of my homeschooling career, I decided to sit for a while at the starting line. I felt the traumatic "missing out syndrome" several times, with my friends all excited about proms and worried about schoolwork. I was staring down a blank and yet incredibly exciting path. I think that when you are told only one way, and then you realize there is a different way, and make the conscious decision to choose that different way, a way that calls to you but yet is much less traveled, your heart can skip a beat or two. It wasn't until I became immersed in my new way, my new and different path, that the world opened up to me. For the first time since I was a child, I saw the tremendous beauty and the endless options. The first six months to a year after I quit school, I knew no other unschoolers in real flesh and blood and hanging out with my high school friends seemed easy and familiar.

It was a slow transformation, and as my interests took me over, my path unfolded before me. I decided to become a vegetarian and quickly found an organization dedicated to teaching people how to become one. I jumped onboard their Core Team and started helping and meeting lots of people in my area who believed in the same things I did. I wanted to dance and found a swing dance troop and learned not only about Haitian dance and movement, but about the people and culture of Haiti. I was interested in sculpture and art, so I took a sculpture class at the local junior college and found an amazing teacher. The list continued as my true interests sparked and were finally set free. I no longer gained anything from drinking beer with my "friends," and I actually wanted to share my story with the adults who thought I was either a genius, a drop out, or on medication.

Homeschooling has given me a path with a big, bright light everywhere that school never gave me. I imagine that if everyone, especially every teenager, was given the choice to go to school, we, as teenagers, would have more self-confidence than most 40-year-old adults. Once you begin to work towards a goal you set for yourself, instead of a goal that your parents and/or society has set for you, your eyes see life the way it really is, as you make it!

—Danielle, 21, California

CHAPTER SIX

After seven years of having been enrolled in school, it was easy to see that home-schooling helps to open one's mind more so than conventional schooling. It seems to encourage people to search out knowledge in their own ways. I've noticed that most homeschooling and unschooling families encourage learning whatever interests the child, opening doors for that person whenever possible. When anyone sets out to do something that they want to do, rather than something being forced upon them, the mind is immediately more open and accepting towards the information being presented.

While in school, I found it to be somewhat "numbing." Conventional schooling presses a strict curriculum and a "don't ask, don't tell" attitude. Kids are told to do a set amount of work and are graded on it. However, the average person in school lacks massive amounts of motivation so they often just do the bare minimum. The only moti-vation there is the desire not to get into trouble or get detention. They do just enough to get by.

Since I have been out of school, I have been able to pursue things that I enjoy more than textbook learning. I was able to learn how to cook, hold a steady job on "school days," learn photography, and take art classes that a school would not be able to provide. These things were so much easier to learn than anything in school because I wanted to be there and I wanted to learn them. My mind just seemed to grasp things easier.

I've seen that homeschooling can open doors towards the world and towards careers more than traditional schooling. I know future writers and performers and people that don't know what they want to do yet, but are trying everything just for the experience. We have all been finding things that we love and things to learn, despite not having someone shoving assignments down our throats. We still learn tons—just not in a con-ventional way.

Mitch, 18, Oregon

WHAT ABOUT THE TEEN YEARS?

There's a Buddhist philosophy that states that life is based upon great change. Without change and evolution, nothing can ever reach its true potential. School made me tunnel-visioned, and deciding to leave it knocked the tunnel down. It was the biggest and most positive change I've ever made, and it continues to ripple outward into the tiniest crevices, making everything about my life wide open and wonderful.

There was never anything wrong with traditional school: in fact, I rather fancied it. Ambition was always my thing, so I strove for pitch-perfect grades and made it my driving force. At age 13, I was acing classes and clamoring around the city with my bundle of grade-greedy girlfriends and feeling pretty on top of my game. It was at this pinnacle of my preteen sassiness that my mother confronted me: we were moving. The idea of a school transfer was frustrating—crushing even—and a new city, even worse. We fought. And fought. And finally, searched for compromise.

That compromise was homeschooling. A temporary change, my mother assured me, and one we would have plenty of control over. It would be structured. I could even get ahead of the game and earn extra credits. I consented reluctantly.

After I left public school, the walls and boundaries I had put up began to blur and melt down softly. A year was no longer nine months of work and a summer. A project was no longer about the notes I took, or the mark I got on it when it was done. Because Mom had trust in my own self-motivation, the structure we talked about was only loosely put together and soon, I was floating about in this strange new freedom. It made me wide-eyed and curious. I found writing was pleasurable—not grunt work, and discovered poetry and playwriting. I found theatre didn't need to be done in an "acting class;" I could go out and volunteer for a company all on my own. I saw that one's world did not need to be so segmented, scheduled, and measured. It could move about freely like water, instead of wood.

For me, transitions and changes have become a welcome and wonderful part of living. Without this great change, I probably wouldn't know or care about Buddhism (let alone philosophies contained within it) unless, of course, it was included in some special assignment. To my mother and to homeschooling, I owe my outlook on life and what learning should be—a study in freedom and personal evolution.

Maggie, 17, New York

CHAPTER SIX

I have been homeschooled all my life. Sometimes I think about going to school, but I wouldn't want to give up the freedoms that I have.

One of the nice things about homeschooling is that you can avoid bullies. You don't have anyone picking on you (unless it's your sister). You can pick and choose who you hang out with, and you aren't forced to be with people you don't like or don't get along with.

Some other cool things about homeschooling:
- I can have sleepovers in the middle of the week.
- I have more time to follow my own interests.
- I don't have to get up and get ready to go to school everyday.
- I have more say in what subjects I learn or don't learn about.

Another cool thing about being homeschooled is that you have more time to go on fieldtrips and outdoor activities. That's really important to me because I feel that a kid should spend more time outdoors than they do in school. I have been able to go fishing and visit hatcheries on school days, which is awesome because it's fun and I get a lot of science that way. I want to go into fishery sciences as an adult and I can start now. If I were in school, I wouldn't have these opportunities. All in all, homeschooling is pretty cool for a teenager.

Ethan, 12, Oregon

WHAT ABOUT THE TEEN YEARS?

*"They will say you are on the
wrong road if it is your own."*
~Antonio Porchia

From the Experts

Traveling, Homeschooling and Learning to Relax
~ Jasmine Orr

Jasmine Orr is the author's sarcastic, brilliant, independent, and beautiful daughter. She is also her mother's favorite walking audio-visual material.

I remember my tee shirt being stuck to my back with dense Las Vegas sweat as I sat on my jam-packed maroon bag on the floor of the Greyhound bus station. The woman to my left kept asking me if I wanted to come and play the slot machines with her before the bus came. The woman to my right was making her hot dog say, "No, please don't eat me!" before shoving it in her mouth. And I still had two hours left to wait.

I love traveling.

It was the last day of September, and I'd already been gone for a little over a month. I'd left my home in northern Indiana, spent the night at a friend's house in Minnesota, driven the rest of the way out to Oregon, spending the night in various hotels along the way; I'd already stayed in three hotels in Eugene, Oregon, two friends' houses, and had been to two weeks of camp. I'd taken a road trip down to Southern California with another friend and stayed there for a week and then early that morning, I had taken a Greyhound bus out of Los Angeles to finally come to this resting point—mid-afternoon in Las Vegas, sitting on the gritty ground in a heat wave listening to some crazy woman make her hot dog screech in pain.

CHAPTER SIX

And I still had almost three months left.

Here in Las Vegas, I was searching for something to do. Finally, I pulled out my road atlas and began paging through it, all the dog-eared pages, all the little notes along the margins. Soon, I was circling all the places I'd been to on a list on the contents page. Much to the amazement of the talking hot dog lady, it was over half of the country.

"Where do you get all the time?" she asked in admiration, her hot dog momentarily silent. "You know, with school and all?" I just grinned and kept circling.

After my layover in Las Vegas, I spent five weeks in Colorado with a most wonderful boy, then two and a half weeks in Minnesota working at a Christmas farm, then two more weeks in Colorado, before driving out to my new home in Oregon. I was gone for four months. In some ways, it seemed like forever. At the same time, it didn't come close to quelling my obsession with traveling. Now, after being home only a month, I'm already pining to leave again. Time to mark another state off the list, time to get some more ticket stubs for my wall collage, time to experience somewhere new.

I've been traveling sporadically since I was 12—various summer camps, train rides, flights, road trips, and more often than anything else, Greyhound Lines Incorporated excursions. Now, five years later, I have an entire wall collage of ticket stubs, itineraries, baggage claims, and bus schedules. I have another wall collage full of photographs of all the places I've been, the people I've met, the things I've seen, and each object is a piece of evidence that I am living "out of the box."

As a lifetime homeschooler, it has become a somewhat necessary part of my life to explain things (like where I get all my time) to what seems like everyone. The amount of ignorance so many people think I have is nothing compared to the ignorance people have about homeschooling. The majority of people blindly accept the stereotypes—that all of us homeschoolers are religious, that we are stuck all day doing textbook work, that we are sadly removed from all possibilities of socialization. Sometimes, these ideas

WHAT ABOUT THE TEEN YEARS?

are so deeply ingrained in people's minds that even after I explain thoroughly the actual truths about my education style, they still retain their beliefs. And people call me stubborn!

A huge discrepancy in the information that most people have is that we are going to miss out... not to mention fall behind with our grades, end up friendless and lonely all through our adolescence, be unable to attend college later in life, etc. On the bad days, it seems like simply everybody is loaded with misconceptions like these. I can't believe sometimes where these ideas originated. While most children are removed from the "real world," I was thrown headfirst in the middle of it, innocent and blinking with wide eyes, full of the drive to learn hands-on—not post-graduation—but right from birth. What's the point of waiting, of allowing my mind to be shaped and molded to the whims of another? Shouldn't it really be my own choice how my mind evolves? There is no better way to reach new and fascinating ideas than through boredom, and although school gives plenty of that, kids are left with no drive to learn outside of school. After years of being force fed knowledge that they will never use by some person somewhere who deemed that it was part of the appropriate curriculum for a grade, they are burnt out.

There are days when it's easy to get angry. These are the days when people seem to be constantly at your throat about your educational decision, leaving you thinking that there isn't a single open-minded person left on the whole planet. We homeschoolers get crazy, completely uninformed questions like, "Are you still smart?" "Don't you miss seeing other kids?" "What's two plus two?" and my personal favorite, "How will you ever learn to answer the phone?" At times, it just takes too much energy to sit and explain that OF COURSE I'm still smart; I see a more diverse group of people than they ever did. Can't you ask me a **real** question (and what does not being in school have to do with learning how to answer the phone)? But at the end of the day, when I can spend my evening doing anything but homework, when I am halfway across the country from home, when I am just sitting on my bed thinking, I have never once regretted the way in which I learn.

CHAPTER SIX

It is incredible the options and new opportunities homeschooling or unschooling can present. But can't people just stop worrying? When I sit down and attempt to explain things, I am hit with the same series of questions, each one like a slap of ignorance across my face. Instead of weighing the advantages and disadvantages, there is only all the worries, all the assumptions, all the misconceptions people refuse to relinquish. There are times when I've sat down and gone over each and every detail, and the conclusion is always to stop worrying. Removing yourself from school is the easiest way to pull out all the stops. My lack of textbook learning will never do anything to obstruct my going to college or having a busy social life. I have the resourcefulness and wherewithal to pursue the exact areas of study I find exciting and to begin working towards my desired occupation. While I watch dozens of school buses haul kids away, I am tying my shoes to go to work that earns me the paychecks that I save up to buy tickets to go and explore other states. Everything I do is building on my life experience—experience that I am racking up in the hours that all the other kids my age are sitting in neat rows of desks, studying things they'll forget as soon as the test is over. Kids look gray colored as they pass by me, while I feel like brilliant technicolor.

In not going to school, a few doors have been closed. I will not go to a school prom. I will not play on a school sports team. I will miss out on having a huge graduation ceremony with a cap and gown. But yet, in closing these few doors, I have simultaneously thrown open dozens more. Not being in school, I have been given the opportunity to have many different part-time jobs, meet people of all ages and from all over the country, not to mention the world, gone to over half of the states and fallen in love with writing and theatre. I've been forced to build my own education, and in doing so, found a love for learning. I have found heroes and poets; I've encountered opposition and discovered ways to always get around someone telling me "no." I am living proof that there is hope in the world. I've read

WHAT ABOUT THE TEEN YEARS?

hundreds of books, filled dozens of notebooks, and taken insane amounts of photographs. I have time to sit and think about the world, to consider ways to change it, how things might be some day, and at the same time, play with a barrel of monkeys and make magazine clipping collages. I know where my priorities are.

The best available advice is relax. When out in the midst of freedom, everything is so much easier. There is an added level of excitement; there is the newfound pursuit of something new everyday and the urge to absorb everything. It is a wide-eyed, hands on approach to poetry, traveling, lights, and words. It is like a present at the foot of your bed every morning when you awake, a box filled with ideas that thrill, concepts that amaze, opportunities that ignite something within. Just imagine having your entire life to yourself. Imagine your eyes opening one morning and realizing that it isn't just an eternal summer vacation, it is eternal freedom. Never once have I been forced to miss out on anything by not going to school, because in being in control of myself, I've been handed the world.

Just the Facts

- Options for teaching your teen's high school subjects are constantly increasing. If your teen is interested in going on to college, you might have to slant your curriculum differently or do a little more preparation.

- Getting a diploma is rarely a problem for homeschooling families. Many of them create their own from forms that they either design or purchase. Others use GEDs or receive diplomas from umbrella or independent study schools.

- Graduation and prom are often more important traditions to parents than to teens. If your teen is interested in either or both, create your own. Also check to see where else these ceremonies are offered, as in conferences or camps.

CHAPTER SIX

- Getting a job is often easier for homeschoolers because of the inherent flexibility of their schedules. If a job is not what one or both of you want, a viable and valuable alternative is volunteering. Many homeschooled teens have the entrepreneur spirit also, so don't be surprised if they want to start their own businesses or surprise the world with an all new invention.

- Apprenticeships and internships are an excellent way for teens to learn about different kinds of jobs as well as what the work world is really like. Resources for these types of programs range from web sites to asking the next door neighbor.

- Colleges and universities are opening up their doors to homeschoolers at a rising rate. Instead of looking at high school transcripts, they are focusing more on portfolios, an area where homeschoolers can really shine. Scholarships are available for homeschoolers; just read the fine lines to see what the exact requirements are. Keep in mind also that college isn't always the only option for teens. They may want to take some time off first, or they may simply find their life journeys taking them in a direction that doesn't require a college education.

- Activities like band, choir, and sports are available to homeschoolers through some school systems. They can also frequently be found in other resources within the community. Driver's education can be obtained through some schools or through private companies and homeschool programs.

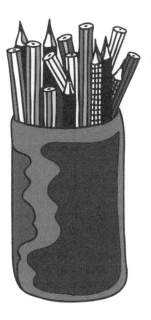

CHAPTER SEVEN
The What Ifs and the What Abouts

"We must not allow other people's limited perceptions to define us."
~ Virginia Satir

There is little within the realm of parenting that doesn't cause moments of self-doubt, and homeschooling is certainly no exception to the rule. There will be moments where even the most veteran parent will stop and wonder if he/she is doing the right thing, responding the right way, providing the right material, etc. This simply means that your children and their education are important to you, and you want to make sure you are doing the best job that you possibly can. This doesn't imply perfection; none of us can reach that level (although there are moments we feel pretty darn brilliant!) and shouldn't attempt to try. Don't let yourself fall into the trap of comparison either. Just because the homeschooling family down the block has made a life size rocket in their back yard which they are planning to fly to Mars when the weather improves, or the other homeschool-

CHAPTER SEVEN

ers around the corner have children who have each invented something that recently sold a million copies, it doesn't indicate that you are doing a bad job because you haven't done the same. It just means that you are doing different things. Not all homeschooled children go on to become rock stars, millionaires, best selling authors, or Nobel Prize winners; instead they just tend to be happy, educated, intelligent, and fulfilled people—not a bad goal to aspire to at all.

This chapter is all about those questions that pop up in your head in the middle of the night when you are supposed to be sleeping. That "what if this happens"or "what about this situation"question that can often create a healthy case of insomnia for us parental figures. Just as with any parenting question, there are answers that will fit you and your children, and ones that won't. Hopefully, these suggestions and ideas will, at least, give you something to think about and a new option to consider.

What if my child doesn't have any friends?

We all want our children to have friends. It's easy to be parent and playmate when your children are still small, but the older they get, the more they will yearn for others closer to their age to relate to. For some, making friends just seems easier than for others, whether in public school or homeschool. Shy children, or those who just appear to be loners, can be more challenging than the outgoing, talk-a-mile-a-minute kind of kid. Your location will make a big difference too; obviously, larger cities are going to have more opportunities than smaller ones. Some of the places you can find peers for your kids include 4-H clubs, Girl Scouts, Boy Scouts, church groups, YM/YWCAs, sports groups, and naturally—homeschool groups. Enroll your child in local classes, workshops, and volunteer organizations. Each one will open up the chance to meet new people and perhaps to make more friends in the process.

THE WHAT IFS AND WHAT ABOUTS

Remember too, that homeschoolers can often make friends in places you wouldn't have thought of. Because they have not been put in school and segregated by age and grade level, they commonly do not carry the concept that you can be buddies only with people your own age. These children are frequently as able to make friends with a child three or four years younger or with an adult 20 years older. They might love playing with toddlers who idolize them, or enjoy the conversations and games they play at the local nursing home.

If you live in a remote area, it's going to be harder to find others to talk to, play with, and just hang out with. Choices here might have to include email and Internet buddies, pen pals, and some long distance trips to friends' houses.

If your child is struggling to meet kids, don't let yourself fall into the trap of thinking that putting him into public school is the solution either. He may have just as much trouble there, if not more, or he may make the kind of friends that you certainly wouldn't have wished for at all.

Some children have a very strong drive for friends, and for these children, you will need to seek out new opportunities for them to meet others. Some want to know a lot of children on a lighter level; others crave close relationships with just one or two people. Other children either enjoy alone time, or have a sibling that fills a good portion of the need for friends. It will change in each family, depending on location, personality, and other factors. Rest assured, however, it is a very, very rare child that doesn't have any friends at all.

CHAPTER SEVEN

What if we have to move?

The most important thing to investigate, if you are going to move, is what the homeschooling laws are in the state (or country) you are going to live in. If they are more lenient, smile and be grateful. If they are stricter, start talking to other homeschoolers in that area (the Internet can help with this) and see what they have to say. Reading the law alone isn't enough; check to see how much is enforced, what loopholes exist, and so on. Also consider this: most likely the state you are moving to will not know of your existence—for a while or forever—so how much you want to comply is up to you.

Go on the Internet or check with homeschooling magazines and find out where the support groups are in the area where you're moving. Join their chat room or group if you can, and start asking important questions. What are the libraries like there? What is the overall homeschooling environment? What activities are available? What are some of the best ways to get connected with others? When and where do support groups meet? If you move to a new area with this information, it will make the transition easier for everyone. You will have the information you need, and your kids will have a head start on meeting new friends and finding new opportunities.

What if my child wants to go to school?

The answer to this depends greatly on the age and experience of the child. Small children may want to go to kindergarten because they hear so much hype about it on television commercials, preschool, friends' houses, and other places. They usually have a pretty idealistic picture of what school is like— lots of time to play, new toys, tons of other kids; they aren't aware of all the downsides of school. Taking time to discuss this with your young child will help; just knowing you have to have permission to go to the bathroom may be enough to change their minds. Older children, on the other hand, may feel pressured to go to public school by friends or by all the promo each fall for back to school supplies, back to school wardrobes, etc.

THE WHAT IFS AND WHAT ABOUTS

The first step to addressing this situation is pinpointing what it is your child really wants; it is rarely going to school, but new clothes, new friends, the excitement of a new year or many other choices. If you can figure out what it is they truly want, then you can begin to address it. If they are lured by 'Back to School' supplies, why not go to the store and let them get new folders, pen, notebooks, and pencils? Even if they use them for non-educational related purposes (are there any truly non-educational related purposes?), what is the harm? If it's new clothes they are really wishing for, try to budget them in.

If the main reason they want to go to school is curiosity (and it often is), consider having them shadow another student at school for a day or two. Pick a neighbor child, friend, cousin, etc. whom your child can follow around to classes and see what different aspects of school are like. (You will need to check in with your local school system first to make sure this is permitted.) Be prepared for a variety of responses. One woman who allowed her 15-year-old to shadow a friend at the local junior high says she spent most of the day with fingers crossed that her daughter wouldn't like it. What relief she felt when her teen walked in the front door, plopped down on the couch, and exclaimed that she had never seen a group of people waste that much time in her life. She was shocked at the amount of busy work involved in a normal school day and couldn't believe anyone would want to spend their days in such a regimented place.

Conversely, if your child spends a few days in school and seems to love it, you are faced with two options. Let him enroll—or don't. If you let him enroll, make sure you talk carefully and at length first about your concerns, and let him know that this is a temporary situation; he can always come back home. You might talk with the school also and see if you can enroll your child part time as somewhat of a compromise and slower introduction to the public school world. If you choose not to put him into school despite his desire, be up front with your reasons why, and be willing to listen to his thoughts and ideas. Younger children will cope with your decision far better than the older student who doesn't want you picking out his socks anymore, let alone tell him where he can and cannot go to school. It can be a difficult time, and if his insistence continues month after month, be prepared to reconsider your homeschooling decision.

CHAPTER SEVEN

What if my child never learns to read?

Can't you just see yourself lying awake at 3 a.m. asking yourself this very question? It's just part of that "what if" mindset that we parents can get ourselves into sometimes. Of course your child will learn to read if you follow a few basic steps: (1) read to them, (2) have books easily available, and (3) read yourself. Will your child read at six? Perhaps; perhaps not. What does it matter? Just because school has trained us to think that children must read at six doesn't mean it's true. Did your child take a step on the day he turned one year old? Or was it at nine months? Or 15 months? Did that mean he was gifted or challenged? No! It just meant that he did it when HE WAS READY. Same thing goes for reading, writing, math, or any other subject at hand. They do it when they are ready. It might be before or after you are ready, but children need to go by their own timetables, not yours.

Homeschooling will not necessarily guarantee that your child will be a voracious reader, but not having it forced on him when he isn't ready, as can happen in public school, will certainly increase his chances. Allowing your child to learn to do things at his own pace and style isn't always easy; your experience keeps telling you that a child of "X" years old MUST know how to do "Y." You have to prepare for your kids when you homeschool; you need to understand that a child learns something when he is interested and capable; doing it before is only a lesson in frustration and coercion.

THE WHAT IFS AND WHAT ABOUTS

What if my child has to take a test?

If your state mandates that your child take a test on certain years, be sure to prepare him. Do many trial runs first so that he understand the process, what is required, what, if any, his time limits are, and all the other details. You may have a child that knows the material inside and out until he goes to write it down on a test, at which point, he freezes. By practicing with him, you can show him how to relax as best he can. If you have a child that reads or writes slowly, you can focus on ways to speed up, since some tests are timed. Many homeschooled children are unaccustomed to testing procedures, institutional settings, and unfamiliar teachers. Help run through different scenarios with your child (what if he has a question, what if his pencil breaks, what if he has to go to the bathroom, etc.), and if possible, use a test administrator that is either a homeschooler or an advocate of homeschooling, so she has a better grasp on how your child might be feeling.

As far as the results of the tests go—sometimes they are never even gathered; some are recorded, and then never commented on; some result (if the child's score is low enough) in a letter. Rarely does a test score cause trouble for homeschooling families, and by now, you are most likely aware that they certainly are not an accurate measurement of what your child does and does not know.

CHAPTER SEVEN

What if my child—or I— hate homeschooling?

Three words: find out WHY. There's a reason and you have to search it out. Do you hate the material? Change it. Do you hate the schedule? Change it. The perk here is that you and your child are the ones in control; if something isn't working, then change it until it does. The more structured your teaching, the more risk of unhappiness and dissatisfaction on both your parts; consider relaxing your methods. Listen to each other; validate what each of you are feeling. Search for a solution together.

Is she lonely? Focus on more group activities. Are you swamped with all of the responsibilities of life? Give up those you can, delegate those you will, and reorganize those you still have to do. Is he bored? Find out what is interesting to him and focus on that for a while. There are solutions out there, and the last one on the list should be giving up and going to public school. Find the reason and find an answer. Ask other homeschoolers; call your state support group; read a homeschooling magazine; attend a conference. Find the solution.

What if my child is ADD/ADHD (Attention Deficit Disorder/Attention Deficit Hyperactivity Disorder)?

This topic could fill up a book all by itself; perhaps even a series. However, this is going to be the abridged version. If this a concern in your family, check out the resources section for lots of places to contact and books to read.

Picture something for a moment. You are rested, energetic, and surrounded by people you would like to be interacting with. It's a beautiful day and in an hour, you get to go outside and feel the sunshine and MOVE. But right now, you have to sit at a desk. Be quiet. Don't talk to anyone around you. Sit still. No fidgeting. No tapping your pencil. No humming. Have to go to the bathroom? Too bad. It's not time and you don't have per-

THE WHAT IFS AND WHAT ABOUTS

mission. Oops—the teacher is talking. She is telling you and everyone else about something you recognize as some kind of math. You listen for a moment, but then a gorgeous bluebird flies by the window and you follow it with your eyes as it disappears into the trees. Back to the teacher. Now, you're lost. You missed something, and you really didn't care in the first place. It's hard to follow her when she talks about new stuff. You would much rather read about it or do a worksheet. Actually, right now you really want to tell someone about the great book you read last night or get up and show the class your latest cartwheel. You start to daydream about becoming cartwheel champion in the 2004 Olympics. Your legs start bouncing and your fingers are twitching. You can feel the energy running through your muscles. Sorry to tell you this but you might have a problem; you might have ADD.

ADD (Attention Deficit Disorder) and ADHD (Attention Deficit Hyperactivity Disorder) are very popular labels to put on an increasing number of kids today. Definitions of what it truly is vary from one end of the spectrum to the other. Scientists have defined it as a mental disorder due to a lack of certain chemicals called neurotransmitters in the brain. On the other hand, experts in the world of alternative education have labeled it as "a teaching disability," "a condition created by schools to shirk accountability," and "superior intelligence coupled with inferior self-esteem." So, what is it? A genuine medical problem requiring medication, or just a different way of learning and relating to the world?

CHAPTER SEVEN

The symptoms of ADD are listed below. A child is often diagnosed as having this condition if they have six or more symptoms that last six or more months. Look down the list. Remind you of anyone you know?

Symptoms of ADD

- Fidgets
- Restless
- Inability to stay seated
- Short attention span
- Can't wait for a turn
- Loud, noisy, disruptive
- Accident prone
- Daydreams

- Impulsive
- Loses things
- Forgetful
- Driven
- Talks a lot, interrupts often
- Low self-esteem
- Fails to finish things
- Can't concentrate

THE WHAT IFS AND WHAT ABOUTS

A great many of these symptoms look to many parents like normal child-like behaviors. Is it too much of a surprise that boys are diagnosed with this condition three times more than girls? If you have a son, you might be shaking your head right now. If you had to write a description of his daily behavior, how many of these symptoms would you list? Does this mean he is disabled, has a deficit, or a disorder, or does this just mean that your child is normal? How many of these symptoms are actually signs of being just plain bored?

Consider, for a moment, other possible causes for this type of behavior. Putting aside the concept of a lack of neurotransmitters, how about:

- This is normal child behavior (read that one several times—think it over).

- Diet – too much sugar, caffeine, and artificial preservatives. They can all affect behavior.

- Learning styles – each child learns in his own way. What happens if that isn't how the school/teacher is teaching?

- Allergies – sensitivities to environmental factors.

- A phase – his behavior might just be a phase he is going through that will pass.

The fact that some children behave differently in school or learning settings isn't being disputed; the question is how did this get turned into a 'disability?' Are we seeing a brand new epidemic among this generation's children or is it something else? Could the schools themselves be playing a role in this diagnosis as they are faced with more children who refuse to—or are unable to—sit still, listen, and learn like the typical child?

CHAPTER SEVEN

Whether or not this type of behavior should be called a disability, it is often treated as such, and many of the children who display such behavior are now being medicated. If you have a child on Ritalin or if you are thinking that might be a solution, consider this:

- The Drug Enforcement Agency's "Drugs of Concern" lists Ritalin right there next to cocaine, LSD, and ecstasy.

- Ritalin, or methylphenidate, is a stimulant that is stronger than caffeine.

- The number of preschool children being treated with medication for ADHD tripled between 1990 and 1995.

- The majority of children who receive stimulants for ADHD do not fully meet the criteria for ADHD.

Do you want to try to figure out how to tell your kids not to use drugs, but be sure and take their Ritalin before they go to school? Ritalin may not be the answer for your child's behavior and the consequences of its use can be severe. As parents, it is your right and responsibility to decide whether the doctors and schools are correct and your child does indeed have a condition that requires medication. That's a heavy burden: prepare yourself with as much knowledge as you can. Read, research, and look at both sides of the controversy, and keep in mind two important things: in almost every case the schools are operating out of concern for the best interests of your child as they see them; and, the schools can be wrong. It's essential that you figure prominently in the decision. There's something else to take note of: For many children diagnosed with ADD, schools set up or create an Individualized Education Program (or IEP—discussed below). School systems commonly receive *twice* the state and federal funds for each child with an IEP than they do for a child who is merely 'normal.'

THE WHAT IFS AND WHAT ABOUTS

Homeschooling a child that has been labeled ADD can be one of the best steps you will ever take as a parent. The vast majority of parents who have made this decision report the same thing: within weeks of coming home, nearly every symptom of ADD disappears. They are gone; the parents have found the solution without turning to drugs. The problem wasn't the child. The problem was the child being put into an environment that was damaging, difficult, and draining.

Parents who homeschool their ADD children have reported that these are the best techniques to use:

- Giving simple, repeated instructions.
- Teaching material in the *child's* learning style.
- Giving immediate feedback.
- Working one-on-one.
- Providing regular and frequent breaks.
- Incorporating motion into most activities.
- Using a child-centered curriculum based on interest.
- Learning everything you can about your child's learning style so you can understand it better.
- Keeping the house clear of clutter and excessive noise.
- Creating a schedule that a child can understand and follow.

CHAPTER SEVEN

Thomas Armstrong, in his book *The Myth of the A.D.D. Child*, offers many different ways to cope with a child with this label. His list includes:

- Find out what interests your child.
- Limit television and video games.
- Provide opportunities for physical movement.
- Provide hands-on activities.
- Use touch to soothe and calm.
- Give your child choices.
- Provide a balanced breakfast.
- Discover your child's multiple intelligences.

Often, the child that is labeled with some kind of learning disability in public school is not the victim of a disorder; he simply wants to do something else or at least, wants to do it in another way. That isn't wrong; it's an alternative. Here is a list of some people who have been diagnosed or who have been shown through history to have exhibited many of the classic symptoms of the condition. What do you think of when you read their names? Are these people disabled or just talented? What would the world have missed out on if these people had been drugged instead of allowed to explore and use their abilities?

- Albert Einstein
- Galileo
- Leonardo da Vinci
- Walt Disney
- John Lennon
- Stephen Hawkings
- Jules Verne
- Alexander Graham Bell
- Hans Christian Anderson
- Thomas Edison
- John F. Kennedy
- Woodrow Wilson
- Louis Pasteur
- Prince Charles
- Beethoven
- 'Magic' Johnson
- Mozart
- Wright Brothers
- Winston Churchill
- General George Patton

THE WHAT IFS AND WHAT ABOUTS

Listen to the perspectives of others: Dr. Martha Denckla, Director of Developmental Cognitive Neurology at John Hopkins, said this about ADD, "Think of an absentminded professor who can find a cure for cancer but not his glasses in the mess on his desk. These are the inventors, creators, poets—the people who think creative thoughts because they don't think like everyone else." Thomas Armstrong, Ph.D. writes, "These children are not disordered. They may have a different style of thinking, attending, and behaving, but it's the broader social and educational influences that create the disorder, not the children. I'm alarmed to think that modern science may be turning creativity into a medical disorder." Psychologist Dr. Kathleen Nadeau says, "ADD people are high-energy and incredibly good brainstormers. They will often happily work 12 to 15 hours by choice. The business community should not fear ADD. Instead, they should see that they have a potential gold mine here."

A child that thinks differently, who processes information in more unusual ways, can struggle in public school. There is rarely the time, the resources, and the budget to meet his needs effectively. On top of this, he will have to deal with the negativity that his unique perspective creates from fellow classmates. The different are not tolerated well in public school; he may be labeled different or weird by his classmates, he may be teased, and his self-esteem may suffer. It becomes a Catch-22 situation as his low self-image contributes to his behavior, and his behavior contributes to how he is treated. By bringing this child home, he will have a chance to be himself without labels and criticism. Think of what this could mean in how he sees himself; by spending his days in a nurturing, loving environment, he may well blossom in ways you could never have imagined.

Keep in mind that your child just may not be ready for a structured school setting of any kind yet. Cindy Wade, editor of *Right at Home* newsletter and author of *The Vermont Homeschoolers Directory* says, "I'm also convinced that children under the age of ten shouldn't be forced to attend any kind of institutionalized training such as preschool or public school... (they) are not psychologically, biologically, emotionally, or physiologically ready

CHAPTER SEVEN

for structured learning." If they aren't ready, how can they behave the way the school wants them to? It's like trying to potty train a one year old. He isn't trying to be difficult or obstinate; he isn't able to do what you are demanding of him.

The controversy over ADD continues to rage and you need to do your own research and reading on the topic to figure out how you feel. The key is to become familiar with a variety of perspectives and most of all, to observe your own child closely to see if there is a problem or not. For many children, the best therapy for their so-called disorder is just bringing them back home.

What if my child is special needs?

There are, of course, children who have definite learning issues like autism, Down's syndrome, and other physical conditions. The process here is different, and your best resources for information are local and national support groups (see resources in the Appendix). They will help direct you to local organizations, conferences, workshops, publications, and other important information. However, here is some general information to get you started.

Laws regarding teaching special needs children are different in most states. You will need to find out what they are and how to work with them if they are not particularly lenient. If your children are under the Individual with Disabilities Education Act (IDEA), or you want access to your local school's special services, you must have an Individualized Education Program (IEP).

The first step in this process is the evaluation. A panel of experts, with your permission, will examine your child. Usually this group consists of a psychologist, a speech pathologist, a social worker, and various medical personnel, depending on your child's needs. They should each discuss their assessments with you. It's helpful to brush up on the terminology they are going to use before you meet with them, be sure that you know your rights, and be ready to take notes.

THE WHAT IFS AND WHAT ABOUTS

If the group deems your child to be disabled, then they will partner with you (hopefully) in creating an IEP. In this, they will list your child's present level of educational performance, annual goals for your child, specific ways to determine if objectives are being met, specific services that are to be provided and by whom, when the education will start, how long it will last, and how and when they will evaluate for progress.

As you enter into this process, be sure to talk with other homeschoolers in the area for their advice and suggestions. Ask them to recommend books to read, and what they wish they had known before they started homeschooling. Other places to go to for help and/or support include the Developmental Disabilities Planning Council, your state Department of Mental Health, Mental Retardation and Health and Human Services. You might also want to check in with your local chapter of the National Academy for Child Development or the Learning Disabilities Association of America.

Marsha Ransom, author of *The Complete Idiot's Guide to Homeschooling* writes, "The most important thing you need to know about providing an education program for your child with special needs is to know your child." For additional information, you might want to also contact Pete and Pam Wright (**www.wrightslaw.com**). He is a special education attorney and she is a psychotherapist. They specialize in the rights of homeschoolers to receiving public school services. Check out their site or contact The Special Education Advocates at P.O. Box 1008, Deltaville, VA 23043. Their number is 804-257-0857.

CHAPTER SEVEN

What if my child is gifted?

Have you ever noticed the incredible similarity between a child who is diagnosed ADD and a child that is considered to be gifted? If you put the lists of behaviors and traits next to each other, it is amazing how much they overlap. Mariaemma Pelullo, a professional learning styles analyst from Reflective Educational Perspectives wrote, "All children are gifted! In our culture, we define areas in which we think children should be smart and then call them 'gifted' when they show the 'right' kind of intelligence, and 'learning disabled' when they don't."

A child that is labeled "gifted" has usually shown an exceptional ability in one or more areas; whether it be in reading, art, math, music, or whatever subject. They might exhibit an extraordinary vocabulary, superior reasoning skills, or excellent recall. These children are often extremely bored in school (hence the fidgeting, daydreaming, etc.) and like their special needs counterparts, they are labeled as "brains," "eggheads," and other terms for being "too smart."(Remember, the law of the school world is that "different"equals WEIRD.)

Homeschooling a gifted child is wonderful; once again, you can tailor their education to their unique needs. Most children who excel in some areas do not excel in all areas, so you might be introducing your 10-year-old to college reading material, and then switching over to learning the multiplication tables. If your child is gifted in an area where you are not, or is already beyond your level, you can attempt to reach her level, or perhaps hire a tutor or find a mentor. Distance learning programs over the Internet, community college classes, and internships are other possibilities. Teaching them may be a combination of helping them with some of their weaker areas and sitting back to marvel as they take off in their strongest areas.

At home, these bright children can accelerate as need be without having to pretend to be slower for the sake of their classmates; they can feel normal instead of strange; they can follow their interests and begin to reach their incredible potential.

THE WHAT IFS AND WHAT ABOUTS

"What does education often do?
It makes a straight-cut ditch of a free, meandering brook."
~ Henry David Thoreau

In the Trenches

Some Say
~ Melanie Walenciak

Some might say he is impulsive. I say he is eager to try new things. Some might say he is into everything. I say he is curious and loves to discover. Some might say he lacks common sense. I say he is a dreamer and is thinking of things I couldn't even imagine. Some would label him ADD. I named him Cody, and he is my son.

From the start I knew he was different. As a child, he was extremely sensitive to stimuli. He startled at even the slightest of sounds. Trips to the mall were out of the question. His little nervous system simply couldn't handle it.

As he got older, he seemed to require more attention and less sleep. He constantly "read" books about heavy machinery and, at the age of two, would hold captivating, articulated conversations on dump trucks and tunnel boring machines. I received several compliments on my clever little boy.

Somewhere along the line, Cody's strengths began to look more like weaknesses, especially to those that didn't know him. I heard fewer compliments, and more "helpful" suggestions from those who understood my child even less than I did.

"Does he ever stop talking?"

"Have you tried time outs?"

"A good spanking will cure him."

"Maybe he eats too much sugar."

During one particularly stressful week, my husband and I were asked on three separate occasions if Cody had been tested for Attention Deficit Disorder. The idea was shocking, and I refused to accept it. I didn't want to have him tested. I didn't want to limit him with a label. I wanted to focus on what was right, not search for what was wrong.

I made the decision to homeschool well before Cody was born. As his personality emerged, I knew there was no other choice. I could not in good conscience send him to school. He could not sit still for 15 minutes, let alone an hour. On the rare occasion he was able to still his body, his mouth would kick in gear. He would click his tongue and pop his lips. I knew a traditional school would kill his spirit and take away his confidence. I knew he would be told day after day, hour after hour, that something was wrong with him.

CHAPTER SEVEN

So our homeschool journey began.

For a while, things went smoothly. I chose a well-known, expensive curriculum for math and phonics, and used a hands-on unit study approach for all the rest. Cody loved his math manipulatives and played with them everyday. He enjoyed discovering all he could do with them. Phonics was a different story. He knew his letters, but when it came time to code and blend them, frustration levels went through the roof.

I distinctly remember one day we were both close to pulling our hair out. His constant motion wore my patience thin. I knew there was nothing to be done about it at the time. I could expect him to be still or expect him to learn. To do both was entirely out of the question and quite impossible.

On this day, with nerves already frazzled, I asked him a simple review question; he hemmed and hawed and tapped his pencil on the table. He was a very capable staller, but there was no reason to stall this time. I knew he knew the answer, but he would not say it. I became angry and sent him to his room. School was dismissed.

That very evening I had a revelation that changed everything. My husband had cut his finger sharpening a knife. When he asked me where the bandages were, I could not tell him. I could see the box, sitting in the first aid kit under the sink in the bathroom. I knew exactly where they were, but when I tried to tell him, the words would not come out in any kind of sensible order. In frustration, I finally went to the bathroom and got them myself. The realization hit me hard. This is how Cody feels every day. He knows the answer, but he can't figure out how to get the answer out of his head. And worst of all, it seems he's inherited this dysfunction from me.

Cody took a break from school for a while, and I went back to school, so to speak. I studied learning styles and learning modalities. I studied how the brain works and how our dominant hemisphere affects the way we think and the way we learn.

Most students are left brained convergent thinkers. That is to say, they are logical and analytical. They appreciate detail and can focus easily on one idea at a time. They thrive on repetition and structure.

It did not take much investigation to discover that Cody was right brain dominant and his thinking was divergent. He prefers the whole picture to the details and lives in a constant state of brainstorm. One idea sparks another, then another, then another. But when he does focus on one thing, he uses hyperfocus. Whether it is heavy machinery at the age of two, or Legos at eight, when Cody is passionate about something, nothing else matters.

THE WHAT IFS AND WHAT ABOUTS

I used my newfound knowledge to make several curriculum changes in our home. I sold my phonics curriculum and opted for a whole language approach instead. The coding details of phonics made him hate books, but when I introduced whole words to him, he was able to break down the words and discover patterns for himself. He is now in third grade and reads at a sixth grade level. In fact, he has turned into a voracious reader.

We used his strength in divergent thinking to build his math program. Instead of asking him what 6+6 equals, I asked him to list all the different ways he can come up with the answer 12. In less time than he could focus on 6+6, he brainstorms and comes up with 8+4, 5+7, 10+2, 11+1, 3X4, and 6+6. It is amazing to watch him work.

When learning a new concept, I always present it to him according to his strengths. After he has mastered it, we continue to work with it in a more traditional way, to help him build up his convergent thinking, or focusing skills. He is excelling in ways I never thought possible.

I recently did an Internet search for "divergent thinking" to see what kind of information is available to frustrated parents. What I found surprised me. People are making money teaching others how to think divergently. What is considered a handicap in schools, is now thought of as a commodity in the business world. My heart breaks when I think of all the children in our schools who have this gift, but are told it is wrong and taught to suppress it.

Thomas Alva Edison is a wonderful example of a divergent thinker. As a child he was kicked out of school for being inattentive and a dreamer. His mother knew better and taught him at home. Edison's brilliant mind was nurtured and he became a prolific inventor. He once credited his mother with his success, saying, "She was the only person who truly understood me."

Cody says the same thing about me.

CHAPTER SEVEN

In the Trenches
A Mother and Son's Journey
~ Margaret Helmstetter

When my son was in second grade, I approached his teacher with a concern. He still could not read, not even his name. I was told that he was still within normal limits, and that some children were slower than others. I was told not to push him; that he would learn at his own pace. There was nothing I could do with him at home that would help. I went against the teachers and read to him more, helped him sound words out, and started to teach him phonics, something he had not had previously.

When my son was in third grade, I was told he needed "resource" since he still didn't read, but there was no problem. A school psychologist examined him and found he had an unspecified learning problem. When I asked for more specifics about it and what could be done to counteract it, I was told the learning problem was minor and it didn't really matter what it was, since "resource" would teach him. His strong points were numbers and an excellent memory; his weak points—poor reading and visual skills.

When my son was in fourth grade, he still could not read more than simple three letter words. After having his eyes checked, we found that one of the problems was poor vision. The doctor said he suspected that he also had some dyslexia because of difficulties during the exam. When I questioned people at the school, I was told there was no need to have him tested for dyslexia, since a diagnosis would not change his "unspecified" learning problem, that dyslexic or not, his "resource" classes would not change. That year he was placed in resource for math and reading. I asked how they could possibly test his math skills when he was given word problems to check his ability to compute numbers. I was told that it wasn't important; he would be given the same lessons as his peers and the additional resource class would provide more funding for the school system as a whole.

When my son entered fifth grade, it was against my wishes. He had improved; he could now read a second grade book and do addition and subtraction, but he was slow and his handwriting frequently had the numbers and letters of his answer backwards. Word problems still gave him problems, but mainly because of his reading problem. I had requested and argued with the school about passing him to fifth grade. The stock response was that keeping him back would damage his self-esteem, and that he should stay with his peers. He would catch up; some children were just slower to mature than others.

THE WHAT IFS AND WHAT ABOUTS

When my son was in sixth grade, he was in constant trouble with teachers. He was frequently suspended from school for fights, for disrupting class, and for failure to do his work. He was still reading at a second grade level. His resource work consisted of adding, subtracting, and writing his name. Occasionally he would do a worksheet, coloring the balloons a specified color, or drawing a line between bigger and smaller objects. Nothing whatsoever was done that was geared towards teaching him to read better, or to progress in math.

When my son was in seventh grade, he was reading at a second grade level and doing simple addition and subtraction. He was in resource class again. When I questioned the teachers on ways to help him, it was the same answer: there was nothing I could do to help him learn. They said that when he started high school, their goal would be educating him to a functional level.

After talking to various people and researching what I needed to do, I pulled my son from public school and began homeschooling him. In three months, he could read third grade books slowly and he could comprehend what he was reading. His math skills were also increasing and in six months, he could do multiplication. In a year, he was doing three-digit multiplication and simple division and was working on a few fourth grade books. In two years, he was tackling pre-algebra, reading classics, and considering what he would do upon graduation.

He still occasionally writes letters, numbers, and even whole words backwards; he still has a problem with left and right. He is a normal teenager now, slightly behind his peers, but catching up rapidly. I still don't know what his learning disability actually is; I suspect he has mild dyslexia, along with problems processing words. However, this isn't important; what is important is that he now loves learning. He has set goals for the future and can see a way to reach them. He may work slower and more deliberately than others his age, but the work will be done, and it will be correct.

CHAPTER SEVEN

In the Trenches
Homeschooling Your Special Needs Child
~ *Deborah Bradshaw*

My son, Curtis, has Down's Syndrome. School was not working for my child for a variety of reasons. He wanted to learn, but he was not learning what he could have been, nor did the school understand how to best meet his needs. My husband saw my frustration and my rising blood pressure and came to the conclusion that we should homeschool.

Although I had personal experience as a schoolteacher and had taught a little bit of everything—preschool through college, including special education, I was nervous about this prospect and unsure of my ability to teach my own child. Somehow the thought of being solely responsible for his education had me sweating bullets.

I researched the subject and while I found a great deal of information on homeschooling, specific information on homeschooling a special needs child was much more difficult to obtain. I wanted specifics. I finally developed a personal plan based upon my experience as a teacher, but more importantly—on what my child has taught me about the way he learns. These techniques apply to any child, but especially to the child with special needs including Down's Syndrome.

When considering any project it is wise to develop a plan. So it is with educating your special needs child. You need a series of steps to determine what your plan will be. Below is a list of suggestions that will help you get started. You will, after working on your plan, find other steps to help you fine tune.

The first step is to determine how your child learns. There are many great books available on learning styles. Some authors list seven styles of learning; others three: visual, auditory, and kinesthetic. I believe there are three basic styles and the remainders are a compilation of these styles and include other factors about the child. Without knowing what style of learning a child has, it is difficult to know how best to present the material.

Visual means the child learns better by a demonstration, or seeing what you are talking about. People who are visual often have trouble remembering people's names but usually remember their face. Visual learners have vivid imaginations, use colors, and often think in pictures. A visual learner will often tell you how they are feeling by their facial expressions.

Auditory learners focus more on hearing. They learn well from verbal instruction but are easily distracted by outside noises, people talking, and background music. Auditory learners benefit from listening and then by retelling.

THE WHAT IFS AND WHAT ABOUTS

Kinesthetic learners need to be part of the action. They learn by experiencing, participating in, and doing. Kinesthetic learners are often physically active and impulsive. Manipulatives (e.g. items such as counters, labeled photographs, sand paper letters, etc.) and games work well for this style of learner.

The next step in the process is determining what to teach. If the child has been in a public school they will have an IEP or IFSP, Individualized Education Plan or Individual Family Support Plan, respectively. It depends on the child's age as to what plan is typically used. Some states may use different acronyms, but the concept is the same—what does this individual child need to learn to help them best succeed. If your child has been part of the public education system, you are probably familiar with this process.

I was not particularly keen on the idea of an IEP for my homeschooled child. The IEP process was a painful memory for me. It was an experience of telling the school what I wanted for my child and being told it couldn't be done or they did not have the resources, the program, the personnel, and so on. I eventually realized I now had control of the education plan for my child. I could decide what he needed to learn, write my own goals and objectives, and then decide how best to implement the plan—but where would I start?

I needed to determine what my child knew, and more importantly, what he was comfortable enough to use. Sometimes our children know information, they will even repeat it back to us when asked, but being comfortable enough to use it on a daily basis may be a goal yet to be achieved. An example might be, I "know" how to make a chocolate cake. I can list the ingredients and can tell you how hot the oven should be, even how long to bake it. I would, however, not want to make a chocolate cake without the recipe. The same is true for kids with special need—sometimes they know the "ingredients" it takes to use a particular skill, but they aren't quite sure how it all goes together, they don't quite have the "recipe" memorized.

A child who seems to know how to say words and name objects, but is still unable to carry on a conversation, may have a problem of not having all the building blocks in place to succeed at the task. Sometimes it is okay to use a support until the skill is achieved. In some areas your child may continue to use a support. As adults, we use calculators, encyclopedias, or the Internet to help us with the information we need. It is acceptable for our children to use the tools they need to accomplish the task at hand. Some tools for math might be a calculator, a number line for addition and subtraction, or a printed times table. Use your imagination to come up with creative ideas to help your child further develop their own skills or "recipe."

As adults, our brains are developed to the point we do not often think of the steps involved in learning a new skill. We may even think that we "just learned it." This is because basic skills are learned in a building block pattern. We first learned the basic skills in order to achieve the level we have reached today. An infant does not learn to

CHAPTER SEVEN

walk overnight. Human infants typically take nine to thirteen months to learn the incremental skills it takes to achieve the larger goal. First they must learn to control their bodies: roll over, crawl, stand, and so on. The fear of falling may then keep them from moving on to walking when they are physically ready.

Determining a child's current level of skill and confidence can be accomplished in several ways. An assessment test can be given to the child by a licensed psychologist or other qualified professional. An achievement test can be administered depending on the child's level of communication and understanding. It may be simpler, however, to simply observe the child through play and daily life. Keep a record of what the child routinely says, does, and plays. For example, what words does the child use? Is the child able to use scissors or other household objects? Can the child tell you their full name?

This need not be a lengthy project, but one of simple, yet careful, observation throughout the natural day of the child. It is best to observe these skills for at least a few weeks. We all have good and bad days. Some children with special needs are particularly susceptible to days when skills seem to come and go. Do not give up! Simply list those skills as ones to be worked on. I suggest three categories in your observations. Skills already attained (those the child is comfortable in using), skills to be practiced (those which seem to fade in and out), and skills to be attained (skills to yet be achieved). Your observation will provide you with the goals and objectives you need to determine what you will teach. An excellent book that provides lists of incremental and developmental steps is **Behavioral Intervention for Young Children with Autism**, edited by Catherine Maurice, published by PRO-ED, Inc. While this book was specifically written for children with autism in mind, I have found the lists of incremental steps and the suggestions for teaching those steps to be invaluable.

Once you have decided what to teach, you need to find curriculum and materials to accomplish your goals. There are many excellent programs and textbooks on the market. Books, which were previously available primarily to schools, have recently been made more affordable for the homeschooler. Look around; talk to friends about what they use.

Keep in mind that if something doesn't work, it does not mean that the child cannot learn that subject or skill. It may be that the particular method used is not incorporating the student's learning style. It may be the child is not developmentally ready to learn that skill or the building block is not yet in place. Don't give up! It is easy to get discouraged for both you and your child. If something is not working, take a break from it. Be creative. Try something else and come back to it later.

Deuteronomy 11:19 says, "And ye shall teach them your children, speaking of them when thou sittest in thine house, and when thou walkest by the way, when thou liest down, and when thou risest up." This verse makes a good point. If you want your child to truly absorb what you are teaching them, learning must be a continual process.

THE WHAT IFS AND WHAT ABOUTS

Learning takes place throughout the day, no matter where you may be. It is not confined to the hours we set aside for school.

My son, Curtis, has gained many new skills through our daily life experiences. When we were trying to learn directional words such as up and under, Curtis would help me in the kitchen. I would ask him to get me the pan that is under the stove, bring me the bowl on top of the cabinet, and find the jar that is beside the breadbox. While working on fine motor skills, he cut open packages and helped sort small objects. By having him actually experience these skills, they became part of his working knowledge.

Homeschooling has been a series of ups and downs. Sometimes I think Curtis is not grasping a concept or skill, or that the learning is going too slowly. Some subjects I thought I presented well, but I did not explain as well as I could have. Progress has seemed slow at times, but then when I look back at what he was doing when we began, and when I look at the records from the school, I see just how far we have come. His accomplishments in reading, math skills, and language development have been impressive. More importantly, his self-confidence has increased dramatically. He carries himself differently, he carries on conversations with people he never would have before, and he even walks differently!

You are your child's best teacher and advocate. You have the God-given ability to know your child like no one else can. Do not be discouraged. It is frustrating and difficult at times, but each and every skill gained, and every step accomplished, is worth the effort. As I look back over the past two years and see how much Curtis has gained, I know the decision to homeschool was the best one we could have made.

Just the Facts

- Every parent experiences the "what ifs" and "what abouts," usually late at night when the rest of the house is quiet. Each one is valid and almost always has a solution.

- Homeschooled children will find friends through a variety of ways—including groups, clubs, organizations, volunteering, church, camps, and the Internet.

- If you have to move, check out the legal situation of home education in the city you are going to, and make contacts before you move, so that you are involved with the homeschooling community as soon as you arrive.

CHAPTER SEVEN

- If your child wants to go to school, pinpoint the reason why and see if that individual issue can be addressed. If not, consider letting him shadow another student to get firsthand exposure. Take the time to talk about it and outline your reasons for deciding to homeschool.

- Your child will eventually learn to read. It may not be the way or the time you think it should be, but it will happen.

- If your child has to take a test, take time to prepare them. Make sure they understand and learned the material and take them through some practice runs to eliminate problems of freezing, going too slow, etc.

- If one or both of you hate homeschooling, you must figure out the main reason and then see how it can be resolved.

- ADD is a label given to far too many children, and many do not even believe it exists. Most parents who choose to teach their ADD children at home find that many of the symptoms of learning disorders disappear.

- Special needs children can be taught at home, but it will mean extra research to find out how the homeschooling laws differ with these children. You will also have to consider creating an Individualized Education Program with a team of specialists.

- Gifted children can be taught at home and often find themselves blossoming there without the labels and difficulties they would have had in the public school setting.

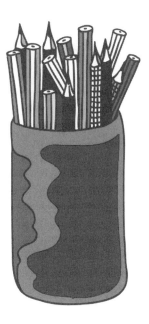

CHAPTER EIGHT
What Are the Legalities Involved in All of This?

"When we lose the right to be different, we lose the right to be free."

~ *C.E. Hughes*

To be perfectly honest, this was my least favorite chapter to put together. The other chapters are so much more full of fun and excitement and new ideas and endless possibilities; in comparison, this chapter seemed dry and dull. However, the information in it is necessary stuff for you to know. (A special thanks for the Kasemans who helped make all these issues clearer and much more interesting in their essay at the end of the chapter.)

CHAPTER EIGHT

If you are thinking about homeschooling or just getting started, please do not let anything in this chapter change your mind. Some states make homeschooling a little more challenging than most of us would want, but as they said in the turbulent 1960s, "The times, they are a'changin.'" The laws are changing; the world is opening up to the concept of homeschooling, and the states will reflect that more and more as time goes by. Already those in the know have seen some radical changes to laws as states recognize that this is the way of the future for many, many families.

If you don't like your state's homeschooling laws, work to change them. Write letters to your newspaper, your school districts, and your state representatives; attend conferences, get politically active. Our children's educational rights are vital to the future, so don't be afraid to fight for them.

How do the laws differ from state to state?

Charting the national homeschooling laws is more than a small challenge because each state is vastly different from the others in their requirements, and even more so in the details of those requirements. The chart in this chapter gives you the generic information, but it can, in no way, give you the full picture of what homeschooling is like in your state. This is a beginning, the tip of that proverbial iceberg. Take this information and then do some investigating on your own to find out exactly what your state requires.

To demonstrate how diverse the requirements can be, consider this:

- If a state requires testing, it may be every year, every other year, or only once. Some states allow parents to administer them; others allow another family member or friend. Still others insist on a certified teacher. Many times, these tests are not necessary if you fulfill other odd requirements, like one parent is a certified teacher, or you are

WHAT ARE THE LEGALITIES?

part of a registered support group. Also, there are states that accept alternatives to standardized tests like portfolios, journals, and so on. In other words, if you look at your state in the chart and it says "YES" under testing, don't be discouraged. Get the details.

- If a state requires equivalency, it simply means that their law requires you to homeschool for a minimum number of days per year. It usually ranges from 132 to 188. Sometimes the law will even dictate how many hours a day you have to spend "in school." Don't worry about this; every minute of your child's day can be translated to something educational, and meeting this minimum is never a problem.

- If a state requires that you keep records of some kind, it may mean attendance records, or a portfolio, or something in between. And, simply because they are required does not mean that anyone will ever ask to look at them. You keep them just in case!

- If a state requires that you register, it might mean registering with the state department of education, or with your local school superintendent. It might mean an official letter, or just a note.

- If a state requires a notification of intent, it might just be a casual letter, or a routine form that you need to fill out and sign. Some states ask for it once, some every year. Some require little to no information, while others ask a lot of questions.

CHAPTER EIGHT

- If a state requires a certain curriculum, it almost always means they want to ensure that you are covering the primary subjects: language arts, math, science, social studies, health, music, art, and physical education. Sometimes they want particular subjects added, and occasionally, the state can be selective about what actual materials you use, although this is rare. Again, this is not usually a problem; how you cover those subjects is up to you most of the time.

- If a state requires parents to have some kind of competency level, it usually means they have to have the equivalent of a high school diploma or GED. Some states require nothing; some require a college degree; others require that a parent's education level be at least several levels higher than those they are teaching.

- Some states consider homeschools private schools; others do not.

- Some states allow individual school districts to set the requirements of their homeschooling families. This can be complicated and crazy.

WHAT ARE THE LEGALITIES?

Which states are the best (and which are the worst) for homeschooling?

Some states make homeschooling easy; some make it more difficult. None of them make it impossible. A state on the best list is there because it requires little to nothing from the parents and does not interfere with the family's homeschooling choices. If it is on the worst list, it is because it has the opposite: lots of requirements and interference. For instance, in the case of Massachusetts, each school district is allowed to make its own requirements, and this creates some complications. Despite this, many families homeschool in Massachusetts. If you see your state's name on the worst list, don't throw out the entire notion of homeschooling; just start getting in contact with local support groups and get their advice and insight early on.

Best States for Homeschooling

- Alaska
- California
- Florida
- Idaho
- Illinois
- Indiana
- New Jersey
- Oklahoma
- Texas
- Utah

Worst States for Homeschooling

- Georgia
- Massachusetts
- Minnesota
- New Mexico
- North Carolina
- North Dakota
- Tennessee
- Virginia
- Washington

CHAPTER EIGHT

It is interesting to compare this list to an article that appeared in *The Wall Street Journal* on September 20, 2000. Titled "Grading States on their Education Freedom," this article listed the top ten 'most free' and 'least free' states. Their determination was based not just on the attitude towards homeschooling, but also on tax voucher credit availability and the number of charter schools. Some of the states on our lists above overlap with *The Wall Street Journal* lists. Georgia and Virginia are on both 'worst lists,' and New Jersey and Texas are on both 'best lists.' Conversely, Minnesota is one of our 'worst,' and the newspaper's 'best'; we give Alaska a great rating, but it's almost at the bottom on *The Wall Street Journal* list.

How do I know what the laws are in my state?

The chart on the following pages is an attempt to answer that question. The laws pertaining to homeschooling are changing often enough and fast enough, however, that it's almost impossible to keep on top of it all. While you can certainly refer to this chart for valuable and helpful information, before you face down a school truancy officer or your irate mother-in-law, check the Internet sites listed in the resource section and check with your state homeschool association to make sure there haven't been any changes since this went to print. Keep up-to-date with what is happening through the web and through reading homeschooling publications and talking to your support group. Do not—let me repeat that—do not call your local school system or state department of education and ask them. Stop. Read that statement one more time. Most likely they will not know and will only give you incorrect information or no information at all, or they will tell you the laws and/or requirements they WANT homeschoolers to follow rather than what the actual law states.

WHAT ARE THE LEGALITIES?

Before you start scanning for your state, here's a little more explanation on each column heading:

- **State**: that one is pretty obvious.
- **Ages of Compulsory Attendance**: these are the ages that children are required by law to go to some kind of school.
- **Required Curriculum**: does this state mandate certain classes, textbooks, or subjects?
- **Parental Competency/Education**: does the state require homeschooling parents to have any specific amount or level of education?
- **Testing**: does this state require testing of kids somewhere during the homeschooling years?
- **# of Days Equivalency**: does the state require that a certain number of days are spent 'in school' each year?
- **Attendance or Other Records**: does this state require parents to keep some kind of records?
- **Notification of Intent**: are you required to send in an official notification of your intention to homeschool to your school district?
- **Registration with DOE/School Superintendent**: does this state require that you register with either the department of education or your local school superintendent before homeschooling begins and/or regularly thereafter?
- **Contact group**: this is the information for your state homeschool association. It is rarely the only one and smaller regional and local groups abound. This is just a starting place.

Please note: This material is not intended to be legal advice and is here for informational purposes only. Check for updates and changes with your state support group.

CHAPTER EIGHT

Alabama

Ages of Compulsory Attendance	7-16	HEART – Home Education of
Required Curriculum	NO	Alabama Round Table
Parental Competency/ Education	YES	P.O. Box 55182
Testing	NO	Birmingham, AL 35255
# of Days Equivalency	NO	www.heartofalabama.org
Attendance or Other Records	YES	
Notification of Intent	NO	
Registration with DOE/ School Superintendent	NO	

Alaska

Ages of Compulsory Attendance	7-16	APHEA – Alaska Private & Home
Required Curriculum	NO	Education Association,
Parental Competency/ Education	NO	P.O. Box 141764,
Testing	NO	Anchorage, AK 99514
# of Days Equivalency	NO	www.aphea.org
Attendance or Other Records	NO	
Notification of Intent	NO	
Registration with DOE/ School Superintendent	NO	

Arizona

Ages of Compulsory Attendance	6-16	AFHE – Arizona Families for
Required Curriculum	NO	Home Education
Parental Competency/ Education	NO	P.O. Box 2035
Testing	NO	Chandler, AZ 85244-2035
# of Days Equivalency	NO	www.afhe.org
Attendance or Other Records	NO	
Notification of Intent	YES	
Registration with DOE/ School Superintendent	NO	

Arkansas

Ages of Compulsory Attendance	5-17	HEAR –
Required Curriculum	NO	Home Educators of Arkansas
Parental Competency/ Education	NO	P.O. Box 192455
Testing	YES	Little Rock, AR 72219
# of Days Equivalency	NO	
Attendance or Other Records	NO	
Notification of Intent	YES	
Registration with DOE/ School Superintendent	NO	

WHAT ARE THE LEGALITIES?

California

Ages of Compulsory Attendance	6-17	HSC – Home School
Required Curriculum	NO	Association
Parental Competency/ Education	NO	of California
Testing	NO	P.O. Box 2442
# of Days Equivalency	NO	Atascadero, CA 93423
Attendance or Other Records	NO	www.hsc.org
Notification of Intent	NO	
Registration with DOE/ School Superintendent	NO	

Colorado

Ages of Compulsory Attendance	7-16	Concerned Parents of Colorado
Required Curriculum	NO	P.O. Box 547
Parental Competency/ Education	NO	Florissant, CO 80816
Testing	YES	
# of Days Equivalency	NO	
Attendance or Other Records	NO	
Notification of Intent	YES	
Registration with DOE/ School Superintendent	NO	

Connecticut

Ages of Compulsory Attendance	5-17	CHEA – Connecticut
Required Curriculum	NO	Home Educators Assoc.
Parental Competency/ Education	NO	101 Mansfield Ave.
Testing	NO	Waterbury, CT 06705
# of Days Equivalency	NO	www.cthomeschoolers.com
Attendance or Other Records	NO	
Notification of Intent	NO	
Registration with DOE/ School Superintendent	NO	

Delaware

Ages of Compulsory Attendance	5-16	DHEA – Delaware Home
Required Curriculum	NO	Education Association
Parental Competency/ Education	NO	P.O. Box 415
Testing	NO	Feaford, DE 19973
# of Days Equivalency	NO	www.dgeaonline.org
Attendance or Other Records	NO	
Notification of Intent	NO	
Registration with DOE/ School Superintendent	NO	

CHAPTER EIGHT

Florida

Ages of Compulsory Attendance	6-16	Florida Parent Educators Assoc.
Required Curriculum	NO	P.O. Box 50685
Parental Competency/ Education	NO	Jacksonville Beach, FL 32240
Testing	YES	www.fpea.com
# of Days Equivalency	NO	
Attendance or Other Records	YES	
Notification of Intent	NO	
Registration with DOE/ School Superintendent	YES	

Georgia

Ages of Compulsory Attendance	5-17	GHEA – Georgia Home
Required Curriculum	NO	Education Assoc.
Parental Competency/ Education	YES	141 Massengale Rd.
Testing	YES	Brooks, GA 30205
# of Days Equivalency	YES	www.ghea.org
Attendance or Other Records	YES	
Notification of Intent	YES	
Registration with DOE/ School Superintendent	YES	

Hawaii

Ages of Compulsory Attendance	6-17	Hawaii Homeschool Assoc.
Required Curriculum	NO	P.O. Box 893476
Parental Competency/ Education	NO	Mililani, HI 96789
Testing	YES	
# of Days Equivalency	NO	
Attendance or Other Records	YES	
Notification of Intent	YES	
Registration with DOE/ School Superintendent	NO	

Idaho

Ages of Compulsory Attendance	7-16	CHOIS – Christian
Required Curriculum	NO	Homeschoolers of Idaho State
Parental Competency/ Education	NO	P.O. Box 45062
Testing	NO	Boise, ID 83711
# of Days Equivalency	NO	www.chois.org
Attendance or Other Records	NO	
Notification of Intent	NO	
Registration with DOE/ School Superintendent	NO	

WHAT ARE THE LEGALITIES?

Illinois

Ages of Compulsory Attendance	7-16	HOUSE – Home Oriented
Required Curriculum	NO	Unique Schooling Experience
Parental Competency/ Education	NO	2508 E. 222 Place
Testing	NO	Sauk Village, IL 60411
# of Days Equivalency	YES	
Attendance or Other Records	NO	
Notification of Intent	NO	
Registration with DOE/ School Superintendent	NO	

Indiana

Ages of Compulsory Attendance	7-17	Indiana Assoc. of
Required Curriculum	NO	Home Educators
Parental Competency/ Education	NO	8106 Madison Avenue
Testing	NO	Indianapolis
# of Days Equivalency	YES	IN 46227
Attendance or Other Records	YES	www.inhomeeducators.org
Notification of Intent	NO	
Registration with DOE/ School Superintendent	NO	

Iowa

Ages of Compulsory Attendance	6-16	IDEA – Iowans Dedicated to
Required Curriculum	NO	Educational Alternatives
Parental Competency/ Education	NO	200 E. Grand Avenue
Testing	SOMETIMES	Des Moines, IA 50309
# of Days Equivalency	NO	
Attendance or Other Records	YES	
Notification of Intent	NO	
Registration with DOE/ School Superintendent	NO	

Kansas

Ages of Compulsory Attendance	7-18	CHECK – Christian Home
Required Curriculum	NO	Educators Confederation
Parental Competency/ Education	NO	of Kansas
Testing	NO	P.O. Box 3968
# of Days Equivalency	NO	Wichita, KS 67201
Attendance or Other Records	YES	www.kansashomeschool.org
Notification of Intent	NO	
Registration with DOE/ School Superintendent	YES	

CHAPTER EIGHT

Kentucky

Ages of Compulsory Attendance	6-16	KHEA – Kentucky Home
Required Curriculum	NO	Education Assoc.
Parental Competency/ Education	NO	P.O. Box 81
Testing	NO	Winchester, KY 40392
# of Days Equivalency	YES	
Attendance or Other Records	YES	
Notification of Intent	YES	
Registration with DOE/ School Superintendent	NO	

Louisiana

Ages of Compulsory Attendance	7-17	Louisiana Home
Required Curriculum	NO	Education Network
Parental Competency/ Education	NO	P.O. Box 700
Testing	NO	Lake Charles, LA 70601
# of Days Equivalency	YES	www.la-home-education.com
Attendance or Other Records	NO	
Notification of Intent	YES	
Registration with DOE/ School Superintendent	NO	

Maine

Ages of Compulsory Attendance	7-17	MHEA – Maine Home
Required Curriculum	NO	Education Assoc.
Parental Competency/ Education	NO	P.O. Box 421
Testing	YES	Tapsham, ME 04039
# of Days Equivalency	NO	
Attendance or Other Records	YES	
Notification of Intent	NO	
Registration with DOE/ School Superintendent	YES	

Maryland

Ages of Compulsory Attendance	5-16	Maryland Home
Required Curriculum	NO	Education Assoc.
Parental Competency/ Education	NO	9085 Flamepool Way
Testing	NO	Columbia, MD 21045
# of Days Equivalency	NO	
Attendance or Other Records	YES	
Notification of Intent	YES	
Registration with DOE/ School Superintendent	NO	

WHAT ARE THE LEGALITIES?

Massachusetts—unique state - depends on the district

Ages of Compulsory Attendance	7-16	Massachusetts Home
Required Curriculum	POSSIBLY	Learning Assoc.
Parental Competency/ Education	POSSIBLY	P.O. Box 1558
Testing	POSSIBLY	Marston Mills, MA 02648
# of Days Equivalency	NO	www.mhla.org
Attendance or Other Records	NO	
Notification of Intent	NO	
Registration with DOE/ School Superintendent	NO	

Michigan

Ages of Compulsory Attendance	6-16	Homeschool Support Network
Required Curriculum	NO	P.O. Box 2457
Parental Competency/ Education	NO	Riverview, MI 48192
Testing	NO	
# of Days Equivalency	NO	
Attendance or Other Records	NO	
Notification of Intent	NO	
Registration with DOE/ School Superintendent	NO	

Minnesota

Ages of Compulsory Attendance	7-16	Minnesota Homeschooler's
Required Curriculum	NO	Alliance
Parental Competency/ Education	YES	P.O. Box 23072
Testing	YES	Richfield, MN 55423
# of Days Equivalency	NO	www.homeschoolers.org
Attendance or Other Records	YES	
Notification of Intent	NO	
Registration with DOE/ School Superintendent	NO	

Mississippi

Ages of Compulsory Attendance	6-17	Mississippi Home
Required Curriculum	NO	Educators Assoc.
Parental Competency/ Education	NO	P.O. Box 855
Testing	NO	Batesville, MS 38606
# of Days Equivalency	NO	www.mhea.net
Attendance or Other Records	NO	
Notification of Intent	YES	
Registration with DOE/ School Superintendent	NO	

CHAPTER EIGHT

Missouri

Ages of Compulsory Attendance	7-16	Families for Home Education
Required Curriculum	NO	P.O. Box 800
Parental Competency/ Education	NO	Platte City, MO 64079-0800
Testing	NO	www.fhe-mo.org
# of Days Equivalency	YES	
Attendance or Other Records	YES	
Notification of Intent	NO	
Registration with DOE/ School Superintendent	NO	

Montana

Ages of Compulsory Attendance	7-16	Montana Coalition of
Required Curriculum	NO	Home Educators
Parental Competency/ Education	NO	P.O. Box 43
Testing	NO	Gallatin Gateway, MT 59730
# of Days Equivalency	YES	www.mtche.org
Attendance or Other Records	YES	
Notification of Intent	NO	
Registration with DOE/ School Superintendent	NO	

Nebraska

Ages of Compulsory Attendance	7-16	Nebraska Christian Home
Required Curriculum	NO	Educators Assoc.
Parental Competency/ Education	NO	P.O. Box 57041
Testing	YES	Lincoln, NE 68505
# of Days Equivalency	NO	www.nchea.org
Attendance or Other Records	NO	
Notification of Intent	NO	
Registration with DOE/ School Superintendent	NO	

Nevada

Ages of Compulsory Attendance	6-17	Silver State Education Assoc.
Required Curriculum	NO	888 W. 2nd Street
Parental Competency/ Education	YES	Suite 200
Testing	NO	Reno, NV 89503
# of Days Equivalency	NO	
Attendance or Other Records	NO	
Notification of Intent	YES	
Registration with DOE/ School Superintendent	NO	

WHAT ARE THE LEGALITIES?

New Hampshire

Ages of Compulsory Attendance	6-16	New Hampshire Home
Required Curriculum	NO	Schooling Coalition
Parental Competency/ Education	NO	P.O. Box 2224
Testing	YES	Concord, OH 03304
# of Days Equivalency	NO	
Attendance or Other Records	YES	
Notification of Intent	YES	
Registration with DOE/ School Superintendent	NO	

New Jersey

Ages of Compulsory Attendance	6-16	New Jersey Homeschool Assoc.
Required Curriculum	NO	P.O. Box 1386
Parental Competency/ Education	NO	Medford, NJ 08055
Testing	NO	
# of Days Equivalency	NO	
Attendance or Other Records	NO	
Notification of Intent	NO	
Registration with DOE/ School Superintendent	NO	

New Mexico

Ages of Compulsory Attendance	6-16	New Mexico Family Educators
Required Curriculum	NO	P.O. Box 92276
Parental Competency/ Education	YES	Albuquerque, NM 87199
Testing	YES	
# of Days Equivalency	NO	
Attendance or Other Records	YES	
Notification of Intent	NO	
Registration with DOE/ School Superintendent	YES	

New York

Ages of Compulsory Attendance	6-16	New York Home
Required Curriculum	NO	Education Network
Parental Competency/ Education	NO	P.O. Box 24
Testing	YES	Sylvan Beach, NY 13157
# of Days Equivalency	NO	www.nyhen.org
Attendance or Other Records	YES	
Notification of Intent	YES	
Registration with DOE/ School Superintendent	NO	

CHAPTER EIGHT

North Carolina

Ages of Compulsory Attendance	7-16	North Carolinians for
Required Curriculum	NO	Home Education
Parental Competency/ Education	YES	419 N. Boylan Avenue
Testing	YES	Raleigh, NC 27603
# of Days Equivalency	NO	www.nche.com
Attendance or Other Records	YES	
Notification of Intent	YES	
Registration with DOE/ School Superintendent	YES	

North Dakota

Ages of Compulsory Attendance	7-16	North Dakota
Required Curriculum	YES	Homeschool Assoc.
Parental Competency/ Education	YES	P.O. Box 7400
Testing	YES	Bismarck, ND 58507
# of Days Equivalency	NO	
Attendance or Other Records	YES	
Notification of Intent	YES	
Registration with DOE/ School Superintendent	NO	

Ohio

Ages of Compulsory Attendance	6-18	Ohio Home Educators Network
Required Curriculum	YES	P.O. Box 38132
Parental Competency/ Education	YES	Olmstead Falls, OH 44138
Testing	NO	
# of Days Equivalency	YES	
Attendance or Other Records	NO	
Notification of Intent	YES	
Registration with DOE/ School Superintendent	NO	

Oklahoma

Ages of Compulsory Attendance	8-16	Home Educator's Resource
Required Curriculum	NO	Org. of Oklahoma
Parental Competency/ Education	NO	302 N. Coolidge
Testing	NO	Enid, OK 73703
# of Days Equivalency	NO	www.oklahomahomeschooling.org
Attendance or Other Records	NO	
Notification of Intent	YES	
Registration with DOE/ School Superintendent	NO	

WHAT ARE THE LEGALITIES?

Oregon

Ages of Compulsory Attendance	7-18	OHEN – Oregon Home
Required Curriculum	NO	Education Network
Parental Competency/ Education	NO	P.O. Box 218
Testing	YES	Beaverton, OR 97075
# of Days Equivalency	NO	
Attendance or Other Records	NO	
Notification of Intent	YES	
Registration with DOE/ School Superintendent	NO	

Pennsylvania

Ages of Compulsory Attendance	8-17	Pennsylvania Home
Required Curriculum	NO	Education Network
Parental Competency/ Education	YES	285 Allegheny Street
Testing	YES	Meadville, PA 16355
# of Days Equivalency	NO	www.phen.org
Attendance or Other Records	NO	
Notification of Intent	YES	
Registration with DOE/ School Superintendent	YES	

Rhode Island

Ages of Compulsory Attendance	6-16	Parent Educators
Required Curriculum	YES	of Rhode Island
Parental Competency/ Education	NO	P.O. Box 782
Testing	NO	Glendale, RI 02826
# of Days Equivalency	NO	
Attendance or Other Records	YES	
Notification of Intent	NO	
Registration with DOE/ School Superintendent	YES	

South Carolina

Ages of Compulsory Attendance	5-17	S.C. Home Educators Assoc.
Required Curriculum	NO	P.O. Box 3231
Parental Competency/ Education	YES	Columbia, SC 29230
Testing	SOMETIMES	www.schea.org
# of Days Equivalency	YES	
Attendance or Other Records	NO	
Notification of Intent	NO	
Registration with DOE/ School Superintendent	YES	

CHAPTER EIGHT

South Dakota

Ages of Compulsory Attendance	6-16	South Dakota Home
Required Curriculum	NO	School Assoc.
Parental Competency/ Education	NO	P.O. Box 882
Testing	YES	Sioux Falls, SD 57101
# of Days Equivalency	NO	
Attendance or Other Records	NO	
Notification of Intent	NO	
Registration with DOE/ School Superintendent	YES	

Tennessee

Ages of Compulsory Attendance	6-17	Tennessee Home
Required Curriculum	NO	Education Assoc.
Parental Competency/ Education	YES	3677 Richbriar Court
Testing	YES	Nashville, TN 37211
# of Days Equivalency	YES	
Attendance or Other Records	YES	
Notification of Intent	NO	
Registration with DOE/ School Superintendent	YES	

Texas

Ages of Compulsory Attendance	6-17	Texas Homeschool Coalition
Required Curriculum	YES	P.O. Box 6747
Parental Competency/ Education	NO	Lubbock, TX 79493
Testing	NO	www.thsc.org
# of Days Equivalency	NO	
Attendance or Other Records	NO	
Notification of Intent	NO	
Registration with DOE/ School Superintendent	NO	

Utah

Ages of Compulsory Attendance	6-18	Utah Home Education Assoc.
Required Curriculum	NO	P.O. Box 1492
Parental Competency/ Education	NO	Riverton, UT 84065
Testing	NO	www.utah-uhea.org
# of Days Equivalency	NO	
Attendance or Other Records	NO	
Notification of Intent	YES	
Registration with DOE/ School Superintendent	NO	

WHAT ARE THE LEGALITIES?

Vermont

Ages of Compulsory Attendance	7-16	Vermont Assoc. of
Required Curriculum	YES	Home Educators
Parental Competency/ Education	NO	P.O. Box 165
Testing	YES	Hartland, VT 05048
# of Days Equivalency	YES	www.vermonthomeschool.org
Attendance or Other Records	NO	
Notification of Intent	NO	
Registration with DOE/ School Superintendent	YES	

Virginia

Ages of Compulsory Attendance	6-18	Home Educators Assoc.
Required Curriculum	YES	of Virginia
Parental Competency/ Education	YES	1900 Byrd Avenue
Testing	YES	Suite 201
# of Days Equivalency	NO	Richmond, VA 23230
Attendance or Other Records	NO	www.heav.org
Notification of Intent	YES	
Registration with DOE/ School Superintendent	NO	

Washington

Ages of Compulsory Attendance	8-18	WHO – Washington
Required Curriculum	YES	Homeschool Organization
Parental Competency/ Education	YES	6632 191st Place
Testing	YES	Suite E100
# of Days Equivalency	NO	Kent, WA 98032
Attendance or Other Records	NO	www.wahomeschool.org
Notification of Intent	YES	
Registration with DOE/ School Superintendent	NO	

West Virginia

Ages of Compulsory Attendance	6-16	West Virginia Home
Required Curriculum	NO	Educators Assoc.
Parental Competency/ Education	YES	P.O. Box 3707
Testing	YES	Charleston, WV 25337
# of Days Equivalency	NO	www.wvhea.homestead.com
Attendance or Other Records	YES	
Notification of Intent	NO	
Registration with DOE/ School Superintendent	NO	

CHAPTER EIGHT

Wisconsin

Ages of Compulsory Attendance	6-18	Wisconsin Parent's Assoc.
Required Curriculum	YES	P.O. Box 2502
Parental Competency/ Education	NO	Madison, WI 53701
Testing	NO	www.homeschooling-wpa.org
# of Days Equivalency	NO	
Attendance or Other Records	NO	
Notification of Intent	NO	
Registration with DOE/ School Superintendent	YES	

Wyoming

Ages of Compulsory Attendance	7-15	Homeschoolers of Wyoming
Required Curriculum	YES	339 Bicentennial Court
Parental Competency/ Education	NO	Powell, WY 82435
Testing	NO	
# of Days Equivalency	YES	
Attendance or Other Records	NO	
Notification of Intent	NO	
Registration with DOE/ School Superintendent	NO	

WHAT ARE THE LEGALITIES?

In the Trenches

A Unique Opportunity

~ Carolyn Hoagland

Families educating their children without public school have a unique opportunity to think about how children learn to understand themselves and how they come to know what they want and like. When parents and children spend a lot of time together, the parent sees and experiences many of the same things the child does. The child's questions about those experiences can get answered in a relaxed way that comes from having no deadlines and having no need to accommodate a large group of other children while the question is explored.

Compare, for example, the typical nature walk a third grade class might take, to the spontaneous outdoor walk that can happen often in a family setting. The difference in quality and quantity is obvious. The spontaneous walk is more likely done just for the enjoyment of being outside, to notice how things have changed. Family members may comment how the "oak buds look like red felt today," or a child may ask, "Does the pocket guide have a picture of these leaves that look like mittens?" or "Why does that squirrel jerk his tail like that?" The classroom trip, on the other hand, is probably designed with an objective in mind, perhaps collecting different types of leaves and identifying trees. Consider the result of an intense desire of a child to study a squirrel's actions instead. You can almost hear the teacher yelling, "Henry! Why are you chasing that squirrel? I don't see any leaves in your hand!" The assumption that tree taxonomy is more important than squirrel behavior is the direct result of the limited amount of time scheduled for the event; there simply isn't time to do both. The teacher may even get the erroneous idea that Henry isn't interested in trees, when he is simply expressing a preference for squirrels at the moment. My guess is that most teachers would like to allow such a child to enjoy observing the squirrel without comment or rebuke, but administrative pressures and curriculum demands require him/her to keep everyone "on task" as much as possible.

Compulsory school attendance, school commuting, and homework devour about 20,000 hours of a child's life. This might be a fair trade if it produced a citizen in possession of a useful trade, an ability and desire to learn new things, and critical thinking skills. But, as many businesses are quick to point out, many high school graduates are barely employable. John Taylor Gatto, a New York State Teacher of the Year and

CHAPTER EIGHT

author, has written, "Reading, writing and arithmetic only take about 100 hours to transmit as long as the audience is eager and willing to learn. The trick is to wait until someone asks and then move on fast while the mood is on." The problem with moving children through a predetermined curriculum in age-based herds is that you can't wait until they ask. There is much valuable material to be covered at least three years in a row so that the slower, middle, and faster learners all get a chance to absorb it when they are able and ready. In addition, there are a host of administrative events that distract from actual learning. There are lines to stand in, forms to fill out, and tests to take and grade. The sheer volume of students to be processed changes the nature of the learning event. One or two adults cannot safely take a group of 20 children to a large park without assuming the roll of drill sergeants. "Everyone get in line! Let's stay together. Don't go over by the bushes or get near the creek!"—even though that is probably the most interesting part of the park.

It almost seems as though one of the goals of compulsory schooling is the crippling of true initiative. Compulsory schooling rewards the kind of initiative that stays within the lesson plan and daily schedule. When people admonish me that my own children must "Go to school, learn to take orders or how else will they ever get a job?", I find myself asking are those really my goals for my children? What I hear in that admonishment is a well-trained person who has been conditioned to believe that it is better to be secure than satisfied (as though they were mutually exclusive!) As a self employed computer programmer, I've learned that my security depends on listening to people's problems, estimating a solution, and then following through—finding that solution— no matter what it takes. In public school, children are rarely given the chance to back track and try a different approach when they fail.

One thing that is stymied during those 20,000 hours is the development of self-discipline. When most of your waking hours are watched, planned, graded, and measured, there isn't much time to get into the thousands of little, troublesome situations that require creative solutions. Self-knowledge comes from experiencing an open-ended problem, creating a solution, and then reflecting on the outcome and consequences of your earlier actions. The truthfulness of the words written in a journal about a personal failure has a different impact that a required essay about a successful or "planned to succeed" experiment to be read aloud in front of the class.

The drain of hours spent on compulsory schooling may also prevent community service and household chores. Sullen narcissism is the logical outcome of a situation where everything is done for the child and nothing is asked or required in return. All people, even young, short ones, seek the kind of respect that comes from contributing to the group in a way that is public and undeniable. Self-esteem is the logical outcome of successfully completing a task when your help is truly needed. The process of completing a variety of chores and community service tasks is a good start on the questions of "What do I like?" and "How can I make a difference?"

WHAT ARE THE LEGALITIES?

When I began educating my children without public school, I looked forward to controlling their lives in order to shelter them and ease their transition into the wider world. It didn't take long to realize the impossibility and error of that idea. I should have known better. I had just finished growing some plants from seed and had accidentally left some exposed to a draft in the greenhouse. Buffeted by the rush of fresh air coming in, they developed roots and stems that were twice as thick and strong as the pampered plants. At transplant time, they began growing immediately, while the sheltered plants took several weeks to adjust from the shock of transplanting. Children require a similar experience in their community in order to develop their own sturdy disposition, one that can bend and isn't shocked by new situations.

My state, Tennessee, requires parents to provide four hours of instruction for 180 days per year. The states does not tell us what subjects are to be taught, or which methods to use. Because our children are still in grade school, we find that reading, writing, and arithmetic are easily covered in two hours per day. That leaves another two hours for the arts, history, science, and physical activities. Our best use of this flexible schedule is getting out into the community to engage in apprenticeships, to explore the local landscape, and to follow adults around and see what they do all day and to help whenever possible. Some adult routines will be so immediately boring or distasteful to one of the children that he/she will know in an instant they could never make a living that way.

The child who dreams of becoming a forest ranger may decide differently after being caught outside in a storm and having to walk through several miles of wet, soggy forest in order to get home and into dry clothes. A math hater may develop an intense desire in that direction after 15 minutes of programming and operating a Computer Numerically Control Led milling machine under the direction of a skilled tool and die maker. The young rider who dreams of being a jockey may learn that cleaning out a stable isn't half bad if you get a free riding lesson afterwards. The child who begrudgingly attends a political rally or demonstration may see a different law making process than the one diagrammed in a social studies textbook.

Most teens go through a period of questing—comparing what they feel to what someone else dictates they should want to learn or do. Yet, their questing is limited by their experience. Do they enjoy growing food, doing legal research, composing music, building long chain polymers, observing animals, or making prosthetic devices for injured persons? How many of these things have they had an opportunity to experience? If most families who educate their children without sending them to school use about four hours a day to get through the "book learning" part of their educational goals, that leaves about 12,000 hours of free time for self directed experiments, apprenticeships, and service to the community.

CHAPTER EIGHT

In the Trenches
Thoughts on Moving from Homeschooling to Public School
~ Bev Eshleman

My husband and I homeschooled three of our four children till they were ready to go into fourth grade. Our fourth child went into school when he was ready for third grade. When I was teaching Daniel, our oldest, kindergarten, our next son was born. When I was teaching Daniel first grade, our daughter was born. I encouraged myself with the thought that when I was teaching Tim and Beth, I would not have a baby; however, son Marc was born the following year.

Teaching at home is a joy. It is wonderful to be able to enjoy your children in the learning environment. There are so many things that you miss when you send your children off to school. When you homeschool, you get lots of homework with love notes on it. You get to share the joy of accomplishment when the child finally understands what you are teaching, and you relish the moment when their eyes light up and their enthusiasm grows.

Homeschooling can also be emotionally taxing when you are teacher as well as mother. You are with the child all day, with no breaks. That can be draining on a mom of more than two children, and it's easy to become tired. If you wish to continue, you need to find a support group that supports, not just gives you more things to do and more directions to go. You need to find one that fits your needs. Tired moms do not need to be in charge of field trips; they need a place they can relax and share with other mothers the joys and frustrations, and come away encouraged. They need playmates for their children, so they do not have to fill that need. Mother, teacher, and only playmate is way more than many mothers can emotionally give and have anything else left.

Our family's goal in homeschooling was to give our children time to develop who they were without peer pressure. It has worked very well. None of our children are inclined to follow the crowd. They are all individuals and clear thinkers. We are very pleased with the results.

Daniel was my first, and therefore the most rigidly schooled. We spent two and a half hours in the morning on academics, and two hours in the afternoon on art, music, and drama. Things slid a little when he was in first grade and his second sibling was born. It took us two years to complete the first grade. By the time he was in third grade, I had a two-year-old and a three-year-old wanting and needing attention from Mom. As I needed to continue to keep Daniel on a schedule, it became difficult to divide my time. Toddlers are not interested in divided time.

My husband and I began to think about putting Daniel into public school. I felt I needed to be spending more time with the little ones. Also, we are Christians, and we felt that Daniel needed to be in the culture he was trying to reach. We wanted to do it while we could be an influence and a help to him. We chose fourth grade because we didn't want

WHAT ARE THE LEGALITIES?

him to have to deal with adjusting to public school and puberty at the same time.

Daniel's difficulty going into public school was primarily with other students. He was teased because he was new. He was also used to going to the authorities, i.e. mom and dad, when there was a problem at home. However, he found when he went to the school authorities, unless a teacher actually saw something happen, they would not act on one child's story. This was an adjustment all my children have had to make when they went into public school.

Teaching Tim and Bethany was very relaxed; far different from the strict regimen that I'd used with Daniel. Some days we didn't have time for school; other days we did only an hour or so. The basics were covered and the kids learned without any major difficulties.

When Tim entered public school, the only problem he had with the academics was his cursive writing; I had taught him a style different from the school's and they insisted that he learn their method. Tim turned out to be the teacher's pet and he had a good school year. He dealt with less teasing than his older brother had. Bethany's only problem when she entered public school was making friends. She forms fewer, but much deeper friendships.

Daniel, Tim, and Bethany were all up to par academically. They had no problems with the work or keeping up with the class. The only adjustment they had was with the homework. They were used to school being completed in the afternoon, with nothing to do on their own later. I sat with them for the first three months of school to help and encourage them as they did their homework. After that, they had the confidence to do their work on their own with occasional questions.

Marc, our youngest, had more difficulties. When we started with the alphabet, I noticed that it took him longer to catch on than the others. I would start with the letter A. We would talk about the sound that it makes while he was writing a page of upper and lower case A's, and at the end of the lesson, I would ask him the name of the letter and he wouldn't know it. By Christmas he knew how to print all the letters in upper case and lower case, but he still didn't know the names of the letters. At the end of first grade, he didn't know how to read. At the beginning of second grade with no summer schooling, he could read. I realized that with Marc, things have to simmer a while before they make sense to him. In math, I made some mistakes; I emphasized the addition facts time test, instead of making sure he understood the basics. I discovered that he was using the clock to do his addition facts and removed the clock. DO NOT DO THIS! If you find your child is using the clock to do addition facts, allow it to continue. He will get to the point where he won't need it. Because of my mishandling this, Marc had little confidence in his math ability.

CHAPTER EIGHT

Marc is a very intelligent boy, and we were both extremely frustrated with his difficulties. He was reluctant to do math; he had problems focusing on his work; he did not like school. We had recently moved to the country, and there are no playmates in the area. We decided to put Marc into third grade, even though we had waited until fourth for the others. We knew he was a little behind, but we felt confident that he would be able to catch up.

Third grade was a transitional year for him. The principal said that if they gave an award for the most improved student, Marc would win it hands down. He jumped way ahead of his class in reading, steadily improved in spelling, and thoroughly enjoyed history. Math continued to be a problem and a source of frustration, as was homework. Marc had trouble staying focused and would tend to walk away before he was done.

Fourth grade has been a good year so far for Marc. He has become much more independent in getting his homework done, many times completing it before supper. He is doing better in math and has found that he loves equations. I think that by the end of this year, he will be totally caught up with his classmates in every area.

The most important thing to remember when you put a child who is up to par academically into school is to support and encourage him/her as he makes the adjustment to a completely different situation. If your child is having academic difficulties, it is vital that you have good communication with the teacher. Most teachers are willing and glad to be able to work with you. If you do not communicate, you will not understand the problems your child is having in school, and the teacher will not be aware of the unique perspective that you as a parent have regarding your child. My husband and I determined after several years that Marc was process oriented in his thinking, just like his father. This meant that he was not interested in the answer to something unless he first understood the process. We explained this to Marc's third and fourth grade teachers, and they were both excited to have this insight into Marc.

If your child comes home crying about something that he says the teacher did unfairly, be sure to talk to the teacher about it and get some clarification on the situation. Communicate with your child also. Always seek to understand his perceptions of school and let him know that you and the teacher are working together in his best interest. Give your child the support he needs as he adjusts. Be creative as possible in trying to help him understand the work, the teacher, and himself. Be willing to spend time helping him with homework, giving him ideas on projects, and letting him know how proud of him you are.

Most of all, know that you are not responsible for all the teaching going on in his life and always take time to laugh, read books, and tickle together. Keep all the good stuff going, so you do not lose touch with your child and his needs and wants. He needs a mom who loves him even when he doesn't do everything right. Actually, isn't that what we all need?

WHAT ARE THE LEGALITIES?

"Self-education is, I firmly believe, the only kind of education there is."

~ Issac Asimov

From the Experts

Is Homeschooling Legal?
~ Larry and Susan Kaseman

Larry and Susan Kaseman have been learning through homeschooling with their children since 1979 and are very active in an inclusive state-wide grass-roots homeschooling organization in Wisconsin. They write a regular column for **Home Education Magazine** and are the authors of **Taking Charge Through Homeschooling: Personal and Political Empowerment**.

"Is homeschooling legal?" This is the question most frequently asked of pioneers of the modern homeschooling movement back in the 1970s and early 1980s. The short answer is, "It's always been legal. There have never been statutes prohibiting homeschooling." The long answer is, "The right and freedom to homeschool rest on very firm foundations." (See below for an overview of these foundations.)

To be sure, during the 1980s the question of how homeschoolers complied with compulsory school attendance laws became the subject of a few court cases. It was taken up by legislatures in many states. (Individual states rather than the federal government have authority over schools, although typically state governments play a relatively minor role in regulating private schools, including homeschools.) The legislation that was passed resulted in widely varying degrees of regulation of homeschooling by different states. Reasonable statutes require only that parents inform the state that they are homeschooling. Other states require that homeschoolers take standardized tests, have their curriculum reviewed and approved by public school officials or certified teachers, report periodically to their local school district or the state, or a combination of these.

Parents who are considering homeschooling and want accurate and reliable information about the legal requirements in a given state find it helpful to talk with experienced and informed homeschoolers in that state by con-

CHAPTER EIGHT

tacting a homeschooling organization listed in one of the directories that are widely available. Such an inquiry works much better than asking or relying on state departments of education or experts from outside the state, even so-called "homeschooling experts." Experienced homeschoolers who live and homeschool under a given state's law are much more likely to understand the history, intent, and interpretation of legal requirements and the ways in which they are implemented and applied. They can provide more helpful and supportive information than can state departments or outside experts.

Why Homeschoolers Work Hard to Maintain Their Freedoms

How tempting it is for homeschoolers to think, "We'll take care of our own family and figure out how we're going to homeschool. Then when we have everything going smoothly, we can use some of our extra time, energy, and money to work for homeschooling freedoms." Unfortunately, the world just doesn't work that way. It is much easier for parents to figure out how to homeschool if they live in a state that has reasonable homeschooling laws and policies. It is much easier for homeschoolers to decide how much emphasis to put on conventional academic subjects and when to work harder on reading, spelling, or algebra when they can focus on their family's goals and priorities and on the needs of each individual child, without also having to worry about how well the children will do on state-mandated tests, or what the parents will write in quarterly or annual reports to public school officials. Therefore, figuring out how to homeschool and working to maintain homeschooling freedoms have to go hand in hand.

If homeschoolers don't work to maintain their freedoms, they will certainly lose them. Why is this loss inevitable? Because, despite the fact that families choose to homeschool for personal reasons and not to undermine the educational establishment, the educational establishment nevertheless sees homeschooling as a threat. Think about it. Simply by deciding, for whatever reasons, not to send their children to conventional schools, home-schoolers have become a scapegoat for one of the largest and most pow-

WHAT ARE THE LEGALITIES?

erful interest groups in our society. As a result, this interest group is using some of its power and resources to try to increase its control over homeschooling by requiring that homeschoolers take state-mandated standardized tests, submit their curriculums for review and approval, etc. By requiring that homeschools become substantially equivalent to conventional schools, the educational establishment will reduce the threat homeschools represent. It will also give parents less reason to bother to homeschool. That is, if children have to do essentially the same things at home as they would have to do at school, why not simply let the schools educate them and force government standards on them. (Of course, there are many other reasons to homeschool and many parents would homeschool even under these dire circumstances. But just think how different their lives would be!)

To make matters even worse, many members of the general public are willing to surrender the primary responsibility for learning to conventional schools. Therefore, it seems reasonable to them to have public schools controlling homeschooling. In order to get the support that homeschoolers need from non-homeschoolers so they can have reasonable homeschooling laws, homeschoolers need to keep explaining to legislators and to the general public what is wrong with having public schools control homeschools. In other words, there is no one but homeschoolers to resist the efforts of the educational establishment to control homeschools.

In short, homeschoolers cannot simply stay where they are. If they don't work actively to maintain their homeschooling freedoms, they will lose them.

There are also more personal reasons to work for homeschooling freedoms. When parents do, they realize they are more in control of their own lives. They forge connections with other homeschoolers and increase the support they give each other. They increase their awareness of the importance of maintaining freedoms in other areas of their lives and in our society. They learn how to work effectively for these freedoms, even against seemingly overwhelming obstacles. They set a good example for their children and help them learn the importance of working to maintain freedoms. And they sleep better at night.

CHAPTER EIGHT

An Overview of the Foundations of Homeschooling Freedoms

The right to homeschool and homeschooling freedoms stand on solid, sure foundations. It is sometimes challenging to recognize the strength and power of these foundations, because doing so requires clear, long-range perspective and a willingness to question common assumptions such as "Children need to go to school to learn." However, it is the responsibility of homeschoolers to understand these foundations, to educate others (homeschoolers, legislators, the media, and the general public), and to prevent these foundations from being lost.

Among the most important of these foundations:

- *The primacy of the family*: The family is the basic unit in all known societies. It is widely understood and acknowledged that parents have the right and the responsibility to help their children learn. This fundamental fact persists, even though today most parents turn much of this responsibility over to a conventional school.

- *Private education*: Families have always been able to comply with the compulsory school attendance law by sending their children to private schools, which are much more independent of state regulation than are public schools. Homeschools are private schools.

- *Legal foundations*: These foundations include rights that amendments to the U.S. Constitution guarantee to homeschoolers and others. In addition, rulings by the U.S. Supreme Court and federal, state, and local courts interpret and expand on the Constitution. Important for homeschoolers are the U.S. Supreme Court cases *Pierce v. Society of Sisters* (268 U.S. 510 [1925]) and *Farrington v. Tokushige* (273 U.S. 284 [1927]) in which the court ruled that

WHAT ARE THE LEGALITIES?

parents have a right to secure for their children an education consistent with their principles and beliefs and that the state may not have a monopoly in education. Important note: Although these two cases have been very helpful to homeschoolers, it is generally not a good idea for a small minority without a broad base of support to initiate court cases because courts generally uphold the beliefs, values, and interests of the majority and/or power centers.

It is important to realize that the *compulsory school attendance law requires school attendance but does not require that children become educated*. This is an extremely important distinction. For one thing, the only laws that can be enforced are those that require behavior that can be described, observed, and evaluated. It is not very difficult to enforce compulsory school attendance laws. It is pretty clear whether or not children who are enrolled in conventional schools are attending them. Classroom teachers take attendance, and children who are absent without acceptable excuses are reported to the truant officer. Similarly, attendance can be checked for children who are enrolled in private schools, including homeschools. (Homeschooled children who are participating in their family's educational plan and program are obviously attending that homeschool, whether the instruction at any given time is being presented at home or at a museum, nature center, library, or any one of a large number of other places where children can and do learn.) Therefore, if a society feels it must pass and enforce laws about schools, laws that require compulsory attendance are not difficult to enforce.

By contrast, laws that require compulsory education would be very difficult, if not impossible, to enforce. First, the state would have to develop a clear set of definitions and criteria for what it means to be educated—what people need to know, and be able to do, in order to be considered educated. This would be very difficult because neither professional educators, nor lay people, can agree on what it means to be educated. Developing such criteria would require agreement about what people should think and do, and about what attitudes and beliefs they should have. Opinions about such topics vary widely.

CHAPTER EIGHT

Then the state would have to find or devise a series of tests that would accurately determine which people have acquired the required facts and skills, and which people have not. This, too, would be difficult because tests do not show what people actually know. Tests only tell how well a given person did on a given test on a given day. Some people are good at taking tests, even about subjects they know very little about. Many more people do not do well on tests, even in subjects they know a great deal about. Therefore, finding ways in which people could demonstrate that they have, in fact, met the requirements that were agreed upon would also be very difficult. Again, laws requiring compulsory education would not work well. If schools laws are necessary, laws requiring compulsory attendance are much better.

Another reason that the distinction between compulsory attendance and compulsory education is so important is that compulsory education would cost us, the citizens of the United States, our freedom. If the state were to require compulsory education, we would lose our freedom of education, and learning, and even our freedom of thought. A society cannot require compulsory education and remain a free society. To even begin to set definitions and requirements for compulsory education would quickly violate our rights and freedoms. Under compulsory education, people would be required to learn, and think, and believe certain ideas, the ideas that had been chosen as proof that a person is educated. In addition, people might not be allowed to learn other ideas that conflicted with the required ones. Without freedom of education and freedom of thought, we could not continue to have a free society in any meaningful sense of the word.

Courts have ruled that schools cannot be held accountable if children attending them fail to become educated. These rulings support the prohibition of compulsory education. Education simply cannot be legislated, and it cannot be legally required. This fact has important ramifications, beginning with strong limitations on the state's ability to dictate curriculum or content of educational programs.

WHAT ARE THE LEGALITIES?

Principles from common law include "Innocent until proven guilty," which means homeschoolers should not have to prove they are educating their children; the state should have to show that they are not. "Hard cases make bad law" means that a law designed to take care of the worst possible hypothetical case is almost certain to be long, difficult to enforce, and more likely to prevent good people from doing good than bad people from doing bad.

When considering the *legal foundations* of homeschooling freedoms, it is important to understand that statutes are not foundations of homeschooling freedoms. Statutes are NOT the source of freedoms, homeschooling or otherwise. Homeschooling freedoms come from nature, God, and our rights and responsibilities as parents. By contrast, statutes are generally used to limit freedom. The power of statutes to take away freedoms can be seen in the language of the First Amendment to the U.S. Constitution, which reads, "Congress shall make no law respecting an establishment of religion, or prohibiting the free exercise thereof; or abridging the freedom of speech, or of the press; or the right of the people peaceably to assemble, and to petition the government for a redress of grievances." Even statutes which seem to grant parents permission to homeschool are actually only restating the obvious, that parents have the right to educate their children. Rather than giving us our freedoms, these statutes list the conditions under which families can homeschool, thereby restricting our freedoms.

In addition, statutes can be changed relatively easily. They do not have the strength, reliability, or staying power of foundations. Minorities that lack a broad base of support, such as homeschoolers, almost always lose big time when they deal with statutes, whether trying to get favorable legislation passed, or have unfavorable laws overturned in court. Legislatures and courts uphold the beliefs and interests of the majority and the power centers of our society.

Among the *logical foundations* of homeschooling freedoms are the following: statutes that regulate homeschooling are unnecessary. Homeschooling is working well in all states, and some states do not have such statutes. Homeschooling statutes do not improve homeschools. In fact,

CHAPTER EIGHT

regulations can harm homeschools and limit their effectiveness. In addition, it is widely held that parents of children who attend conventional schools have stronger influence on them than do the schools. Such a claim is often made by schools when students are having difficulty and schools want to get off the hook by blaming parents. Homeschooling provides children with better opportunities for positive social experiences and interactions with people of varying ages in their communities than attending a conventional school.

Practical foundations of homeschooling include the fact that homeschooling works for many, many families. Homeschools save taxpayers money. Some children who do not learn well in a conventional school setting do well as homeschoolers, preventing or solving problems for themselves, their families, and the schools.

Moral foundations include the fact that our society has an obligation to try to provide children with an education that works for them as individuals. A society that believes in freedom of thought, and freedom of belief, must allow parents to choose for their children an education consistent with their principles and beliefs, and allow people to choose alternative approaches to education without unreasonable regulation.

Religious beliefs and principles are very important to many homeschoolers and provide strong support for homeschooling. Under our federal and state constitutions, the state may not pass laws or engage in practices that would either establish a religion, or interfere with the free exercise of religion, including parents' instructing their children in religion.

WHAT ARE THE LEGALITIES?

Conclusion

Although homeschooling freedoms rest on very solid foundations, home-schoolers need to be alert to the continuing challenges to their freedoms and work to maintain them. Working for homeschooling freedoms is definitely an opportunity, although it may sometimes also seem like a chore. Through such work, homeschoolers learn a great deal. They strengthen themselves, their families, and our society. They prevent the inevitable erosion of homeschooling freedoms that will occur if they do not work to maintain their freedoms. And they increase the opportunities they have to decide how best to homeschool their children. Then homeschooling can be a joyful way of life!

CHAPTER EIGHT

Just the Facts

- It is legal to homeschool in every state of the United States.

- Every state in the country has different homeschooling laws; some even differ within separate districts.

- Requirements vary from state to state.

- One source is not enough for understanding the homeschooling laws for any state; families must also contact their state, regional, and local support groups for details and keep up on any legislative changes.

- Homeschoolers must work to keep, maintain, and improve their homeschooling rights.

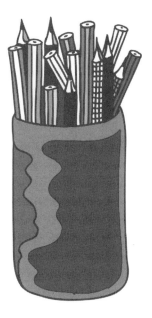

Appendix A

Home Based Learning in Canada

~ Wendy Priesnitz

Home-based education is alive and well in Canada. In fact, over the last 20 years, the phenomenon has grown almost by 2,000 percent! In 1980, there were an estimated 5,000 home educating families. Currently, approximately 100,000 Canadian families educate their children at home, and this number continues to grow at an estimated 15 percent per year.

Home-based education is legal right across Canada. Education is a provincial matter and the laws that regulate home-based learning vary from province to province. The provinces of British Columbia, Alberta, and Ontario have the most home educating families.

APPENDIX A

Some home educating families across the country have been able to arrange part-time attendance, use of school libraries, participation in physical education activities or music programs, and provision of special services for special needs students. These arrangements are generally subject to negotiations between parents and individual schools or school boards.

Wendy Priesnitz is a Canadian deschooling pioneer. She and her husband helped their two daughters (now 28 and 30) learn at home when it was almost unheard of in Canada. In 1979, she founded the Canadian Alliance of Home Schoolers and continues to share her experience and long-term perspective through workshops, speeches, articles, and books. Among the nine books she has authored are **School Free—The Home Education Handbook** (1987, The Alternate Press), which is a Canadian bestseller, and a follow-up book about deschooling society, entitled **Challenging Assumptions in Education** (2000, The Alternate Press). As an award-winning journalist and owner of Life Media, a 25-year-old publishing company, Wendy edits **Natural Life**, a magazine focusing on personal and grassroots efforts leading to economic, political, and social change. In the mid-90s, she was also leader of the Green Party of Canada.

At the other end of the spectrum, a significant proportion of Canadian home educators would rather have nothing to do with the public education system. For their own philosophical reasons, these parents may avoid contact with education authorities—which in some jurisdictions is perfectly legal—and/or refuse to comply with the regulations.

The reasons why Canadian families choose home education are as varied as they are anywhere else. They include religious beliefs; the pursuit of a higher quality academic education; a fear of schoolyard violence and bullying; the pursuit of a learner-driven, non-coercive style of education; travel; and participation in elite sports.

In a survey I first conducted of Canadian home educating families in 1989 and have updated regularly since, I have found that most parents attribute their choice of home-based education to academic concerns or philosophical beliefs. These range from concerns about peer pressure, lack of individual instruction, and insufficient stimulation, to wanting to spend more time with young children and enjoying watching them grow up. Many Canadian home-based educators also keep their children out of regular

HOME BASED LEARNING IN CANADA

schools for religious reasons. These parents generally use a Bible-based curriculum and feel they are better able than any school to teach their children the values and morals that are fundamental to their religion.

The survey results also show that home-based education is not limited to one socio-economic group or educational background. Approximately two-thirds of the families surveyed have at least one parent with college or university education. One quarter of parents have only high school diplomas, and a few parents never even graduated from high school.

Although some parents have teaching certificates, most do not. In fact, less than one quarter tend to be teachers, librarians, or professors. The remaining parents are employed in various fields ranging from technology and trades, to agriculture and sales. Approximately one-third are self-employed.

As much as it is possible, many families use an informal home education style, which is sometimes referred to as 'unschooling.' This unstructured type of education utilizes neither a formal curriculum nor text books and testing. Parents act as facilitators, taking their lead from the children's interests and learning styles.

As for higher education, Canadian universities are increasingly realizing that home-educated students generally thrive in the post-secondary environment. A group of parents in Ontario has begun a program of informing and educating universities about home-based learning in order to facilitate their acceptance of the growing number of teenaged self-sufficient learners.

Throughout Canada, there are a variety of home-based education support groups—at both the provincial and local levels. These vary from the extremely informal to the highly organized. Families often feel more comfortable with those of similar philosophy (Christian versus secular, curriculum-based learning versus "unschooling"). While each group develops its own personality, they all offer activities for children, and support and information for parents.

APPENDIX A

In most provinces, these groups of parents have also been instrumental over the past decade in helping their provincial governments create new home education friendly regulations and/or in preserving existing rights. In some cases, school authorities overstep their bounds—either through ignorance of the law, or through the personal convictions of individual employees—and insist on compliance with rules that do not actually exist.

The Laws

Please note: This material is not intended to be legal advice and is here for informational purposes only. Check for updates and changes with provincial and national support groups.

British Columbia

All children in B.C. are required by law to be provided with what the law calls an "educational program." In the case of home-based learning, this means an organized set of learning activities that the parent believes is designed to develop the learner's potential and acquire the knowledge needed to contribute to society. Families are not required to explain or describe their program to anyone. However, they must register their home-educated child with either a public or private school, or the province's correspondence branch, preferably before September 30. Funding is allotted to schools on the basis of the number of children enrolled (or registered as homelearners) as of that date. This money is supposed to be used to provide services such as the loan of resource materials and evaluation or assessment.

Alberta

A parent of a student in Alberta may provide, at home or elsewhere, a home education program for the student if the program meets the requirements of the regulations, and is under the supervision of a school board or an accredited private school. Families must complete a Home Education Regulation Notification Form and submit it to the supervising board or

HOME BASED LEARNING IN CANADA

school. Boards or schools then share with parents a small amount of funding to help pay for the learning program. If a parent chooses to register the student in a program or courses through the Alberta Distance Learning Centre or through Distance Education Consortia operated by school boards or funded private schools, the entire program is paid for.

Saskatchewan

Home educated children in Saskatchewan may be exempted from attendance at a school if they are receiving instruction in a registered home-based education program. Parents or guardians who present a written educational plan that outlines their home-based education program can register with their resident board of education. While educational plans must be consistent with the goals of education for the province, and appropriate for the age and ability of the students, parents retain the freedom to base their home-based education program on a religious or philosophical perspective different from that of the public education system. School authorities may require two meetings a year, usually in the fall during registration, and in the spring for monitoring. The Provincial Regulations, which were negotiated by the home education community, are extensive and limit the power of local school boards. They do not require home visits, curriculum approval, or parent teacher qualifications. Assessment is done by the parent—not the school board.

Manitoba

In Manitoba, home educating families must register with the provincial Department of Education and Training Home Schooling Office. A child may be removed from a public or private school at any time by parents or legal guardians as long as the Home Schooling Office has been informed of the decision. No reason for home schooling need be provided to the office or the school, although a form must be submitted, and an education plan must be in place. Parents are periodically asked to supply progress reports on home educated children. Provincial correspondence materials are generally expensive and out-of-date, so not used much by home-based learners.

APPENDIX A

Ontario

Children not attending school in Ontario must receive "satisfactory instruction at home or elsewhere." There is no definition of the term "satisfactory instruction," nor is it clear who must be satisfied. Ministry of Education policy is that local school boards should monitor home-based learning. In practice, this means that school boards tell families they must request permission to home school, submit a curriculum document, participate in home visits by school authorities, and test their children. However, these practices have no basis in law, and are not required. The provincial correspondence courses are not made available to home-based learners. Home educating families have been included in new legislation that provides a tax credit for parents with children enrolled in private schools.

Quebec

The Quebec Education Act excuses students from attending public schools if they are provided with instruction and a learning experience, which, according to an evaluation made by or for the school board, are "equivalent" to what is provided at school. As in Ontario, there are guidelines that require a parent to have his or her teaching methods approved by a school board, but this policy does not carry the weight of law.

New Brunswick

Home educating parents in New Brunswick are required to provide "effective instruction," which is based on a learning plan. A form, which is available from local School District offices, must be filled out annually for each child who is learning at home. An interview is then conducted with the family, at which their learning plan is discussed for the coming year. This meeting, which is not necessarily a home visit, is followed by a letter of permission from the Minister of Education. Testing or further visits are not required, although they are usually strongly suggested by school district authorities.

HOME BASED LEARNING IN CANADA

Prince Edward Island

A PEI family must seek authorization for its home education program from the Minister of Education via a "notification of intent" form. The program must be monitored by a licensed teacher twice a year. Testing is not mandatory, but the teacher is supposed to send reports to the Minister of Education who may terminate a home education program if he or she thinks that the program no longer meets the requirements of the regulations, or that the student is not achieving acceptable educational progress.

Nova Scotia

A parent providing home education in Nova Scotia must register the child with the Minister of Education for each academic year. They must also report the child's progress to the Minister at least once a year, in June. The Minister may require the parent of a child in a home education program to provide evidence of the child's educational progress by providing results of a standardized test administered by a school board; and/or an assessment from a qualified assessor (a teacher or a faculty member of a University education faculty); and/or a portfolio of the child's work.

Newfoundland & Labrador

Newfoundland parents are responsible for ensuring that they receive written approval from the Director before starting to educate at home and that this approval is renewed annually. Home educated children are also supposed to be enrolled in a public school.

APPENDIX A

Northwest Territories

A home-based learning program in the NWT must fulfill the curriculum standards set by the Minister of Education and be approved by the principal of the local school at the beginning of the school year. The parent and the principal must agree on a method of assessment that is consistent with the education program. At least twice during the academic year, the parent must provide to the principal a sampling of assessments that show the progress of the student, and discuss the student's progress. Access to school facilities and support is mandated in the regulations. A home educating parent can request reimbursement for education program costs up to one quarter of the amount of funding received for a regular student.

Yukon

In the Yukon, home educated students must be registered with the Minister of Education prior to starting their program and on an annual basis thereafter. An educational plan covering a minimum period of three school years must be provided to the Minister. Either parents, or the Minister, can require that tests be administered to the student at any time.

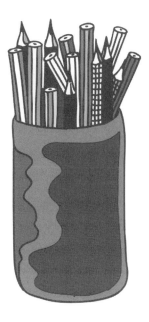

Appendix B
Selected Chapter by
Chapter Resources

"He is educated who knows how to
find out what he doesn't know."
~ George Simmel

Please note: The following resources are referenced in the text of the book itself and are collected here for quick reference. Appendix C: Additional Resources contains an exhaustive listing of books, journals, websites and organizations for the new homeschooler and as well as the veteran.

APPENDIX B

Chapter One
How Did Homeschooling Begin—
and Where Is It Going?

Resources for those interested in publicly funded alternative education.

- National Coalition of Education Activists, PO Box 679, Rhinebeck, NY 12572-0679; 914-876-4580.

- *Rethinking Schools: An Urban Educational Journal*, 1001 East Keefe Ave., Milwaukee, WI 53212

- National Coalition of Alternative Community Schools (NCACS—address below)

- Charter Schools Development Corporation, 1725 K. St. NW, Suite 700, Washington, DC 20006; 202-739-9629

- Some publicly funded alternatives may be found in the two directories: *The Almanac of Education Choices* and *National Directory of Alternative Schools*, listed below under "Books."

- An interesting story of an alternative school within a school is *The Learning Community: The Story of a Successful Mini-School*, by James Penah and John Azrak. For information about this book, contact Bob Knipe, 40-18 21st Ave., Astoria, NY 11105.

CHAPTER BY CHAPTER RESOURCES

Other helpful organizations and publications.

- Alliance for Parental Involvement in Education (ALLPIE), PO Box 59, East Chatham, NY, 12060-0059; 518-392-6900, **allpie@taconic.net**. Mail-order lending library, resources catalog, newsletters, workshops, and conferences.

- Alternative Education Resource Organization (AERO), 417 Roslyn Road, Roslyn Heights, NY 11577; 516-621-2195. Newsletter, books, and videos.

- Association for Experiential Education, 2305 Canyon Blvd., Suite 100, Boulder, CO 80302; 303-440-8844, **www.aee.org**

- Association of Waldorf Schools of North America, **www.awsna.org**. This organization publishes *Renewal: A Journal for Waldorf Education.*

- Creating Learning Communities, an on-line publication, conversation, and resource center, **www.CreatingLearningCommunities.org**

- Folk and People's Education Association of America, Goddard College, 123 Pitkin Road, Plainfield, VT 05667 or c/o Merry Ring, Women's Center, Lakeland Community College, 7700 Clocktower Dr., Kirkland, OH 44094

- Friends Council on Education has a directory of Quaker boarding schools: **http://forum.swarthmore.edu/fce**

APPENDIX B

- Informed Birth and Parenting, Box 3675, Ann Arbor, MI 48106 or PO Box 1733, Fair Oaks, CA 95628. Sponsors workshops and conferences on Waldorf education and parenting.

- International Montessori Society, 912 Thayer Ave. #207, Silver Spring, MD 20910; 301-589-1127. Has listing of Montessori schools.

- Journal of Family Life, 22 Elm Street, Albany, NY 12202; 518-471-9532

- National Coalition of Alternative Community Schools, 1266 Rosewood #1, Ann Arbor, MI 48104; 734-668-9171, **www.ncacs.org**

- North American Montessori Teachers' Association, 13693 Butternut Road, Burton, OH 44021; 440-834-4011. Listing of Montessori schools.

- Paths of Learning: Options for Families and Communities, PO Box 328, Brandon, VT 05733-0328; **www.great-ideas.org**

- Paths of Learning Resource Center, **www.pathsoflearning.org**

- Pendle Hill Publications, Wallingford, PA 19086 has Quaker-related publications and information; 610-566-4507, **www.pendlehill.org**

- Waldorf Early Childhood Association, 1359 Alderton Ln., Silver Spring, MD 20906; 301-460-6287

CHAPTER BY CHAPTER RESOURCES

Books

- *The Almanac of Education Choices: Public and Private Learning Alternatives and Homeschooling*, Jerry Mintz, ed. (Macmillan, 1995)

- *Creating a Cooperative Learning Center: An Idea-Book for Homeschooling Families*, Katharine Houk (Longview, 2000)

- *Creating Learning Communities: Models, Resources, and New Ways of Thinking About Teaching and Learning*, Ron Miller, ed. (Solomon Press, 2000)

- *Deschooling Our Lives*, Matt Hern, ed. (New Society Publishers, 1996)

- *National Directory of Alternative Schools*, National Coalition of Alternative Community Schools (NCACS, 2001)

APPENDIX B

Chapter Three
How Do I Get Started?

Organizations and Info Online

Legal Information (see also Chapter Eight)

About.com homeschooling site
http://homeschooling.about.com

HSLDA Legal Information by State
www.hslda.org

Online Support Groups

About Support Groups & Associations
http://homeschooling.about.com/library/weekly/aa072999.htm

National Home Education Network
www.nhen.org/support/index.htm

Finding Curriculum Online

Homeschoolers Trading Zone
http://forums.about.com/ab-homeschool2/start/

VegSource
www.vegsource.com/homeschool

Ebay
www.ebay.com

Half.com
www.half.com

CHAPTER BY CHAPTER RESOURCES

Online Classes

Online Unit Study Directory
>http://homeschooling.about.com/cs/unitonline

Distance Learning
>http://homeschooling.about.com/cs/distancelearning

News & Info Online

Homeschooling in the News
>http://homeschooling.about.com/cs/homeschoolnews

NHEN-Announce
>http://groups.yahoo.com/group/NHEN-Announce

Chapter Seven
The What Ifs and the What Abouts

Assistance for homeschool students with Special Needs

The Special Education Advocates
P.O. Box 1008
Deltaville, VA 23043
804-257-0857
www.wrightslaw.com

APPENDIX B

Chapter Eight
What Are the Legalities
Involved in All of This?

Homeschool advocacy groups by state

Alabama

HEART – Home Education of Alabama Round Table
P.O. Box 55182
Birmingham, AL 35255
www.heartofalabama.org

Alaska

APHEA – Alaska Private & Home Education Association,
P.O. Box 141764,
Anchorage, AK 99514
www.aphea.org

Arizona

AFHE – Arizona Families for Home Education
P.O. Box 2035
Chandler, AZ 85244-2035
www.afhe.org

Arkansas

HEAR – Home Educators of Arkansas
P.O. Box 192455
Little Rock, AR 72219

CHAPTER BY CHAPTER RESOURCES

California

> HSC – Home School Association of California
> P.O. Box 2442
> Atascadero, CA 93423
> www.hsc.org

Colorado

> Concerned Parents of Colorado
> P.O. Box 547
> Florissant, CO 80816

Connecticut

> CHEA – Connecticut Home Educators Assoc.
> 101 Mansfield Ave.
> Waterbury, CT 06705
> www.cthomeschoolers.com

Delaware

> DHEA – Delaware Home Education Association
> P.O. Box 415
> Feaford, DE 19973
> www.dgeaonline.org

Florida

> Florida Parent Educators Assoc.
> P.O. Box 50685
> Jacksonville Beach, FL 32240
> www.fpea.com

APPENDIX B

Georgia

GHEA – Georgia Home Education Assoc.
141 Massengale Rd.
Brooks, GA 30205
www.ghea.org

Hawaii

Hawaii Homeschool Assoc.
P.O. Box 893476
Mililani, HI 96789

Idaho

CHOIS – Christian Homeschoolers of Idaho State
P.O. Box 45062
Boise, ID 83711
www.chois.org

Illinois

HOUSE – Home Oriented Unique Schooling Experience
2508 E. 222 Place
Sauk Village, IL 60411

Indiana

Indiana Assoc. of Home Educators
8106 Madison Avenue
Indianapolis
IN 46227
www.inhomeeducators.org

Iowa

IDEA – Iowans Dedicated to Educational Alternatives
200 E. Grand Avenue
Des Moines, IA 50309

CHAPTER BY CHAPTER RESOURCES

Kansas

CHECK – Christian Home Educators Confederation of Kansas
P.O. Box 3968
Wichita, KS 67201
www.kansashomeschool.org

Kentucky

KHEA – Kentucky Home Education Assoc.
P.O. Box 81
Winchester, KY 40392

Louisiana

Louisiana Home Education Network
P.O. Box 700
Lake Charles, LA 70601
www.la-home-education.com

Maine

MHEA – Maine Home Education Assoc.
P.O. Box 421
Tapsham, ME 04039

Maryland

Maryland Home Education Assoc.
9085 Flamepool Way
Columbia, MD 21045
www.mhea.org

Massachusetts

Massachusetts Home Learning Assoc.
P.O. Box 1558
Marston Mills, MA 02648
www.mhla.org

APPENDIX B

Michigan

Homeschool Support Network
P.O. Box 2457
Riverview, MI 48192

Minnesota

Minnesota Homeschooler's Alliance
P.O. Box 23072
Richfield, MN 55423
www.homeschoolers.org

Mississippi

Mississippi Home Educators Assoc.
P.O. Box 855
Batesville, MS 38606
www.mhea.net

Missouri

Families for Home Education
P.O. Box 800
Platte City, MO 64079-0800
www.fhe-mo.org

Montana

Montana Coalition of Home Educators
P.O. Box 43
Gallatin Gateway, MT 59730
www.mtche.org

Nebraska

Nebraska Christian Home Educators Assoc.
P.O. Box 57041
Lincoln, NE 68505
www.nchea.org

CHAPTER BY CHAPTER RESOURCES

Nevada

Silver State Education Assoc.
888 W. 2nd Street
Suite 200
Reno, NV 89503

New Hampshire

New Hampshire Home Schooling Coalition
P.O. Box 2224
Concord, OH 03304

New Jersey

New Jersey Homeschool Assoc.
P.O. Box 1386
Medford, NJ 08055

New Mexico

New Mexico Family Educators
P.O. Box 92276
Albuquerque, NM 87199

New York

New York Home Education Network
P.O. Box 24
Sylvan Beach, NY 13157
www.nyhen.org

North Carolina

North Carolinians for Home Education
419 N. Boylan Avenue
Raleigh, NC 27603
www.nche.com

APPENDIX B

North Dakota

North Dakota Homeschool Assoc.
P.O. Box 7400
Bismarck, ND 58507

Ohio

Ohio Home Educators Network
P.O. Box 38132
Olmstead Falls, OH 44138

Oklahoma

Home Educator's Resource Org. of Oklahoma
302 N. Coolidge
Enid, OK 73703
www.oklahoma
homeschooling.org

Oregon

OHEN – Oregon Home Education Network
P.O. Box 218
Beaverton, OR 97075

Pennsylvania

Pennsylvania Home Education Network
285 Allegheny Street
Meadville, PA 16355
www.phen.org

Rhode Island

Parent Educators of Rhode Island
P.O. Box 782
Glendale, RI 02826

CHAPTER BY CHAPTER RESOURCES

South Carolina

South Carolina Home Educators Assoc.
P.O. Box 3231
Columbia, SC 29230
www.schea.org

South Dakota

South Dakota Home School Assoc.
P.O. Box 882
Sioux Falls, SD 57101

Tennessee

Tennessee Home Education Assoc.
3677 Richbriar Court
Nashville, TN 37211

Texas

Texas Homeschool Coalition
P.O. Box 6747
Lubbock, TX 79493
www.thsc.org

Utah

Utah Home Education Assoc.
P.O. Box 1492
Riverton, UT 84065
www.utah-uhea.org

Vermont

Vermont Assoc. of Home Educators
P.O. Box 165
Hartland, VT 05048
www.vermonthomeschool.org

APPENDIX B

Virginia

Home Educators Assoc. of Virginia
1900 Byrd Avenue
Suite 201
Richmond, VA 23230
www.heav.org

Washington

WHO – Washington Homeschool Organization
6632 191st Place
Suite E100
Kent, WA 98032
www.wahomeschool.org

West Virginia

West Virginia Home Educators Assoc.
P.O. Box 3707
Charleston, WV 25337
www.wvhea.homestead.com

Wisconsin

Wisconsin Parent's Assoc.
P.O. Box 2502
Madison, WI 53701
www.homeschooling-wpa.org

Wyoming

Homeschoolers of Wyoming
339 Bicentennial Court
Powell, WY 82435

Appendix C
Additional Resources

Please note: The state-by-state legal chart in Chapter Eight contains the information to contact primary support groups across the nation. Look there, or in Appendix B, to find those resources.

Books to Read

This is nowhere near a complete listing of all the books that are out there. Because of the growing popularity of homeschooling, the number of books about it is increasing quickly. Instead, here are some of the books that I think are most influential, plus they cover a gamut of ideas, philoso-

APPENDIX C

phies, experiences, and topics. Don't stop with this list; use it as a starting point. Check your library and bookstore shelves to see what else there is; check in with book-selling web sites like Amazon, Borders, or Barnes and Noble to see what's new.

Albert, David. *And the Skylark Sings with Me: Adventures in Homeschooling and Community-Based Education*. New Society Publishers, 1999.

Armstrong, Thomas. Awakening *Your Child's Natural Genius: Enhancing Curiosity, Creativity and Learning Ability*. J P Tarcher, 1991.

Armstrong, Thomas. *The Myth of the A.D.D. Child: 50 Ways to Improve Your Child's Behavior and Attention Span without Drugs, Labels or Coercion*. Plume, 1997.

Armstrong, Thomas. *In Their Own Way: Discovering and Encouraging Your Child's Multiple Intelligences*. JP Tarcher, 2000.

Beechick, Ruth. *Language Wars and Other Writings for Homeschoolers*. Arrow Press, 1995.

Bell, Debra. *The Ultimate Guide to Homeschooling: Year 2001 Education Book and CD*. Thomas Nelson, 2000.

Block, Mary Ann and May. *No More Ritalin: Treating ADHD Without Drugs*. Kensington Publishers Corp., 1997.

Boyles, Nancy M.Ed. and Darlene Contadino M.S.W. *The Learning Differences Sourcebook*. McGraw-Hill, 1998.

Breggin, Peter R., *Talking Back to Ritalin: What Doctors Aren't Telling You about Stimulants for Children*. Common Courage Press, 1998.

Brown, Teri with Elissa Wahl. *Christian Unschooling: Raising Your Child in the Freedom of Christ*. Champion Press Limited, 2001.

Cohen. Cafi. *And What About College? How Homeschooling Leads to Admissions to the Best Colleges and Universities*. Holt Associates, 2000.

Colfax, David and Mary. *Homeschooling for Excellence: How to Take Charge of Your Child's Education—and Why You Absolutely Must*. Warner Books, 1988.

Deckard, Steve. *Homeschooling Laws and Resource Guide for All Fifty States*. Vision Publishing, 2001.

Dobson, Linda. *The Art of Education: Reclaiming Your Family, Community and Self*. Holt Associates, 1997.

Dobson, Linda. *The Complete Book of Home Education: A Parent's Guide to Education in the Natural Way*. Prima Publishing, 2002.

Dobson, Linda. *The Homeschooling Book of Answers: The 88 Most Important Questions Answered by Homeschooling's Most Respected Voices*. Prima Publishing, 1998.

ADDITIONAL RESOURCES

Downs, Laurajean. *You're Gonna Do What? Helping You Understand the Homeschooling Decision*. Holly Hall Publications, 1997.

Farenga, Patrick. *The Beginner's Guide to Homeschooling*. Holt Associates, 2000.

Freed, Jeffrey and Laurie Parsons. *Right-Brained Children in a Left-Brained World: Unlocking the Potential of Your A.D.D. Child*. Fireside, 1998.

Gardner, Howard. *Frames of Mind: The Theory of Multiple Intelligences*. Basic Books, 1993.

Gardner, Howard. *The Unschooled Mind: How Children Think and How Schools Should Teach*. Basic Books, 1993.

Gatto, John Taylor. *Dumbing Us Down: The Hidden Curriculum of Compulsory Schooling*. New Society Publishers, 1991.

Gatto, John Taylor. *The Underground History of American Education*. Odysseus Group, 2001.

Gold, Lauramaery and Joan Zielinski. *Homeschool Your Child for Free: More than 1,200 Smart, Effective and Practical Resources for Home Education on the Internet and Beyond*. Prima Publishing, 2000.

Griffith, Mary. *The Unschooling Handbook: How to Use the Whole World as Your Child's Classroom*. Prima Publishing, 1998.

Guterson, David. *Family Matters: Why Homeschooling Makes Sense*. Harvest Books, 1993.

Hayes, Lenore C. *Homeschooling the Child with ADD (or Other Special Needs): Your Complete Guide to Successfully Homeschooling the Child with Learning Differences*. Prima Publishing, 2002.

Healy, Jane. *Endangered Minds: Why Our Children Don't Think and What We Can Do About It*. Touchstone Books, 1999.

Healy, Jane. *Failure to Connect: How Computers Affect Our Children's Minds and What We Can Do About It*. Touchstone Books, 1999.

Hegener, Mark and Helen, eds. *The Homeschool Reader: Collected Articles from Home Education Magazine 1984-1994*. Home Education Press, 1995.

Hegener, Mark and Helen, eds. *The Homeschool Reader: Perspectives on Home-schooling*. Home Education Press, 1998.

Hendrickson, Borg. *Home School: Taking the First Step—The Complete Home School Program Planning Guide*. Mountain Meadow Press, 1994.

Hendrickson, Borg. *How to Write a Low Cost/No Cost Curriculum for Your Homeschool Child*. Mountain Meadow Press, 1998.

Hensley, Sharon M.A. *Homeschooling Children with Special Needs*. Noble Books, 1995.

Holt, John. *Teach Your Own: A Hopeful Path for Education*. Delacorte Press, 1989.

Holt, John. *How Children Fail*. Perseus Press, revised edition, 1995.

Holt, John. *How Children Learn*. Perseus Press, revised edition, 1995.

Holt, John. *Growing without Schooling: A Record of a Grassroots Movement*. Holt Associates, 1997.

APPENDIX C

Holt, John. *Learning All the Time.* Perseus Press, 1990.

Hood, Mary. *The Home-Schooling Resource Guide and Directory of Organizations.* Ambleside Educational Press, 1997.

Hood, Mary. *The Joyful Homeschooler.* Ambleside Educational Press, 1997.

Ishizuka, Kathy. *The Unofficial Guide to Homeschooling.* Hungry Minds, Inc., 2000.

Jones, Steve. *Internet for Educators and Homeschoolers.* Etc. Publishing, 2000.

Kaseman, Larry and Susan. *Taking Charge through Homeschooling: Personal and Political Empowerment.* Koshkonong Press, 1991.

Kaufeld, Jennifer. *Homeschooling for Dummies.* Hungry Minds, Inc., 2001.

Kealoha, Anna. *Trust the Children: A Manual and Activity Guide for Homeschooling and Alternative Learning.* Celestial Arts, 1995.

Lande, Nancy. *Homeschool Open House.* Windy Creek Press, 2000.

Lande, Nancy. *Homeschooling: A Patchwork of Days/Share a Day with Thirty Homeschooling Families.* Windy Creek Press, 1999.

Layne, Marty. *Learning at Home: A Mother's Guide to Homeschooling.* Sea Change Publications, 2000.

Leppert, Mary and Michael. *Homeschooling Almanac 2002-2003.* Prima Publishing, 2001.

Llewellyn, Grace. *Freedom Challenge: African American Homeschoolers.* Lowry House Publications, 1996.

Llewellyn, Grace and Amy Silver. *Guerilla Learning: How to Give Your Kids a Real Education With or Without School.* John Wiley and Sons, 2001.

Leistico, Agnes. *I Learn Better by Teaching Myself.* Holt Associates, 1997.

Leistico, Agnes. *Still Teaching Ourselves.* Holt Associates, 1997.

McClaine, L.S. *Physical Education for Homeschoolers: An Easy to Use, Low Equipment Cost Program for Homeschooling Families.* Nutmeg Publications, 1994.

McKee, Alison. *From Homeschool to College and Work: Turning Your Homeschool Experience into College and Job Profiles.* Bittersweet House, 1998.

McKee, Alison. *Homeschooling Our Children, Unschooling Ourselves.* Bittersweet House, 2002.

Meighan, Roland. *The Next Learning System: And Why Homeschoolers are Trailblazers.* Educational Heretic Press, 1997.

Moore, Dorothy and Raymond. *The Successful Homeschooling Family Handbook: A Creative and Stress Free Approach to Homeschooling.* Thomas Nelson, 1994.

Morgan, Melissa and Judith W. Allee. *Homeschooling on a Shoestring: A Jam-Packed Guide.* Harold Shaw Publications, 1999.

Morgan, Melissa and Judith A. Allee. *Educational Travel on a Shoestring: Frugal Family Fun and Learning Away from Home.* Harold Shaw Publications, 2002.

ADDITIONAL RESOURCES

O'Leary, Jennifer. *Write Your Own Curriculum: A Complete Guide to Planning, Organizing and Documenting Homeschool Curriculums*. Whole Life Publications, 1993.

Orr, Tamra. *101 Ways to Make Your Library Homeschooling Friendly*. Scarecrow Press, 2002.

Orr, Tamra. *150 Things Homeschoolers Can Do on the Internet*. Scarecrow Educational Press, 2003.

Pearce, Joseph Chilton. *Magical Child*. Plume, 1992.

Pearce, Joseph Chilton. *Evolution's End: Claiming the Potential of Our Intelligence*. Harper, 1993.

Plent, Mac and Nancy. *An A in Life: Famous Homeschoolers*. Unschoolers Network, 1999.

Priesnitz, Wendy. *School Free: The Home Schooling Handbook*. The Alternate Press, 1995.

Ransom, Marsha. *The Complete Idiot's Guide to Homeschooling*. Alpha Books, 2001.

Rivero, Lisa and Maurice Fisher. *Gifted Education Comes Home: A Case for Self-Directed Learning*. Gifted Education Press, 2000.

Rupp, Rebecca. *Getting Started in Learning: How and Why to Teach Your Kids at Home*. Three Rivers Press, 1999.

Rupp, Rebecca. *Good Stuff: Learning Tools for All Ages*. Home Education Press, 1993.

Rupp, Rebecca. *Home Learning Year by Year: How To Design a Homeschool Curriculum for Preschool through High School*. Three Rivers Press, 2000.

Soyke, Jean. *Art Adventures at Home: A Curriculum Guide for Home Schools*. At Home Publications, 1993.

Whitehead, John and Alexis I. Crow. *Home Education: Rights and Reasons*. Crossway Books, 1993.

Williams, Jane. *Home School Market Guide*. Bluestocking Press, 1999.

APPENDIX C

Books For and About Teens

Asher, Donald. *Cool Colleges for the Hyper-Intelligent, Self-Directed, Late Blooming and Just Plain Different.* Ten Speed Press, 2000.

Callihan, David and Laurie. *The Guidance Manual for the Christian Home School: A Parent's Guide for Preparing Home School Students for College or Career.* Career Press, 2000.

Cohen, Cafi. *And What about College: How Homeschooling Can Lead to Admissions to the Best Colleges and Universities.* Holt Associates, 2000.

Cohen, Cafi. *Homeschoolers' College Admissions Handbook: Preparing Your 12-to-18-Year Old for a Smooth Transition.* Prima Publishing, 2000.

Cohen, Cafi. *Homeschooling: The Teen Years.* Prima Publishing, 2000.

Dobson, Linda. *Homeschooler's Success Stories: 15 Adults and 12 Young People Share the Impact that Homeschooling Has Made on Their Lives.* Prima Publishing, 2000.

Duffy, Cathy. *Christian Home Educators' Curriculum Manual: Junior/Senior High.* Grove Publishing, 2000.

Eikleberry, Carol. *Career Guide for Creative and Unconventional People.* Ten Speed Press, 1999.

Estell, Doug. *Reading List for College-Bound Students.* Arco Publications, 2000.

Grand, Gail. *Free (and Almost Free) Adventures for Teenagers.* John Wiley and Sons, 1995.

Grand, Gail. *Science Opportunities: Your Guide to Over 300 Exciting National Programs, Competitions, Internships and Scholarships.* John Wiley and Sons, 1994.

Gurvis, Sandra. *Careers for Non-Conformists: A Practical Guide to Finding and Developing a Career Outside the Mainstream.* Marlowe and Company, 1999.

Heuer, Loretta. *The Homeschooler's Guide to Portfolios and Transcripts.* Arco Publications, 2000.

Kohl, Herbert. *The Question is College: On Finding and Doing Work You Love.* Heinemann, 1998.

Llewellyn, Grace. *Real Lives: Eleven Teenagers Who Don't Go to School.* Lowry House Publications, 1993.

Llewellyn, Grace. *The Teenage Liberation Handbook: How to Quit School and Get a Real Life and Education.* Lowry House Publications, 1998.

Sheffer, Susannah. *A Sense of Self: Listening to Homeschooled Adolescent Girls.* Heinemann, 1997.

Wood, Danielle. *The Uncollege Alternative: Your Guide to Incredible Careers and Amazing Adventures Outside College.* Regan Books, 2000.

ADDITIONAL RESOURCES

Books for Young Children about Homeschooling

Krames, Brenda. *Homeschool Huskies for Boys* Series. Krames Publications, 1997-1998.
Krames, Brenda. *Homeschool Ponies for Girls* Series. Krames Publications, 1997-1998.
Lurie, Jon. *Allison's Story: A Book about Homeschooling*. Lerner Publications Co., 1996.
Ratner, Susan. *Kandoo Kangaroo Hops into Homeschool*. Master Books, 2000.
Voetberg, Julie. *I am a Homeschooler*. Albert Whitman and Co., 1995.

Magazines

Homeschooling Today
PO Box 1425
Melrose, FL 32666

Jewish Home Educators Newsletter
2122 Houser
Holly, MI 48442

Home Learning Canada
PO Box 3301
Leduc AB T9E 6MI Canada

The Link
587 N. Ventu Park Rd.
Suite F-911
Newbury Park, CA 91320

Right at Home
PO Box 1703
Diamond Springs, CA 95619

APPENDIX C

Home Education Magazine
PO Box 1083
Tonasket, WA 98855

Practical Homeschooling
PO Box 1250
Fenton, MO 63026

Home Educators
    Learning Magazine
4200 Alabama Highway 157
Danville, AL 35619

Home School Digest
PO Box 374
Covert, MI 49043

Life Learning/
    Natural Life Magazine
PO Box 112
Niagara Falls, NY 14304
and
PO Box 340
St. George, ON N0E 1N0
Canada
800-215-9574
www.lifelearningmagazine.com

Dynamic Homeschooling
3419 Bell St.
Norfolk, VA 23513

Teaching Home
PO Box 20219
Portland, OR 9294

Home Educators Family Times
PO Box 708
Gray, ME 04039

Paths of Learning
PO Box 328
Brandon, VT 05733

NATHHAN News
National Challenged
Homeschoolers
Association Network
5383 Alpine Rd. SE
Olalla, WA 32666

Options in Learning
The Alliance for Parental
Involvement in Education
(ALLPIE)
PO Box 59
East Chatham, NY 12060

ADDITIONAL RESOURCES

The Best Web Sites

General Homeschool Resources

researched by homeschooler **Rowena Litzler**

www.homeschool.com/top100

This website links to what they consider to be the top 100 educational websites on the Internet. Indeed there are some excellent sites to check out.

www.midnightbeach.com/hs

You don't want to miss this website! Jon's Homeschool Resource Page is one of the oldest homeschool website resource sites. You will find everything imaginable pertaining to homeschooling. This is a huge site, with over 200 pages of homeschool information.

www.enchantedlearning.com

This website is loaded with so much practical information on many subjects. Look for geography and science pages and activities. Map/quiz printouts, animal printouts, and label me printouts, to name a few of the many available. K-3 themes, nursery rhymes, crafts, preschool and kindergarten activities, and much more.

http://ericir.syr.edu

AskERIC is a federally funded national information system that provides a variety of education-related materials. It includes a virtual library of more than 700 subject-specific lesson plans and a 'Question and Answer' service for educators, including a homeschool section.

http://infotech.fbhs.fortbragg.k12.ca.us/school_resources

This website is a resource for teachers. There are 222 links listed for all of the major subjects taught.

www.hsadvisor.com

This site is for all of you homeschooling families who need questions answered or need a good resource for homeschooling. This website is easy to navigate and has quality information for the new homeschooler and veteran alike. Look for their featured article. Find out what the homeschooling laws are in your state. Do you have a question? Receive your answer from the experts!

APPENDIX C

www.sitesforteachers.com

Sites for teachers featuring the best teaching resource websites on the Net. There are numerous links to help you obtain information for teaching your student.

http://members.tripod.com/~wethepeople/homschl.htm

This is good resource for new homeschoolers looking for information.

Planning, Record Keeping, & Forms

www.donnayoung.org/forms

This is a wonderful website to help you organize your homeschooling days and months. You will find many printable forms and an area to create a custom planner book. Look for printouts for planners, homeschool scheduling, record keeping, homeschool journals, handwriting and graph paper, certificate achievements, and a lot more.

http://teachers.hypermart.net/links/pages/Worksheets/ Homeschool_Forms

Unit Study Library has many links for homeschool forms. Look for links that will help you with record keeping, and portfolios for teachers and students. You will also find a course of study form, test makers, and more.

www.homeschool.com/top100

This website hosts what they consider to be the top 100 education websites on the Internet. Indeed there are some excellent sites to check out!

www.fun-books.com

Fun books on homeschooling resources for unschooling and unit studies.

www.greenleafpress.com

Greenleaf Press

www.classicshome.com

The Helping Hand – Educational Services and supplies

www.insectlore.com

Insect Lore

ADDITIONAL RESOURCES

www.classroomdirect.com
   Classroom Direct
www.ace-educational.com
   Ace Educational Supplies
www.gwbc.com
   God's World
www.rainbowresource.com
   Rainbow Resouce Center
www.LoveToLearn.net
   Love to Learn
www.friendshiphouse.com
   Friendship House – musical gifts, awards and teaching aids.
www.discoveryschool.com
   Discovery Channel School
www.bbhomeschoolcatalog.com
   Builder Books, Inc
www.chinaberry.com
   Educational Books
www.homeschooldiscount.com
   Homeschool Discount material
www.homeschoolcentralmall.com/eduproducts
   Homeschool Central Mall – online resources for teaching.
www.mathconcepts.com
   Math Concepts

APPENDIX C

Lesson Plans, Activities, and Worksheets

http://puzzlemaker.school.discovery.com

Puzzlemaker is a puzzle generation tool. Create and print customized word search, crossword, and math puzzles using your word lists. Build your own maze or print our specialty hand-drawn mazes created around holidays and classroom topics.

www.coastlink.com/users/sbryce/mathwork

MathWork is a website where you can create and print math worksheets for children learning simple arithmetic (addition, subtraction, multiplication, and division).

www.worksheetfactory.com

If you're searching for quality educational software that will give you the tools you need to easily and quickly create targeted worksheets to help students gain proficiency in the basic academic skills, then you will want to visit this website. These programs can be downloaded for a very low cost. There are also two free programs.

www.superkids.com/aweb/tools/math

Make your own math worksheets at SuperKids for free! Make your own worksheets for addition, subtraction, multiplication, division, fractions, greater than, less than, and rounding.

www.eduplace.com/search/activity

Search their database of 400+ original K-8 classroom activities and lesson plans for teachers and parents. You may search for activities by both curriculum area and grade level. You can select more than one item from each list or browse activities by theme.

www.teach-nology.com/web_tools/work_sheets

Worksheet generator – generate crossword puzzles, science lab worksheets, word scramble generator, today in history, word search generator, and more.

www.criticalthinking.com

Building Thinking Skills

ADDITIONAL RESOURCES

All Subjects

www.kn.pacbell.com/wired/bluewebn

What a wealth of information! Plan on taking some time to browse through this site. There are web-based activities, web-based lesson plans, web-based resources, etc. for all grade levels and all subjects.

www.eduhound.com

This website has a wealth of educational value. It is interactive with games and activities on all subjects.

members.aol.com/PegFlint/units_how_to_plan

If you are interested in learning how to create your own unit studies instead of buying them, this website is a good place to start.

www.fairtest.org

For information on standardized testing and the controversies within the field.

Arts and Crafts

www.kinderart.com

Visit the largest collection of free art lessons on the Internet. Enjoy their array of artist ideas from early childhood activities and lessons to crafty ideas and the history of art, plus much more.

www.homeschoolarts.com/main

This site is devoted to providing free art lessons in many mediums to homeschoolers.

home.socal.rr.com/exworthy/art

Studying art can be a pleasure. This website will give you an appreciation for art history. Look for art exhibits, art activities, and crafts.

History

www.kidsites.com/sites-edu/history

KidSites.com has many history links for kids. Come and enjoy a variety of topics.

www.hyperhistory.com/online_n2/History_n2

HyperHistory has over 2,000 files covering 3,000 years of world history.

APPENDIX C

Language Arts

www.homeschoolcentral.com/reading

Another useful homeschool reference website. You will find sites that will help you in your quest to teach reading and comprehension to your child as well as handwriting and spelling.

homeschooling.about.com/cs/langhand

Handwriting and penmanship links. Find the font that you want to use for your student.

Music

www.music-scores.com/composers

Select your music by instrument, composer, or style.

www.si.umich.edu/chico/instrument

This site offers a visual and sound encyclopedia of 140 musical instruments used in cultures throughout the world. You can browse the site for instruments divided into 4 major categories: wind, percussion, string, and electronic. You can also search for an instrument based on geographical location of origin.

Science

kids.msfc.nasa.gov

NASA KIDS offers a fun way for children to learn about NASA's activities and science, using interactive tools. Look for on-line or printable resources designed for kids aged 5 to 14.

www.eps.mcgill.ca/wtp/planets

This is a collection of many of the best images from NASA's planetary exploration program. The collection has been extracted from the interactive program "Welcome to the Planets" which was distributed on the Planetary Data System Educational CD-ROM Version 1.5 in December 1995.

www.chabotspace.org/vsc/planetarium/thesky

This site offers a Virtual Planetarium! View the StarDome and see the sky as it is right now. Learn about constellations and how to locate them. Ever

ADDITIONAL RESOURCES

wonder about the really bright stars in the night sky? Here you will not only find out their names (and learn how to pronounce them!)—but you will learn their location, magnitude, distance, and surface temperature as well.

www.sciencepage.org/general

This site lists many science links that are available on the web. Look for a large variety of science subjects.

http://faculty.washington.edu/chudler/works

This website contains pages of worksheets and lessons about the human body. You will also find word searches, mazes, codes, crossword puzzles, coloring pages, games, and more that are ready for you to print out.

www.webbschool.org/nancy/index

Nature of science, introduction to chemistry, chemical basis of life, cell structure and function, nucleic acids and protein synthesis, cell growth and division. Introduction to genetics, meiosis, genes and chromosomes, human heredity, genetic engineering, and evolution.

Special Interest Support Online

www.egroups.com/group/homeschoolwidow

Homeschooling support for widows and widowers

www.drix.net/jdowling/HUUH.html

Homeschooling Unitarian universalists and humanists and friends

http://members.ncbi.com/trtlgrrl/PaganHomeschool.htm

Pagan Homeschoolers

http://expage.com/page/nahomeschool

Native American Homeschool Association Website

APPENDIX C

Resources for Special Needs Children

Understanding Our Gifted
Open Space Communications, Inc.
1900 Folsom Suite 108
Boulder, CO 80302
303-444-7020

Gifted Child Today
Prufrock Press
PO Box 8813
Waco, TX 76714-8813

Journal for the Education of the Gifted (JEG)
The Association for the Gifted
1920 Association Dr.
Reston, VA 22091

Journal for the Education of the Gifted
University of North Carolina Press
 PO Box 2288
Chapel Hill, NC 27515-2288

Tempo
5521 Martin Lane.
El Paso, TX 79903

Roeper Review
PO Box 329
Bloomfield Hills, MI 48013

ADDITIONAL RESOURCES

Gifted Education Press
10201 Yuma Court
PO Box 1586
Manassas, VA 22110

Creative Child and Adult Quarterly
8080 Spring Valley Drive
Cincinnati, OH 45236

Parents of Gifted and Talented Learning Disabled Children
2420 Eccleston St.
Silver Spring, MD 20902
301-986-1422

The National Research Center on the Gifted and Talented
University of Connecticut
2131 Hillside Rd. U-7
Storrs, CT 06269-3007
860-486-4676

International Dyslexia Association
Chester Building
Suite 382
8600 LaSalle Rd.
Baltimore, MD 21204
410-296-0232

NATHHAN
National Challenged Homeschoolers Association Network
5383 Alpine Rd. SE
Olalla, WA 32666

APPENDIX C

National Handicapped Homeschoolers Association
814 Shavertown Rd.
Boothwyn, PA 19061
215-459-2035

National Down Syndrome Society
666 Broadway
New York, New York 10012
800-221-4602

CHADD
Children and Adults with Attention Deficit Disorder
8181 Professional Place, Suite 201
Landover, MD 20785
800-233-4050

Autism Society of America
7910 Woodmont Ave. Suite 300
Bethesda, MD 28014-3015
301-657-0881

Sensory Integration International
PO Box 9013
Torrance, CA 90508
310-320-9986

The Special Education Advocates
P.O. Box 1008, Deltaville, VA 23043
804-257-0857

ADDITIONAL RESOURCES

Deafness Research Foundation
15 West 39th St.
6th Floor
New York, NY 10018-3806
800-535-3323

American Foundation for the Blind, Inc.
15 West 16th St.
New York, NY 10011
800-232-5463

Special Interest Support Groups

The Adventist Home Educator
PO Box 836
Camino, CA 95709

Catholic Homeschool Network of America
PO Box 6343
River Forest, IL 60305-6343
330-652-4923

Homeschool Association for Christian Science Families
445 Airport Rd.
Tioga, TX 76271

Islamic Homeschool Association of North America
1312 Plymouth Court
Raleigh, NC 27610

APPENDIX C

Jewish Home Educator's Network
2122 Houser
Holly, MI 48442

Latter Day Saint Home Educators Association
2770 South 1000 West
Perry, UT 84302

Muslim Homeschool Network and Resources
PO Box 803
Attleboro, MA 02703

Native American Home School Association
PO Box 979
Fries, VA 24330

Single Parents Educational Children in Alternative Learning
2 Pineview Drive #5
Amelia, OH 45102

Appendix D
Inspiration from the Trenches

Certificate of Empowerment
-Sandra Dodd

Sandra Dodd is the online editor of Home Education Magazine.
www.home-ed-magazine.com

As bearer of this certificate, you are no longer required to depend on the advice of experts. You may step back and view the entire world—not just your home, neighborhood, or town, but the whole Earth—as a learning experience, a laboratory containing languages (and native speakers thereof), plants, animals, history, geology, weather (real live weather, in the sky, not in a book), music, art, mathematics, physics, engineering, foods, human dynamics, and ideas without end. Although collections of these treasures have been located in museums for your convenience, they are to be found everywhere else, too.

APPENDIX D

This authorizes you to experiment; to trust and enjoy your kids; to rejoice when your children surpass you in skill, knowledge, or wisdom; to make mistakes, and to say "I don't know." Furthermore, you may allow your children to experience boredom without taking full responsibility for finding them something to do.

Henceforth, you shall neither be required nor expected to finish everything you start. Projects, books, experiments, and plans may be discontinued as soon as something more interesting comes along (or for any other reason) without penalty, and picked up again at any time in the future (or never).

You may reclaim control of your family's daily life, and take what steps you feel necessary to protect your children from physical, emotional, or social harm. You have leave to think your own thoughts and to encourage your children to think theirs.

Each person who reads and understands this is authorized to extend these privileges to others, by reproducing and distributing this certificate or by creating another of his/her own design. Those who don't feel the need to obtain approval to experiment, to think, or to do things they've never seen others do are exempt, as they didn't need permission in the first place.

Contributors

From the Experts

Foreword

Preface

Website Research

In the Trenches

Dads

Teens

INDEX

INDEX

INDEX

INDEX

INDEX

INDEX

INDEX

INDEX

NOTES

NOTES

NOTES

NOTES

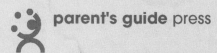

parent's guide press

Good For You.
Good For Your Kids.

A Parent's Guide to THE INTERNET
ISBN 0-9675127-9-4
$19.95 (December 2001)

208 Pages —Trade Paperback—**Available in Library Bindings**
Hundreds of Website Listings, Dozens of Illustrations, Index

• **The project oriented non-technical guide to family Internet use.**
Dozens of hands-on projects for parents and children help de-mystify the
Internet and lay bare issues of privacy, youth-targeted marketing, and safety.

• **Written by Ilene Raymond**, an award winning writer and essayist who
has taught at Temple University and Pennsylvania State University. Her articles and fiction have appeared in numerous national publications, including Good Housekeeping, Redbook, Cosmopolitan, Readers Digest, Ladies
House Journal, and Mademoiselle. She lives outside Philadelphia with her
husband and two sons.

The only book about kids and the Internet to be published in the last two years.

"(An) imaginative, valuable resource"

—*American Library Association*

• **HTML explained.** How building a family
Web site helps parents and children better
understand the Internet (and have fun at the
same time).

• **A brief history of the Internet** (and why the
Internet is more than the World Wide Web and
vice versa).

• **E-mail, Discussion Groups, FTP, IRC Chat**:
the Internet that isn't the Web and the opportunities for enlightenment— and abuse—
they offer.

• **Advice from experts** such as Slashdot
columnist Jon Katz, MaMaMedia.com founder
Idit Harel, researcher Michael Antecol and many
others: Internet developers, child psychology
experts, homeschooling parents, academics,
and involved educators. All share insights on
how best to use the Internet in the home. In
short: Parents need to be involved with their
children's Internet activity. The Internet is not a
teacher, parent, sibling, babysitter or friend,
though it is a powerful communication medium
that can help children, grow, learn, meet,
and explore.

• **Scores of Web sites** to explore and enjoy,
from games to filtering services, online
encyclopedias to blogs.

• **A concise glossary** of common Internet
and computer terms makes the jargon
comprehensible.

• **Indexed** for easy reference.

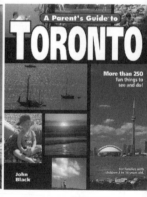